THE
POWER
HANDBOOK

Pamela Cuming

THE POWER HANDBOOK

a strategic guide to organizational and personal effectiveness

CBI Publishing Company, Inc.
51 Sleeper Street
Boston, MA 02210

Production Editor: Linda Dunn McCue
Text Designers: Maureen Harris and Richard Sarabia
Compositor: Commonwealth Graphics

Library of Congress Cataloging in Publication Data

Cuming, Pamela, 1944–
   The power handbook.

    1. Success.   2. Power (Social sciences) I. Title.
HF5386.C899   650.1   80–14039
ISBN 0-8436-0778-5

Printed in the United States of America

Printing (last digit): 10 9 8 7 6 5 4 3 2 1

Dedication

It is with love and gratitude that I dedicate this book and the thoughts it represents to William I. Bechard. Bill was not only my partner in business. He was also my husband until his death on July 1, 1979. Without his emotional support and the challenge of his thoughts, I could not have written this book. He was a truly great person, as is clear in this statement about Bill, made by Francis P. Lucier, one of Bill's most valued friends:

"Bill and I started our careers nearly thirty years ago as sales trainees at the Stanley Works in New Britain, Connecticut. For a few years, our lives—business and personal—moved in tandem until Bill found his home in the people-skills area. High intellect, inquisitiveness, and a passion for understanding others and himself combined to move Bill's career forward.

"Although there were time lapses, we never lost touch with one another. Bill's special skills were critical to me twice in my business career. I am most grateful that his achievements include the help given to me personally and to my company.

"Bill Bechard personally involved himself thoroughly in his work and with those close to him. It was his trademark. This trademark will remain etched in my mind and heart forever."

Contents

Foreword

This is a book about **success**. It will help you define what you want to do with your life and with your career, and then encourage you to go about reaching your objectives in a planned way. Success is not a stable state, nor is it a possession or something external to us. It is a state of mind, a feeling of self-worth and mastery. The mountain climber who conquers Mount Everest is successful. The child who manages the first day in school is successful. The salesman who snares a lucrative account is successful. The division manager who aspires to corporate leadership succeeds when he is named corporate vice president.

This is also a book about **people** and about **power**. The three topics are intertwined. Without power, would-be leaders cannot lead. Without power, people cannot control their lives; they cannot even assume responsibility for their lives. And yet, power has a negative connotation. People deny power, fearing that to be powerful is to be disliked. This is unfortunate. The purpose of the consulting organization to which I belong is to assist organizations and groups within organizations to succeed. Our work with both private and public sector clients has convinced us that inability to use power in a straightforward or nonmanipulative manner is the root cause of both individual despair and organizational immobility. Power is a necessity. As such, it needs to be fully understood and managed properly.

People who manage power properly do so in a way that inspires the commitment and/or cooperation of others. They perceive power not as an end in itself, but as a means to an end. Further, their efforts to get and to use power illustrate their belief that the effective Influence Strategy results in more "winners" than "losers." In short, people who use power effectively are the same people who are effective on an interpersonal level. To exercise power without understanding people is to inspire resentment, fear, and dislike. To develop a refined understanding of people in the absence of power is to become a highly sensitive individual who projects good feelings but accomplishes little. To succeed is to combine a high level of interpersonal skill with an ability to get and to use power appropriately.

People who feel successful have much in common. Most importantly, they feel good about themselves. They are clear about their goals. They know where their strengths lie and use them in an assertive fashion. Further, they are aware of their weaknesses and limitations and are able to complement their own efforts by utilizing the abilities of others in a mutually productive fashion. Their actions are characterized by a "can do" feeling and are backed by a sufficient and appropriate power base. Successful people do not waste their energy complaining about the obstacles and barriers that beset them; they focus on what can be done, rather than what cannot.

This book has been designed for people who want to succeed. However, it does not and cannot impose a definition of what constitutes success. To a paralyzed patient, for example, success is movement. To a scientist, success may be effecting a new cure. To a budding author, success is getting published. Like success, this book should represent a highly personalized experience for you. It offers theories and frames of reference to clarify the available options, and provides further clarification through examples of strategies applied by others in their efforts to succeed in industry, academe, and government.

The numerous planning formats and self-scoring questionnaires should prove especially useful. The formats are designed to help you construct a plan of action that reflects your individual values and that responds to your unique problems and opportunities. The questionnaires are designed to stimulate self-insight and to encourage you to privately challenge old ways and assumptions.

Planning formats and questionnaires are supplied in the Appendices as well as throughout the text to aid your exploration of power and its role in your life. For further copies of the Appendix materials, in particular the Influence Style Profile, please write to:

Dialectics Inc.
695 Summer Street
Stanford, CT 06901

If you hope to get maximum benefit from the book, I urge you to take the time to complete and think about the formats and questionnaires as they appear. By the time you have completed the book, you will have begun your own success story.

Pamela Cuming

Acknowledgments

I would like to thank the following individuals: John Brooman, president of Black and Decker Inc., whose comments and suggestions provided a base as theory was tested against the experiences and perceptions of an individual who has truly succeeded; Barbara Olausen, who patiently and effectively proofread the multitude of pages generated as the manuscript evolved; Jennifer Sherman, who persevered through the typing of four manuscript drafts; Dennis P. Sleven, Ph.D., Graduate School of Business, University of Pittsburgh, whose comments were extremely helpful in separating conjecture from proven fact, and in finding the appropriate balance between theory and instrumentation; Margaret Stevens, Ph.D., consultant, Dialectics Inc., who provided tremendous assistance in doing the extensive research required to substantiate concepts and observations; and Martha Wenz, corporate assistant vice president and director of manpower development at Citytrust Bank, Bridgeport, Connecticut, who provided not only conceptual suggestions, but an ongoing challenge that forced greater precision of thought and clarify of explanation.

I am also grateful to the various business organizations and government agencies that provided an observational base and opportunity to test and refine both the concepts and the questionnaires.

1

Power: A Dirty Word?

What is power? It is the **ability to make happen that which we want to happen** or, conversely, the **ability to block the occurrence of events that are undesirable to us.** More simply, **power is the ability to choose.**

Power is exercised in all human interactions, but to say that one person is "more powerful" than another is overly simplistic. People are only "more powerful" or "less powerful" along a given dimension or within a given situation. A wealthy man who lives in an iron lung may have greater purchasing power than his healthy, less wealthy peer. But he has less power to choose life over death, being vulnerable to the continued functioning of the artificial lung.

Power is not inherently "dirty." While powerful people may be corrupt, it is not their power that corrupts, but their need or desire to win at others' expense. **To feel empowered** is fundamental to leading a healthy, active, fulfilled life. It is not power that is the antagonist, but **powerlessness.** Those who feel they cannot affect others, or control life's events die psychologically, physically, or make life miserable for others. Prisoners of war who are placed in solitary confinement for extended periods of time often die for no apparent physical reason. Their complete lack of interaction with others, combined with a physical inability to control their environment, leads first to mental impairment, and then to physical atrophy. Similarly, infants whose physical needs are met but who are deprived of all direct human touch and interaction will fall prey to Marasmus—a syndrome characterized first by mental lethargy and physical passivity, and finally, by death. The prisoners of war and the infants have in common the total absence of human give-and-take. Lacking the opportunity to interact with others, they are unable to influence others. They are, in effect, physically and psychologically powerless. The result is alienation carried to the point of death.

Orphaned or abandoned infants and prisoners of war are not alone in their feelings of powerlessness. Powerlessness, and the resulting alienation, is a widespread phenomenon in the workplace as jobs are designed to increase predictability for the organization, while diminishing meaningfulness and control by the worker. It is not just assembly-line workers who find their jobs frustrating, dull, and without opportunity for influence or advancement. Powerlessness and boredom on the job are also key contributors to white-collar job dissatisfaction. In one study, a striking 57 percent of white-collar workers stated they would not choose similar work again. There is probably no greater indicator of job dissatisfaction than the desire to be in a different line of work.[1]

Feelings of powerlessness on the job are detrimental to both the worker and the organization. Strikes, sabotage, and high turnover rates are some of the symptoms of personnel fighting for power. Managers who are stripped of autonomy or power often become more political than task-oriented. As part of the politicking, they refuse to provide negative feedback or constructive criticism to their own bosses. It is the empowered person who feels safe enough to take a risk, to say no or ask why or to suggest alternatives at problem-solving sessions.

It is thus powerlessness, not power, that destroys social and commercial institutions. Power becomes a dirty word only when it is used to disempower others and to create situations in which others must unnecessarily lose.

In this chapter, we'll take a closer look at **power** and at **powerlessness**. We'll consider why being empowered is fundamental to success as we discuss the **self-fulfilling prophecy**. We'll also look at the other side of power: power abuses, when they occur, and why.

FEELING EMPOWERED

To feel empowered is to have a strong sense of "can do," a feeling of control and choice over life's events. People who are empowered are fully aware of all their resources—their strengths and weaknesses, their feelings and frustrations, their values and their attitudes. They are clear about what they want to accomplish in life, and are optimistic about their ability to achieve these goals.

How empowered do you feel? The following questionnaire can help you answer that question. Spread a total of five points over the alternative responses to each item. For example, you might select these point spreads:

A. **4**　　or　　A. **5**　　or　　A. **2**
B. **1**　　　　　B. **0**　　　　　B. **3**

Sometimes, you may believe you display the two responses to equal degrees. If this instrument is to be useful to you, it is important that you force yourself to rank one of the options slightly more heavily than the other.

---

[1] Department of Health, Education, and Welfare, *Work in America: Report of a Special Task Force to the U.S. Department of Health, Education, and Welfare* (Cambridge, MA: MIT Press, 1973), pp. 12-23.

Empowerment Profile

1. *When I have to give a talk or write a paper, I ...*
   - ☐ A. Base the content of my talk or paper on my own ideas.
   - ☐ B. Do a lot of research, and present the findings of others in my paper or talk.

2. *When I read something that I disagree with, I ...*
   - ☐ A. Assume my position is correct.
   - ☐ B. Assume what's presented in the written word is correct.

3. *When someone makes me extremely angry, I ...*
   - ☐ A. Ask the other person to stop the behavior that is offensive to me.
   - ☐ B. Say little, not knowing quite how to state my position.

4. *When I do a good job, it is important to me that ...*
   - ☐ A. The job represents the best I can do.
   - ☐ B. Others take notice of the job I've done.

5. *When I buy new clothes, I ...*
   - ☐ A. Buy what looks best on me.
   - ☐ B. Try to dress in accordance with the latest fashion.

6. *When something goes wrong, I ...*
   - ☐ A. Try to solve the problem.
   - ☐ B. Try to find out who's at fault.

7. *As I anticipate my future, I ...*
   - ☐ A. Am confident I will be able to lead the kind of life I want to lead.
   - ☐ B. Worry about being able to live up to my obligations.

8. *When examining my own resources and capacities, I ...*
   - ☐ A. Like what I find.
   - ☐ B. Find all kinds of things I wish were different.

9. *When someone treats me unfairly, I ...*
   - ☐ A. Put my energies into getting what I want.
   - ☐ B. Tell others about the injustice.

10. *When someone criticizes my efforts, I ...*
    - ☐ A. Ask questions in order to better understand the basis for the criticism.
    - ☐ B. Defend my actions or decisions, trying to make my critic better understand why I did what I did.

11. *When I engage in an activity, it is very important to me that ...*
    - ☐ A. I live up to my own expectations.
    - ☐ B. I live up to the expectations of others.

12. *When I let someone else down or disappoint them, I ...*
    - ☐ A. Resolve to do things differently the next time.
    - ☐ B. Feel guilty, and wish I had done things differently.

13. *I try to surround myself with people ...*
    - ☐ A. Whom I respect.
    - ☐ B. Who respect me.

14. *I try to develop friendships with people who ...*
    - ☐ A. Are challenging and exciting.
    - ☐ B. Can make me feel a little safer and a little more secure.

15. *I make my best efforts when ...*
    - ☐ A. I do something that I want to do, when I want to do it.
    - ☐ B. Someone else gives me an assignment, a deadline, and a reward for performing.

16. *When I love a person, I ...*
    - ☐ A. Encourage him or her to be free and to choose for and fulfill himself or herself.
    - ☐ B. Encourage him or her to do the same things I do and to make choices similar to mine.

17. *When I play a competitive game, it is important to me that I ...*
    - ☐ A. Do the best I can do.
    - ☐ B. Win.

18. *I really like being around people who ...*
    - ☐ A. Can broaden my horizons and teach me something.
    - ☐ B. Can and want to learn from me.

19. *My best days are those that …*
- ☐ A. Present unexpected opportunities.
- ☐ B. Go according to plan.

20. *When I get behind in my work, I …*
- ☐ A. Do the best I can, and don't worry.
- ☐ B. Worry or push myself harder than I should.

To get a numerical indication of how empowered you feel, add all your "A" scores. Then, add all your "B" scores. You can get an indication of the depth of your feelings of "can do" by comparing your "A" total with your "B" total:

My A total is ☐   My B total is ☐

"B" greater than "A":   You feel somewhat unempowered; you experience the choices and reactions of others as more critical than your own.

"B" equal or close to "A": Feelings of freedom are matched by feelings of entrapment. Chances are you bet on yourself, but hedge that bet in case you are wrong.

"A" greater than "B":   More often than not, you experience yourself as the prime mover of the events that affect you. Life is experienced more as a series of opportunities than as a series of "must do's" and obligations.

Feeling empowered is critical. Why? Because others cannot make us successful. We have to do it ourselves. The most others can do is to provide opportunities or establish barriers. Only the self-empowered can take advantage of the opportunities and remove the barriers.

To feel empowered is to have confidence in yourself, to trust your feelings and maintain a sense of personal worth **regardless of the reactions of others.** The empowered person likes himself or herself, and makes decisions on the basis of personal values rather than external measures of success imposed by others. The empowered student has a high enough level of self-esteem to take on a course that will enrich his knowledge even though the course's difficulty may cause his grade point average to suffer. The empowered actor maintains an optimistic, "can–do" feeling even while critics pan his performance in a certain role. The empowered parent retains a high level of positive self-regard even if a child elects a life pattern of which the parent disapproves. The empowered manager is sufficiently self-confident to encourage the development of subordinates to a point where their abilities surpass his own. Regardless of rank or status, empowered people value themselves and measure their successes against their own standards, not the standards and values of others.

Feelings of self-empowerment determine life's events more than any other factor—more than our birthright or lack thereof; more than our race; more than our sex; more than our innate intelligence. Our attitudes about ourselves almost always become facts, or **self-fulfilling prophecies.**

The Self-Fulfilling Prophecy

The first ingredient in succeeding is a firm belief that you can succeed. To expect failure is to fail. To expect disaster is to court disaster. To aspire to be "Number Two" is to preclude the possibility of becoming "Number One." **To predict that something will occur is to take a giant step in the direction of making it occur.**[2]

Timothy Gallwey's book, *Inner Tennis: Playing the Game* (Random House, New York, 1976), provides us with a good example of the power of the self-fulfilling prophecy on the tennis court:

> "A tennis player first confronts the Inner Game when he discovers that there is an opponent inside his own head more formidable than the one across the net ... Further, he becomes aware that these same mental obstacles also prevent him from living his best life."

His often proved thesis is that the inner psychological game determines the outcome of the match. By teaching his students to play a strong "Inner Game"—to believe in his or her innate capacity—Gallwey creates tennis pros out of former tennis clowns.

A dramatic example of the self-fulfilling prophecy was provided by a friend who suffered a massive heart attack. The doctors gave him a 2 percent chance of living, and urged his loved ones to pray for death, since (according to the doctors) the extent of oxygen deprivation was so great as to guarantee loss of all mental ability and physical control. This friend, at the time, was a great lover of life and a firm believer in his capacity to build the kind of life he wanted. Today, he is not only alive, but actively engaged in building a new business and re-engaging in sports. The doctors offer no explanation. They fully admit that the outcome cannot be explained by medical science. A miracle? Perhaps. More likely, the outcome was the result of a strong will to live, a self-fulfilling prophecy that "I will live and not die."

Less dramatic but no less significant examples of the self-fulfilling prophecy are evident in our schools and businesses or industries. Students who are placed in "slow track" classes often internalize the expectation of others that they are not as bright and capable as other students. Academic achievement generally bears this out, since the student who expects to perform poorly actually does so. Similarly, manager's expectations are often internalized by subordinates. The subordinate who is repeatedly told his ideas are unworthy may begin to believe it. He or she then stops contributing, and becomes a "yes person." Then, at appraisal time, the manager gives a low rating to the employee on initiative, contribution, and creativity. Opportunities for promo-

---

[2]For an insightful discussion of the self-fulfilling prophecy as it affects the management of employees see J. Sterling Livingston, "Pygmalion in Management." *Harvard Business Review* (July-August 1969).

tion become less frequent. The expectation that "I can't perform" becomes a reality. **To feel unempowered is to be unempowered.**

People who feel unempowered—who lack a strong sense of positive self-regard, and who base their evaluations of themselves on external measures of worth—tend to be those persons who commit power abuses. Lacking an inherent sense of self-esteem, and requiring external reinforcement of their worth, they experience life as a perpetual contest, as a stressful situation in which the only way to "win" is to make others "lose." Choices made by unempowered people tend to generate negative consequences for the self, or others, or both.

THE IMPACT OF OUR CHOICES

As people use power, they inevitably effect any one of four outcomes:

- WIN–WIN
- WIN–LOSE
- LOSE–LOSE
- WIN–NO-LOSE

A win–win outcome occurs when all those involved in a situation or transaction benefit as a result of the power dynamics. When a sales representative sells a prospect something that prospect needs, the persuasive power of the sales representative has been used to effect a win–win outcome. When a manager uses his or her power to promote qualified subordinates, the outcome is win–win, since the productivity of the manager's unit is increased, and the employee benefits from having a better job.

The use of power frequently results in a win–lose outcome. Competitive sports provide a clear example of the power of one individual or group pitted against the power of another individual or group, the result being victory for one and loss for the other. But win–lose outcomes are not always confined to sport and good fun. When two people are competing for the same job, there is inevitably a winner and a loser. When five students apply to the same university, and only three are accepted, there are clearly winners and losers.

Sometimes what at first appears to be a win–lose proposition ends up with a lose-lose outcome. Consider war. While every battle ends with an apparent victor and an apparent loser, both parties suffer significant losses in many cases. Given today's awesome weapons, war is likely to have many lose–lose characteristics. The inability or reluctance to deal openly with a coworker whose behavior is disturbing also leads to a lose–lose outcome. Given no indications of the impact of his or her behavior, the coworker persists in antagonizing others. The associate who chooses to remain quiet, to withhold feedback, continues to suffer. Both lose.

Is it possible to have a winner and no-loser? That depends on your point of view. If I give my son the use of my car for the evening, he is winning—that is, he is in a better position because of my gesture. Am I losing? Only if I experience as a "loss" the extra miles put on the car and perhaps half a tank of gas expended. Volunteerism can be seen as either a win–no-lose proposition, where persons who have time to give (no loss) work to benefit others, or as a win–win proposition, since the volunteers themselves gain the satisfaction of doing something meaningful with their spare hours.)

People who feel fundamentally unempowered are most likely to abuse whatever power they do have, effecting far more win–lose and lose–lose outcomes than the more empowered person who values the win–win. Rarely is the use of power to effect a win–win outcome labeled as abusive. Cries of "power abuse" are almost always triggered by the loss to at least one of the parties involved in the power play.

What Constitutes a Power Abuse?

While people's feelings about power being "dirty" vary greatly, most of us would agree that power abuses do occur. We complain most loudly about power abuses in these situations:

WHEN WE ARE PUT IN THE POSITION OF "LOSER." People usually view power as "dirty" when its use creates an inconvenience that is perceived to be unjust, unfair, or unnecessary. People who sympathize with strikers during the early days of a protest generally begin to view the strike as a form of power abuse when the lack of goods and services starts to affect them directly. For many, the only time it is acceptable to be a "loser" is when we engage in sports or other forms of "friendly competition," and some of us find it difficult to be a "loser" even in that situation.

WHEN THE RESULT OF A POWER PLAY OFFENDS OUR VALUES. Those who embrace the democratic ideal that everyone should be given an equal opportunity perceive an abuse of power in the privileges accorded persons because of race or sex. When power is used to exploit others, those who are exploited as well as those who watch (but do not benefit), tend to feel an abuse of power is occurring. Sympathy strikes occur when one group perceives that another group with similar interests is being exploited. Letters to the editor are replete with arguments that the "underdog" should be more fairly treated.

WHEN POWER IS WASTED AND THE OUTCOME IS LOSE–LOSE OR NO-WIN. Many people would consider the arms race a lose–lose, or a no-win proposition, as significant amounts of the resources of both the United States and the Soviet Union are spent on creating highly destructive weaponry. (Others disagree, perceiving the effort to build bigger and better weapons as necessary to maintaining at least a win–lose position.) People appear to resent what they perceive to be a waste of power. A look at the rules of many sports shows how true this is. In golf, tennis, squash, baseball, and basketball, for example, ties—no-win situations—are unacceptable; play is extended until one player or team wins. The dislike of power- or resource-waste provides a strong stimulant in organizations to match talent and interest with job requirements. Increasingly, companies are establishing skill inventories: they are realizing that employees lose when unable to fully utilize their skills while organizations lose when unable to employ its full human-resource pool.

In general, then, people feel that power is abused when:

- The outcome is win–lose and they are the loser.

- The outcome is win–lose and their values are offended.

- The outcome is lose–lose (or no–win) and power is wasted.

It is unusual, however, to find a situation in which all would agree that a power abuse has occurred. Perceptions of what constitutes a win–win, a win–lose and a lose–lose situation vary tremendously. Many would say that, in defeating Hitler, the world effected a win–lose outcome, with the free world winning and Hitler losing. Others, more concerned with the devastation wrought in so many countries, might argue that the whole event was lose–lose.

When one company acquires another, what is the nature of the outcome? Has a power abuse occurred? The acquirer often protests that the acquisition is a win–win proposition, as stockholders in the acquired entity benefit from a greater sale price of their stock. Employees of the acquired entity who are unfortunate enough to lose their jobs may see the acquisition as win–lose, with their company losing.

Justifying the Use of Power

Most of us spend a great deal of energy attempting to convince ourselves and others that, in exercising our power, we are only striving for win–win outcomes. Companies that cut prices in order to drive out smaller competitors firmly believe they are effecting a win–win. Consumers win as they pay lower prices. Stockholders win as the company gains market share. It is even possible that the unsuccessful competitor wins as it is forced out of a business in which it could not gain significant share of market, and is, therefore, forced to invest its resources in potentially more profitable areas.

Occasionally, it is impossible to label the second party to our power plays as anything other than a "loser," forcing us to rationalize further. In these situations, we often find there is a "win" for a third party (as well as for ourselves) that is so great as to outweigh the "loss" to the second party. Companies that are forced to fire significant numbers of employees (the losers) during recessions do so in the interests of their stockholders (third party winners). Ex-spouses who sue for additional support (making their "ex" lose financially) often do so in the interest of minor children. Employees often justify the spreading of negative information about other employees on the basis of the greater good of the company.

And finally, there is always the moral solace inherent in the knowledge, "It was me or them; I did it in self-defense." Or, if self-defense is not sufficient, comfort may be derived from the belief, "After all, they deserved it." Most managers find it extremely difficult to fire a subordinate. Typically, they delay as long as possible. Between the onset of performance problems and the actual firing, many managers try to avoid contact with the employee in question. As a result, the employee is deprived of performance feedback and, consequently, the opportunity to change his or her behavior in cordance with the boss's expectations. The firing comes as a surprise. The manager attempts to find solace in such thoughts as:

- If the employee were smart enough for the job, (s)he would have been smart enough to figure out that I have been unhappy with his (or her) performance.

- No matter how much time and attention I might have given him (or her), his (or her) performance would not have improved.

- I had too much on my mind keeping solid performers organized to waste my time with a marginal performer.

People, then, are reluctant to admit to themselves or to others that they have abused their power. And, generally, they succeed in convincing themselves (if not others) that, if they were abusive, it was justifiable. Given the number of possible justifications, it is little wonder that few of us feel we have abused our power.

How often have you relied on these rationales to justify behavior that had negative consequences for others? Try to think of three or four persons who have suffered (or who feel they have suffered) directly as a result of your actions. In each case, determine why you did what you did.

☐   I was trying to achieve a win-win outcome.

☐   I was trying to achieve a win-no-lose outcome.

☐   The "win" for the third party was more important than the "loss" incurred by the second party.

☐   I had no choice; someone had to win at another's expense. I couldn't afford to be the loser. (Self-defense.)

☐   They deserved it.

Some of us undoubtedly find it easier to think of instances when someone has "lost" as a result of our actions than do others, and some of us create far more situations in which someone must lose. Part of the explanation lies in the degree to which we feel empowered. Empowered people tend to effect win-win outcomes. People who feel fundamentally unempowered find the concept of "win-win" more difficult to grasp. They regard power as finite. They assume that power is a fixed sum, and that if they are to get a larger piece of the power pie, someone else must go without.

THE POWER PIE

Think of the people you know who demonstrate a need to be continually "one up." These are the people who take every available opportunity to point out or to try to prove that they are better than you, more capable than you, more worthy than you, more perceptive than you, more sensitive than you, smarter than you, etc. People who need to be one up demonstrate the feeling that the only way for them to "win" is for others to "lose." For these people, the amount of power available appears to be finite.

In sharp contrast to those who live life as though it were a "power pie" are those who regard power as unlimited. Those who believe the amount of power available is expandable or infinite will tend to create more win–win outcomes. In attempting to empower others, they empower themselves. In making others more effective, they believe they become more effective in the process. It is difficult, if not impossible, to be an effective parent, teacher, or manager without at least some belief that win–win outcomes are possible. The teachers who inwardly fear that students will surpass them will inevitably fall short of imparting their full range of knowledge. The manager who fails to give subordinates developmental assignments is often attempting to protect a definable piece of the power pie by keeping the subordinate less empowered.

To what extent does your behavior reflect the power pie idea rather than the attitude that power is infinite? The following is a checklist of behavioral traits. Next to each trait are symbols:

SP: for Spouse
C: for Child
B: for Boss
SUB: for Subordinate

Next to each trait, circle the symbol of any person or persons whom you would like to possess the trait. For example, let's assume you want your children and subordinates to do what you say without question. You would respond to item 1 as follows:

| 1. Does what I say without question. | SP | C | B | SUB |

POWER PIE CHECKLIST

1. Does what I say without question.	SP	C	B	SUB
2. Challenges my way of doing things.	SP	C	B	SUB
3. Insists that I recognize his or her rights.	SP	C	B	SUB
4. Points out when I don't do things as well as I could.	SP	C	B	SUB
5. Gives me credit when credit is due.	SP	C	B	SUB

6. Feels (s)he can learn more from me than any-one else.	SP	C	B	SUB
7. Is less smart than I am.	SP	C	B	SUB
8. Thinks that I can do no wrong.	SP	C	B	SUB
9. Is smarter than I am.	SP	C	B	SUB
10. Can outperform me.	SP	C	B	SUB
11. Values my friendship more than anyone else's.	SP	C	B	SUB
12. Leaves me alone; respects my privacy.	SP	C	B	SUB
13. Likes me better than anyone else.	SP	C	B	SUB
14. Thinks (s)he'll never be as clever as I.	SP	C	B	SUB
15. Wants to stand on his or her own and realize his or her own potential.	SP	C	B	SUB
16. Regards me as totally reliable.	SP	C	B	SUB
17. Is dependent on me.	SP	C	B	SUB
18. Feels (s)he couldn't survive without me.	SP	C	B	SUB
19. Is not afraid of angering me.	SP	C	B	SUB
20. Is afraid of my anger.	SP	C	B	SUB
21. Is afraid of losing my affection.	SP	C	B	SUB
22. Recognizes that I can hurt or help him or her as I choose.	SP	C	B	SUB
23. Could function well without me.	SP	C	B	SUB
24. Is good at doing things I am not good at doing.	SP	C	B	SUB
25. Is aware of my weaknesses.	SP	C	B	SUB

26. Is awed by my strengths and abilities.   SP   C   B   SUB

To score your power pie, count the number of times you circled "SP" next to these items: 1, 6, 7, 8, 11, 13, 14, 17, 18, 20, 21, 22, 26. Then, count the number of times you circled a "C," "B," or "SUB" for any of these items. Then, do the same thing around the remaining items.

	COLUMN A	COLUMN B
	No. of the following items used: 1, 6, 7, 8, 11, 13, 14, 17, 18, 20, 21, 22, 26	No. of the following items used: 2, 3, 4, 5, 9, 10, 12, 15, 16, 19, 23, 24, 25
Spouse		
Subordinate		
Boss		
Child		
TOTAL		

Column A indicates your power pie tendencies. Column B indicates the extent to which you behave as though power were infinite.

If your Column A score is greater than or equal to your Column B score, then you have some indication that:

- You may undervalue your own inherent worth, being more concerned about your position relative to others than about the extent to which you are living up to your own values and potential.

- *Therefore,* you may regard the amount of power available as finite and limited.

- *Therefore,* you may engage in more win-lose or lose-lose activities than are truly necessary.

- *Therefore,* you may find it necessary to justify a series of abuses (small or large).

- *Therefore,* you may further undervalue your own worth.

If your Column B score is greater than your Column A score, then it is likely that:

- You have a strong sense of self-confidence and are both aware of and feel good about your true capacities.

- *Therefore,* your self-respect is not dependent on maintaining a "top dog" position nor on being the best at everything.

- *Therefore,* you can enjoy and benefit from interacting with others who can out-perform you.

- *Therefore,* you tend to create opportunities for learning and growth.

- *Therefore,* you continually elaborate your abilities and your successes.

Feelings of unempowerment, then, create a destructive cycle that feeds upon itself, making any kind of success difficult. It is empowered people who realize their goals. Empowered people are secure enough to regard power as infinite, and to seek win–win outcomes whenever possible. Empowered people are clear about their goals and their definitions of success. In the next chapter, you will have a chance to consider what you can do to introduce a greater sense of purpose or direction into your life, thereby taking an important step toward becoming more empowered.

2

Goal Confidence:
How Much Do You Have?

A common characteristic of people who consider themselves successful is a **sense of purpose**. A sense of purpose evolves from clarity about one's **goals** and is accompanied by a feeling of **power**—of being free and able to pursue the objectives of one's choice. **Resilience** is another characteristic of the successful individual. Failure to achieve one goal does not generate a feeling of despair; on the contrary, resilience and flexibility emerge as this person explores and creates alternative ways to satisfy similar ends. His or her goals are not so contradictory as to generate a "damned if I do, damned if I don't" life situation. In short, the successful individual experiences a high degree of **Goal Confidence**.

Goal Confidence suffers when problems arise in any of the following areas:

- **Goal Control:** the extent to which a person feels *able* to pursue goals of his or her choosing.

- **Goal Clarity:** the extent to which there is *clarity* or lack of confusion about goals and priorities.

- **Goal Compatibility:** the degree to which the things an individual wants to accomplish are compatible with each other, or the extent to which the goals of two or more interdependent persons are mutually supportive; the absence of goal conflict.

- **Goal Flexibility:** the degree to which an individual is able to pursue alternatives, to shift the goal focus, and to experience diversity of aim and objective.

In this chapter, each of the factors affecting Goal Confidence will be discussed. Before reading the chapter, complete the Goal Confidence Profile. It will help you identify the extent to which you feel Goal Confident.

To complete the questionnaire, consider one descriptive statement at a time. Think about how accurately the response describes your perceptions of how things are in your life.

Use this scale:

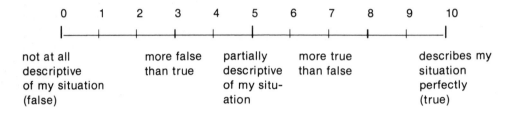

If the response accurately describes your situation, you would record a 9 or 10 in to the right of the item. If the response is not at all descriptive of how you view your situation, put a 0 or perhaps a 1 in the box. If the response is partially descriptive, record a 4, 5, or 6. If the response is more accurate than not, but is not completely true, you might put a 7 or 8 in the box. **Circle whole numbers only.**

There are no "right" or "wrong" answers. There are only your perceptions of what is happening in your life. The questionnaire will be useful to you only to the extent that you are honest in your answers. It is important that you complete every item.

The Goal Confidence Profile

1. The things I want to accomplish are within my power to do or to learn to do.

2. The people whose needs I want to satisfy as a result of my accomplishments are clearly known to me.

3. Location is not a problem for me; I could pursue my chosen field in a number of locations.

4. The methods I want to employ as I pursue my goals are not a problem; others important to me would be pleased by my efforts to learn and apply these methods.

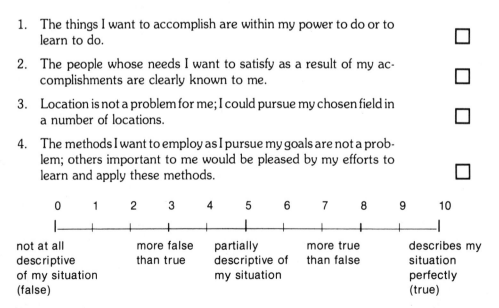

5. The things I want to do with or for those persons most important to me outside my work life are within my power to do. ☐

6. I know exactly what financial resources I'll need to pursue my career goals. ☐

7. Materials and equipment are not a constraint for me; I could use any number of different types of equipment and materials. ☐

8. The people whose help or support I need to reach my career goals have reason to want to provide the support I need. ☐

9. The people with whom I will have to compete in order to achieve my career goals do not constitute a major threat to achieving my objectives. ☐

10. The things I want to accomplish in my work life are very clear to me. ☐

11. My work can be of benefit to many; I am not constrained by being a "specialist" who responds only to unique problems. ☐

12. The location in which I want to work would also be a good place in which to live and to pursue my other interests. ☐

13. The methods I plan to employ in my work represent things I know how to do, or things I can learn to do. ☐

14. I know what I want to do with or for those persons most important to me outside my work life. ☐

15. The financial resources I need to pursue my career goals can be acquired from a variety of sources; if one source falls through, there are others to whom I can turn. ☐

16. There will be no need to sacrifice other life goals in order to get the materials and equipment I'll need to pursue my career goals. ☐

17. I know I can get the help or support of others that I need to reach my career goals. ☐

18. I can identify the people with whom I'll have to compete in order to achieve my career goals. ☐

0	1	2	3	4	5	6	7	8	9	10

not at all descriptive of my situation (false)   more false than true   partially descriptive of my situation   more true than false   describes my situation perfectly (true)

19. The things I want to accomplish in my work life are sufficiently varied so that if one path is blocked, I can happily pursue other goals. ☐

20. There will be no need to make unwelcome sacrifices in other areas of my life if I am to satisfy the needs of persons important to me. ☐

21. I work or know I could work in the location in which I want to work. ☐

22. I am clear about the methods I am going to employ in my work. ☐

23. The things I want to do with or for those persons most important to me outside my work life are sufficiently varied so that if I fail in one area, I can happily devote my energies to other areas. ☐

24. I will not have to make unwelcome sacrifices in order to get the funding I need to pursue my career goals. ☐

25. The materials and equipment that I need to pursue my career goals are available to me, or can be readily obtained. ☐

26. I know who's help and support I'll need if I am to reach my career goals. ☐

27. In order to compete effectively with others in my chosen field, I can elect any one of a number of ways in which to attempt to excel. ☐

28. The things I want to accomplish are such that accomplishing one will make it easier to accomplish another. ☐

29. I know I will be able to "reach" those persons whose needs I want to satisfy as a result of my accomplishments. ☐

30. I can identify the location in which I want to work. ☐

31. I have a number of options as to the methods or technologies I will be able to employ in my work. ☐

32. As I work to accomplish my career objectives, I will be simultaneously doing the things I want to do with or for those persons most important to me outside my work life. ☐

33. The financial resources I need to pursue my career goals are available to me, or can be mobilized by me. ☐

0	1	2	3	4	5	6	7	8	9	10

not at all descriptive of my situation (false)

more false than true

partially descriptive of my situation

more true than false

describes my situation perfectly (true)

34. I know exactly what materials and equipment I'll need to pursue my career goals. ☐

35. I have a great many options as to the relationships I can develop to get the help or support I need to reach my career goals. ☐

36. I won't have to rely on methods I don't approve of in order to compete effectively in my chosen field. ☐

```
   0    1    2    3    4    5    6    7    8    9    10
   ├────┼────┼────┼────┼────┼────┼────┼────┼────┼────┤
```

not at all   more false   partially   more true   describes my
descriptive   than true   descriptive of than false   situation
of my situation   my situation   perfectly
(false)   (true)

To compute your Goal Confidence Index, record all your scores on the following chart in the indicated spaces.

Goal Confidence Computation Chart

ITEM	GOAL CONTROL	ITEM	GOAL CLARITY	ITEM	GOAL FLEXI-BILITY	ITEM	GOAL COMPATI-BILITY
1		2		3		4	
5		6		7		8	
9		10		11		12	
13		14		15		16	
17		18		19		20	
21		22		23		24	
25		26		27		28	
29		30		31		32	
33		34		35		36	
TOTAL							

The maximum possible score for any single Goal Confidence area is 90. If you scored less than 45 in any area, then you may be experiencing a sufficient lack of confidence to hinder your efforts to be all that you can be.

Understanding the source of Goal Confidence problems is the first step in alleviating them. In most cases, we can do a great deal by ourselves to increase Goal Confidence through life or career planning.

CLOSING THE GAPS: INCREASING GOAL CONFIDENCE

Goal Confidence can be increased. Doing so requires that we clarify our **values,** becoming aware not only of what we value, but of the relative degree of importance we attach to each value. **Values** are our beliefs about what constitutes a desirable existence. **Goals** are the translation of our values into action—into objectives that, when achieved, will satisfy our values. In this chapter, you will have an opportunity to clarify your overall values, and to use the results to begin to increase your level of Goal Confidence.

People differ markedly in their values and in the relative importance they place on each. One person, when asked to list his primary values, included:

- Love and mutual trust
- Autonomy
- Honesty
- Self-expression
- Levelheadedness
- Gentleness
- Capacity to change; flexibility
- Believing in something
- Self-respect

Another person created a very different list, including such qualities as:

- National security
- Equality
- Personal security
- Immortality
- Recognition

The first step in clarifying your values is to list them. This can be difficult, but it helps to provide a frame of reference: imagine that you are faced with the task of writing what will appear on your own gravestone. Assume you want the engraving to begin:

During (his or her) lifetime, _____ (your name) _____
valued, prized, held important:

Then, note down up to ten factors that describe what you believe to be a desirable existence. If you have trouble getting started, the list of values that follows the box below might stimulate your thoughts.

During (his or her) lifetime, _____
valued, prized, held important:

1.

2.

3.

4.
5.

6.

7.

8.

9.

10.

Sample List of Values

- Comfort
- Excitement
- Accomplishment
- Peace in the world
- Beauty in the world
- Physical well-being
- Family happiness
- Happiness
- Mature love
- Pleasure
- Salvation
- Self-respect
- Recognition
- Influence, authority
- True friendship
- Wisdom
- Challenge
- Personal growth
- Making a contribution
- Helping others
- Progress
- Honesty
- Fairness
- Justice

Next, try to determine the relative importance of each value you listed. Place a "1" next to the value that is most important to you, a "2" next to the value that is second in importance, etc. If you listed ten values, you would place a "10" next to the value that is least important. While it is likely that you will find this difficult to do, we urge you to make the effort. Only by making these kinds of decisions can we increase Goal Confidence.

The third step in clarifying our values and modifying our goals is to determine how hard we are working to satisfy those values. Write your values in order of importance on the format that follows. Then, place a number next to each to show the extent to which you are satisfied with what you are doing to achieve that value. Use this scale:

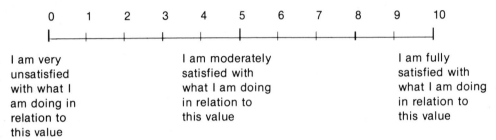

| 0 | 1 | 2 | 3 | 4 | 5 | 6 | 7 | 8 | 9 | 10 |

I am very unsatisfied with what I am doing in relation to this value

I am moderately satisfied with what I am doing in relation to this value

I am fully satisfied with what I am doing in relation to this value

Value Scoring Table

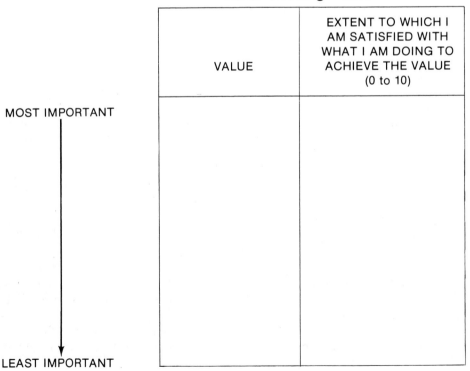

MOST IMPORTANT

LEAST IMPORTANT

VALUE	EXTENT TO WHICH I AM SATISFIED WITH WHAT I AM DOING TO ACHIEVE THE VALUE (0 to 10)

Note here the values you must work harder to satisfy—those important values that yielded a satisfaction score of 6 or less:

_____

_____

_____

_____

By now, you have taken all the steps required to diagnose the source and nature of your goal discomfort. The Goal Confidence Profile provided an indication of the kinds and degrees of blocks you may be experiencing. The values analysis you just finished will help you determine the degree to which your goals are in harmony with your values; of the extent to which the goals you are pursuing are appropriate for you, given the values you hope to satisfy. In the pages that follow, specific ways to minimize each of the blocks to Goal Confidence will be discussed along with ways to simultaneously increase the extent to which you are satisfying your primary values.

ACHIEVING GOAL CLARITY

Place an "X" on the following scale to indicate your own Goal Clarity score (see page 19):

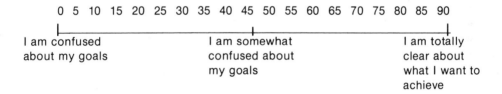

0 5 10 15 20 25 30 35 40 45 50 55 60 65 70 75 80 85 90

I am confused
about my goals

I am somewhat
confused about
my goals

I am totally
clear about
what I want to
achieve

If we are unclear about our values, we will be uncertain about our goals. If preferred "end states" are ambiguous, then objectives will be either nonexistent or unclear; we lack **Goal Clarity.** Clarification of values represents a major first step in reducing **Goal Confusion.** The next step is to translate those "key values" that you are not satisfying into concrete goals.

Failure to satisfy our values generally indicates that the goals we need to pursue are either unclear or not sufficiently well defined or comprehensive. Minimizing Goal Confusion requires that we define what we plan to accomplish, and how; the kind of support from others we'll need; and how we hope others will benefit. If you wish to enjoy a high level of Goal Clarity and a high level of value satisfaction, you need to answer the following questions with regard to all the values that you are not currently working to satisfy. If you scored 60 or lower on Goal Clarity or if you are not satisfied with what you are currently doing to satisfy your values, I suggest you take the time to answer these questions for each of those values you could do more to satisfy (see page 23).

Goals Clarification:
Minimizing Goal Confusion

1. ACCOMPLISHMENT:
    What products can I make or services can I offer that will contribute to the satisfaction of my value?

    _____

    _____

    Of the product and service options available to me, which appeals to me the most?

    _____

    _____

    _____

2. BENEFICIARIES:
    Who would benefit from my accomplishments?

    _____

    _____

    How will they benefit?

    _____

    _____

    In what ways would their benefiting contribute to the satisfaction of my primary value?

    _____

    _____

    _____

3. LOCATION:
    Where do I hope to work?

    _____

    _____

How will my choice of location contribute to my ability to satisfy my value?

_____

4. METHODOLOGY:
   What methods do I need to master or use?

   _____

   _____

   How will mastery in these areas contribute to my value satisfaction?

   _____

   _____

5. SIGNIFICANT OTHERS:
   How will my efforts affect other persons who are important to me?

   _____

   _____

   _____

   Is this impact consistent with my value?

   _____

   _____

   If not, how can I modify my plans so that they will be consistent with their impact on others?

   _____

   _____

6. FINANCES:
   How much money will I need, and how will I get it while satisfying my value?

   _____

   _____

   _____

7. MATERIALS:
   What tools or equipment will I need and how can I secure them in a way that is consistent with my value?

   _____

   _____

8. SUPPORT:
    What kind of support and help will I need from others, and how do I plan to get their commitment, cooperation, or approval?

    _____

    _____

    _____

    In the process of trying to gain their support and help, will I be contributing to the satisfaction of my value?

    _____

    _____

9. COMPETITION:
    Who, if anyone, is likely to try to block my efforts, and how do I hope to deal with them?

    _____

    _____

    _____

    Are my plans in this area consistent with my value?

    _____

    _____

    _____

    If not, what can I do to modify the approach I plan to take?

    _____

    _____

    _____

    Appendix A contains additional Goal Clarrification formats.

ACHIEVING GOAL COMPATIBILITY

Place an "X" at the appropriate point on this scale to indicate your own Goal Compatibility score (see page 19):

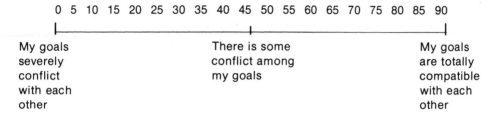

```
0  5  10  15  20  25  30  35  40  45  50  55  60  65  70  75  80  85  90
├─────────────────────────────────────┼─────────────────────────────────────┤
```

| My goals severely conflict with each other | There is some conflict among my goals | My goals are totally compatible with each other |

Reducing **Goal Conflict** and, thereby achieving **Goal Compatibility** requires, first, that you identify the nature of the conflict. Is it an incompatibility between one or more of your goals, or between your goals and the goals of another person? If you frequently find yourself in tug-of-war between two equally compelling activities, then chances are you are experiencing **Internal Goal Conflict**. If, on the other hand, you find yourself resenting another's intrusions into your time or privacy, then chances are the source of your Goal Conflict is **external**.

Are You Effectively Using Your Resources?

To understand the nature and source of Goal Conflict, it is important to specify your current efforts to satisfy your values. Taking each of your values (see page 22), list *all* the things you are doing or plan to do or achieve in order to satisfy that value. For example:

VALUE: INFLUENCE OR AUTHORITY

GOALS:

1. to get elected to a position of prominence in my community

2. to become a department head in the company for which I work

3. to write books that are regarded as the last word on the subject of engineering

---

VALUE: PHYSICAL WELL-BEING

GOALS:

1. to play tennis at least an hour a day

2. to jog every morning before I catch the train

3. to maintain a body weight of 165 pounds

As you list your goals under each of your values, try to be as specific and comprehensive as possible. Complete the blank forms that follow.

Current Efforts To Satisfy Values

VALUE: _____

GOALS:

1.

2.

3.

4.

5.

6.

VALUE: _____

GOALS:

1.

2.

3.

4.

5.

6.

Current Efforts To Satisfy Values

VALUE: _____

GOALS:

1.

2.

3.

4.

5.

6.

VALUE: _____

GOALS:

1.

2.

3.

4.

5.

6.

Current Efforts To Satisfy Values

VALUE: _____

GOALS:

1.

2.

3.

4.

5.

6.

VALUE: _____

GOALS:

1.

2.

3.

4.

5.

6.

Next, consider each set of goals associated with a single value, and **spread 100 points over the goals to indicate the relative importance of the goals to you. In no case should you assign the same number of points to any two goals.** Use whole numbers only. For example:

GOAL	POINTS
to play tennis at least an hour a day	25
to jog every morning before I catch the train	15
to maintain a body weight of 165 pounds	60
	100

GOAL	POINTS
to get elected	20
to become a department head	65
to write books	15
	100

Record your assigned point values on the format you completed on the preceding pages.

Now use the scale that follows to record *all* the goals that support your values next to the point count you assigned. For example:

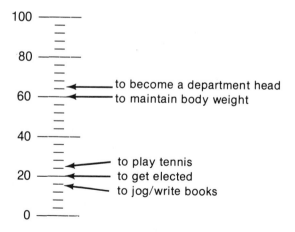

My Goal Importance Scale

```
100  ____
 95  —
 90  —
 85  —
 80  —
 75  ____
 70  —
 65  —
 60  —
 55  —
 50  ____
 45  —
 40  —
 35  —
 30  —
 25  ____
 20  —
 15  —
 10  —
  5  —
  0  ____
```

Sometimes merely constructing this scale will help increase Goal Compatibility as it becomes obvious that you have been investing equal amounts of your resources (time and energy) in the pursuit of goals that are not equally important to you. For example, consider the hypothetical individual whose schedule looks like this:

4:30–5:30 A.M.	Jog
5:30–6:00 A.M.	Shower and dress for work
6:00–6:15 A.M.	Eat a specially prepared diet breakfast

6:15–6:40 A.M.	Drive to station and park car
6:45–7:45 A.M.	Ride train to work
7:45–8:15 A.M.	Take subway downtown
8:30–5:30	**Office time pursuing the goal of becoming a department head**
5:30–6:00 P.M.	Take subway uptown
6:00–7:00 P.M.	Ride train back
7:00–7:20 P.M.	Drive home
7:20–7:30 P.M.	Change into tennis clothes and jog to courts
7:30–8:30 P.M.	Play a set of tennis
8:30–9:30 P.M.	Shower, change, and eat dinner with spouse
9:30–11:00 P.M.	Work on "the book"
11:00–11:30 P.M.	Watch late news on TV with spouse

While this schedule is admittedly hypothetical, it only mildly exaggerates the daily life of many busy people. These individuals often find their enthusiasm and energy running low after a few months of adherence to this type of plan. Not wanting to give up on any of their pursuits, they persist without stopping to ask "why?" Goal Conflict (the opposite of Goal Compatibility) results as resources begin to seem too limited and as goals even out at the same level of importance. Constructing a scale showing relative importance can often reduce this kind of conflict.

If time and energy limitations are the source of your Goal Conflict or Incompatibility, then constructing the scale may have indicated to you ways to shift your resource investment to better match the relative importance of your goals. Another way to better allocate time and energy is to pinpoint those activities that do not contribute to goal achievement and value satisfaction.

To begin, sit back and reflect on the activities that make up a typical week in your life. Write down the ten activities that take most of your time (other than life maintenance activities, such as sleeping and eating). Your list might include:

- Yard work

- Writing

- Reading

- Sales calls

- Filling out trip reports

- Traveling

- Shopping

- Playing with children

- Playing tennis

- Making repairs at home

Next to each activity, note down the value or values the activity helps to satisfy. If an activity satisfies none of your values, write None. Finally, put a star next to those activities that contribute to the values you feel are most important —those that appear in the top half of your list on page 22. Take a few minutes to question the need to engage in time-consuming activities that do not support your values and, in turn, your goals.

Importance of Most Common Activities

ACTIVITIES THAT MAKE UP A TYPICAL WEEK IN MY LIFE	THE VALUES THESE ACTIVITIES HELP TO SATISFY

Resolving Contradictions Between Goals

Resource limitations are responsible for one form of Internal Goal Conflict. A second form of Internal Goal Conflict results from inherently contradictory goals.

Working mothers often complain of the conflict that stems from goal contradiction as they attempt to pursue a full-time career and to also be available to their children whenever needed. Supervisors often experience the same frustrations: "I want to be part of the management team" and "I want to retain the friendship of the workers I supervise." Scan the list of goals you created (pp. 28-30). Do any seem to contradict others? If so, record these contradictory goals here.

Contradictory Goals

THIS GOAL . . .	CONTRADICTS WITH THIS OR THAT GOAL

Sometimes, contradictions in goals are so great that they appear to be unreconcilable. For example, it is simply not possible to "become a ski instructor in Aspen" and to simultaneously "become an archaeologist in Africa." When you face a contradiction in goals, there are two things you can do: give up the goal with the lower priority, or shift your goal focus so that the goal statements become less contradictory.

You shift your goal focus as you consider options to your goal statements. You can do this through asking both "Why?" and "How?" of those statements that appear to be contradictory:

Sample Option List

GOAL STATEMENT →	RESULT OF ASKING "WHY?" →	RESULT OF ASKING "HOW?"
To become a ski→ instructor in Aspen.	So that I can work→ outdoors, and make money while pursuing a sport I enjoy.	Taking any outdoor job that is near snow-covered mountains: - gardening - logging - sports instructor - Himalayas - Andes - Swiss Alps
To become an→ archaeologist in Africa.	So that I can expand→ my awareness of other cultures by living and working with others who lead a life very different from my own.	Living in any foreign culture.

As alternatives emerge, contradictions may often emerge as the result of a failure to consider options in location, method, etc. Consideration of the options available may make it possible to pursue a form of both goals without sacrificing either. The individual in the example would probably experience a high level of Goal Compatibility if he were to become an outdoor sports instructor in Switzerland.

If you are experiencing a lack of Goal Compatibility, I suggest you take a few minutes now to ask yourself "Why?" and then "How?" of the goals you indicated as contradictory on page 35.

GOAL STATEMENT →	RESULT OF ASKING "WHY?" →	RESULT OF ASKING "HOW?"
→	→	
→	→	
→	→	
→	→	

In deciding which option to select, consider those values that you regard as most important, but that you are not fully satisfying. Looking at the notes you made on page 22 and then at your list of options, select the option that would most contribute to satisfaction of your priority values.

Resolving External Goal Conflict

We have looked at ways to resolve two types of Internal Goal Conflict: conflict due to resource limitations and conflict due to inherent contradictions in the goal statements themselves. In both cases, resolution is possible through a consideration of Goal Priorities and Options. Priorities and Options are also important in resolving **External Goal Conflict.**

External Goal Conflict stems from incongruencies between the goals we are pursuing and the goals others are pursuing. This type of conflict is **Self–Other Goal Conflict.** One by-product of the emergence of the "career-oriented mother" has been an increase in familial Goal Conflict. The male spouse finds it necessary to plan his business trips so that he can be home while his equally ambitious wife is on a work assignment in a distant location. Stress might also come from one spouse's academic goals, which interfere with the pursuit of the other spouse's social or leisure time goals. Families with precocious or retarded children often experience an increase in Self–Other Goal Conflict, as the child's special needs require educational experiences that challenge parents' economic goals.

Sometimes, the Self–Other Goal Conflict takes a subtle form and can be subdued, if not resolved, by slight shifts in everyone's daily routine. Other times, decisions must be made that will inevitably favor the goals of one while diminishing the opportunities of the other. Consider the wife who is progressing along a career path that is available only in a large urban area. Then consider her sociologist husband who gets an opportunity to study the lives and habits of the Australian aborigines. If she truly values her career, and if he is genuinely enthusiastic about the research opportunity, the decision that must be made is experienced as a win–lose event. Self–Other Goal Conflict of the win–lose variety is extremely difficult to resolve, and yet must be resolved if the unit (in this case, the couple), is to remain healthy and intact.

It is generally possible to resolve even the most intense Self–Other Goal Conflict if:

- You understand one another's value systems and how the goal or goals at issue fit into those systems.

- The value systems of both you and the other person are such that goal similarity exists in other areas.

- Both of you are willing to problem-solve, to honestly explore alternate means to achieving either or both goals.

- The problem is perceived as being a contradiction in goals, rather than a contest of will or power between two unsupportive, antagonistic persons.

The first step in resolving your Goal Conflict with other people is to make sure you truly understand their value system and that they, in turn, fully understand yours. You might find it helpful to share the Values Clarification process and your results (pp. 24–26) with the individual whose goals conflict with your own. Then, suggest that the other person use the same process to clarify his or her values for both of you. **As you share the results of the values clarification process, it is important that neither of you challenge the value priorities presented as being "true" or "false."** Suspend judgment and try to understand—rather than evaluate or convince—the other person.

After sharing perceptions about and developing a greater understanding of your respective values, work with one another in a mutually helpful way to identify all goals that, if achieved, would lead to satisfaction of "top priority" values. As you go through this process, again, try to suspend judgment. Regard this part of your discussion as an opportunity to expand your thinking and to be creative. Set as your mutual objective the generation of as long a list of goal possibilities as possible.

Developing a list of absolutes, what the chosen goal must do for you, is the next step in resolving external Goal Conflict. In other words, you must now work together to develop a list of criteria for evaluating each possibility. For example, let's consider a couple who needed to decide which of five houses to buy. This couple first listed their "musts" as follows:

- Cost less than $100,000

- Have no fewer than three bedrooms

Next the following "wants" were listed:

- Have a porch
- Be near water
- Have a den
- Be on light-traffic street
- Have a two-car garage
- Be within walking distance of station
- Be within walking distance of schools

The lists could be longer. There is no magic number of "musts" and "wants" for you. Your lists should be extensive enough to include everything you consider critical as well as all "desirables" you would not happily give up. Since one of your objectives is to resolve Goal Conflict, you might include "makes it possible for both of us to pursue our individual goals."

Now let's say our home buyers matched the five possible houses with their "must" criteria, and found that one house did not fit the cost absolute. They would then either have to dismiss that house as a possibility, or reevaluate their financial resources. If they did the latter, they would, in effect, relist one of the "musts" as a "want."

Let's assume our home buyers really couldn't come up with more than $100,000 and so dismissed one house as a possibility. They still had four homes from which to choose, each offering distinct advantages and disadvantages. One house had three bedrooms but only a one-car garage. Another was within walking distance to schools, but not to the station. And so it went. In order to determine which house to buy, they found it necessary to establish priorities among the "wants."

Use of numbers, or "weights" can be helpful as you do this. Assign a number from 1 to 10 to all your "want" criteria, using this scale:

0	1	2	3	4	5	6	7	8	9	10

somewhat desirable, but not important

desirable and somewhat important

extremely important as well as highly desirable

Going through the exercise of "weighting" (assigning numbers to) the criteria can help you to get a fix on their relative importance.

Now, all that remains is to consider the goal possibilities that satisfied your "musts" in the light of the weighted criteria. To do this, you can also make use of numbers:

3 — The alternative totally meets the criterion.

2 — The alternative comes awfully close to meeting the criterion.

1 — The alternative is pretty far afield from meeting the criterion.

0 — The alternative does not meet the criterion at all.

By multiplying the weight you gave to the criterion by the degree to which the alternative meets the criterion, you can get a numerical representation of the "best" goal to pursue. For example, let's say House #4 is located on a dead end and that our couple gave the "light-traffic street" criterion a weight of 8. When you match House #4 (one solution possibility) against the traffic criterion, you get a score of 24. Now, let's say the couple's next criterion was "within walking distance to the station" and that they gave that an importance weight of 7. House #1 is four miles from the station. Well, that's within walking distance, but it's a hefty walk, so House #1 scores a "2"—the alternative comes awfully close to meeting the criterion. The total on this criterion is 2 (score) times 7 (criterion weight) for a total of 14.

All of this is relatively easy to do when you use a chart that lists the criteria and their weights across the top, and the goal possibilities down the side. In the boxes, record the degree to which the alternative meets the criterion identified directly above the box. Using our home buyers again as an example, notice the number in the triangle is the degree to which the alternative meets the criteria multiplied by the criterion weight. To get a total score for each goal possibility, simply add up the scores in the small triangles, going across the page.

The result of this analysis is that the home buyers should consider House #4 as the "best" option (it got a score of 77), assuming the money can be raised. If not, then

House #2 is clearly the best bet. It too, meets all the "musts", and it got a score of 67. A blank format follows for your use.

CRITERIA / GOALS	PURCHASE HOUSE 1 (score / weighted)	PURCHASE HOUSE 2 (score / weighted)	PURCHASE HOUSE 3 (score / weighted)	PURCHASE HOUSE 4 (score / weighted)	
a den — 2	2 / 4	0 / 0	0 / 0	3 / 6	
near the water — 4	0 / 0	1 / 4	1 / 4	2 / 8	
a two-car garage — 2	0 / 0	3 / 6	0 / 0	3 / 6	
a porch — 1	0 / 0	0 / 0	0 / 0	3 / 3	
on a light traffic street — 8	2 / 16	2 / 16	1 / 8	3 / 24	
walking distance to schools — 9	3 / 27	3 / 27	2 / 18	1 / 9	
walking distance to station — 7	2 / 14	2 / 14	0 / 0	3 / 21	
TOTALS (scores × weight)	61	67	30	77	

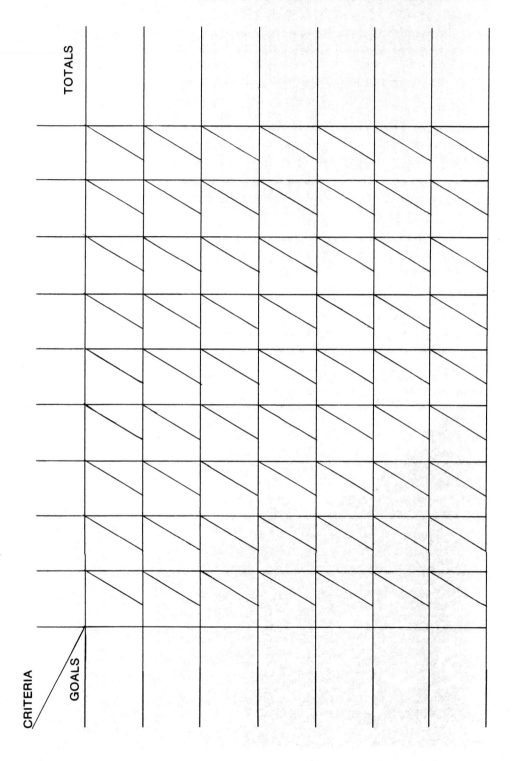

The criteria development and weighting process, in and of itself, can often help alleviate the intensity of Self–Other Goal Conflict. This happens as you involve the other person in the development and weighting of the criteria. Because of this involvement, the alternative that emerges as the "best" genuinely reflects the feelings, needs, and aspirations of both parties to the Conflict.

Goal Conflict in all its forms can be extremely stress-producing. If not resolved, it can create lethargy and despair as the "damned if I do and damned if I don't" feeling begins to overshadow hope and ambition. The lack of Goal Confidence that stems from insufficient Goal Flexibility can be just as detrimental. It too tends to create feelings of entrapment and ennui.

ENHANCING GOAL FLEXIBILITY

Place an "X" at the appropriate point on this scale to indicate your own Goal Flexibility score (see page 19):

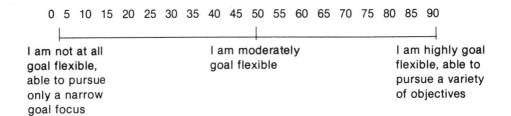

```
0  5  10  15  20  25  30  35  40  45  50  55  60  65  70  75  80  85  90
├────────────────────────────────────┼────────────────────────────────────┤
```

I am not at all goal flexible, able to pursue only a narrow goal focus

I am moderately goal flexible

I am highly goal flexible, able to pursue a variety of objectives

Goal Flexibility refers to the ease and frequency with which an individual can shift energy and focus from one goal to another. The person who is highly goal flexible is able to respond to opportunities and restraints as they appear, realizing the potential inherent in each day.

An individual who experiences tension around Goal Flexibility generally finds it difficult to shift gears and to pursue alternate goals, to experience the stimulation of multiple pursuits. This often leads to a feeling that life is one-sided or limiting.

> **Frustrated Musician:** "I tried to hold down a full-time corporate job and play my music too. After awhile, I stopped playing. Somehow, if I can't be a professional musician, I don't want to play at all. I guess I'm an all-or-nothing person. Now, I don't do anything but work. I probably couldn't play a song from start to finish if I tried."

> **Lethargic Retiree:** "All my life, I was a public relations man. I traveled for the company all the time, hardly giving a thought to my family while I was on the road. I never had a hobby or an outside interest that really meant anything to me. Now, I feel like a nobody. I can't get interested in anything. Oh, I dabble with fixing up the

house, but I can't get serious about it. I have no goals other than staying out of my wife's hair and cajoling the kids and their families to come see me so I can begin to get to know them."

Our frustrated musician experienced Insufficient Goal Flexibility because of a need to be nothing, if not the best. Our lethargic retiree expressed regret combined with a lack of self-esteem. Both are powerful inhibitors to increasing the level of Goal Flexibility. Equally powerful are **Fear of Failure** and **Fear of Success.**

What is Fear of Failure? If I fear failure, I fear being discovered as the essentially weak, incapable, unworthy person that I really believe I am. "I've managed to fool them so far. If I fail, they'll know I'm really not okay." In the last analysis, Fear of Failure stems from a basic sense of personal unworthiness combined with a need to have that unworthiness disconfirmed by others.

Fear of Success is like Fear of Failure in many ways. Consider the fear of success that historically characterizes women. One explanation is that some women fear success because they equate it with aggressive, controlling, and take-charge behaviors—all stereotypically "masculine."[1] In avoiding opportunities to become outwardly successful, such women *may* be attempting to reaffirm their essential femininity. The women who are concerned about being perceived as nonfeminine and who need to have their femininity confirmed by others are expressing a combination of an "I'm unworthy or ineffective" feeling and other-directedness.

Fear of Success is not limited to women, however. Consider someone you know who has repeatedly come very close to "making it happen" only to give up at the last minute ...

- The student who does a great research job, writes 75 percent of the paper, and then surrenders to distractions, failing to complete the assignment.

- The political candidate who runs a fine primary campaign, and then stops making appearances a few short weeks before the election.

- The playwright who never completes the last act.

Why do some people fear success? They often lack self-confidence—confidence in the ability not only to *emerge* on top but to *remain* on top. In a sense, those who refuse to seize opportunities to succeed are saying, "I can't lose what I never had"; "If I don't have the crown, no one else can take it from me"; "If I'm not Number One, there's no chance that I might experience the shame of slipping back to Number Two."

---

[1]Gail Sheehy, *Passages: Predicatable Crises of Adult Life* (New York: E.P. Hutton and Co., Inc., 1976), pp. 114-115.

Another root of Fear of Success is the belief that "Nobody loves a winner." People who believe this may elect to narrow their goal pursuits in order to be loved. The "Third Seed" provides an example:

> **Tennis Pro:** "One of my students has been ranked as Third Seed at our tennis club for years. Each year, I'm convinced that the Third Seed will have no trouble emerging as the Number One match winner. After all, he's in considerably better physical shape than the First Seed, and has a tennis form far superior to that of the Second Seed. But each year the Third Seed comes in third. Why? Because he values the friendship of the First and Second Seeds and is afraid of losing a friend as a result of winning a match."

If the Third Seed had more positive feelings about himself, he would have confidence in his ability to retain the friendship of his tennis friends or to find other friends.

Because of its source, Insufficient Goal Flexibility is difficult, though by no means impossible, to resolve. A significant first step lies in determining **what you are "good at"**—in identifying your **resources** or **positive attributes.** If Insufficient Goal Flexibility is a problem for you, then take a few minutes to list your strengths or resources in *each* of the following areas:

Personal Resources Checklist

KNOWLEDGE (Things I know or understand that I am proud of.)

_____

_____

_____

_____

VOCATIONAL OR AVOCATIONAL SKILLS (Things I can make or services I can provide.)

_____

_____

_____

_____

MANAGEMENT SKILLS (My ability to plan and organize projects involving myself and others.)

_____

_____

_____

_____

INTERPERSONAL SKILLS (Things I do that make people relate well to me; reasons why people might or do like being with me.)

_____

_____

_____

_____

PHYSICAL SKILLS (Things I can do with my body.)

_____

_____

_____

_____

ANALYTICAL, CONCEPTUAL, OR INTELLECTUAL SKILLS (Things I can do with my mind.)

_____

_____

_____

_____

If you experience Insufficient Goal Flexibility, chances are the goals you are presently pursuing are not making adequate use of your resources and your positive attributes. List below those goals you spend the most time and energy pursuing. Then, next to each goal statement, note the resources or positive attributes which are utilized in the process of pursuing the goal.

Resource Utilization in Pursuit of Goals

GOAL STATEMENTS	RESOURCES OR POSITIVE ATTRIBUTES THAT ARE UTILIZED

Next, look back at your resource analysis format. Circle all those attributes that are not being utilized fully. **Consider additional goals you might pursue that make use of these resources while contributing to the satisfaction of your values.**

We've looked at how fear of failure and fear of success can result in Insufficient Goal Flexibility, the inability to shift energies to pursue alternative goals. These are all "internal blocks." Sometimes, "external blocks" arise that deter an individual from shifting his or her focus. Consider the lament of one unfulfilled craftsman:

> "I never even considered trying to become anything other than a carpenter. My father and my father's father were carpenters. Those were the only skills I had. Somehow, it was just the thing to do. Even if I had wanted to follow another trade, there was no money for education. I had to go to work when I was fourteen."

When external barriers result in Insufficient Goal Flexibility, lack of Goal Control is contributing to and exaggerating lack of Goal Flexibility.

ENHANCING GOAL CONTROL

Place an "X" on the following scale to indicate your own Goal Control score (see p. 19):

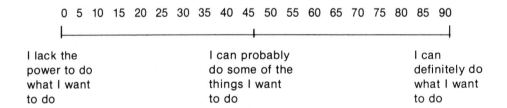

| 0 5 10 15 20 25 30 35 40 45 50 55 60 65 70 75 80 85 90 |

I lack the power to do what I want to do

I can probably do some of the things I want to do

I can definitely do what I want to do

Chapter 1 focused on the immobilization and bitterness that can result from lack of personal empowerment. People who experience tension over Insufficient Goal Control are feeling underempowered: "I can't be what I want to be, or become what I want to become." Enhancing Goal Control really amounts to identifying your goals, analyzing the barriers to reaching your goals and then problem-solving in order to find ways to overcome these barriers.

If you experience less Goal Control than you want, then take the time to identify the barriers. Consider any one of the priority goals that you are having difficulty accomplishing. Ask yourself, "What behaviors should I be displaying that I am not if I am to achieve my goal?"

Sample Barriers Analysis

GOAL: TO BECOME A PRODUCT MANAGER

BEHAVIORS THAT I SHOULD BE DISPLAYING AND AM NOT:

1. learning more about the product and marketing methods

2. giving my boss a reason to like and trust me

3. watching for product manager openings

Several formats for your use follow.

Barriers Analysis

GOAL: _____

_____

BEHAVIORS THAT I SHOULD BE DISPLAYING AND AM NOT:

1.

2.

3.

4.

GOAL: _____

_____

BEHAVIORS THAT I SHOULD BE DISPLAYING AND AM NOT:

1.

2.

3.

4.

Barriers Analysis (cont'd.)

GOAL: _____

_____

BEHAVIORS THAT I SHOULD BE DISPLAYING AND AM NOT:

1.

2.

3.

4.

GOAL: _____

_____

BEHAVIORS THAT I SHOULD BE DISPLAYING AND AM NOT:

1.

2.

3.

4.

Next, list as many reasons as you can as to why the behaviors you feel should be occurring are not. Do this separately for each behavior. Make your lists as long as possible. A sample format follows.

Sample Behavior Analysis

BEHAVIORS THAT I SHOULD BE DISPLAYING AND AM NOT: learning more about the product and about marketing methods

WHY NOT (BARRIERS):

1. I am not on the routing list for periodicals that deal with the product or its marketing.

2. I do not see corporate correspondence dealing with marketing approaches.

3. I don't like to take work home.

A format for your use follows. (Several additional blank formats can be found in Appendix B.)

Behaviors Analysis

BEHAVIOR THAT I SHOULD BE DISPLAYING AND AM NOT:

_____

_____

WHY NOT (BARRIERS):

1.

2.

3.

4.

5.

Often, people stop with an analysis of barriers, feeling that the barriers can never be overcome, and justifying their lack of goal attainment on the basis of the obstacles they face. A more constructive approach is to try to identify **Root Causes**. This happens as we take each barrier in turn and ask, "What could or does this result from?" Again, it is helpful to make these lists as long as possible. Here are a few examples of this process in action:

Sample Root Causes Analyses

BARRIER 1:   I AM NOT ON THE ROUTING LIST FOR PERIODICALS
              THAT DEAL WITH THE PRODUCT OR ITS MARKETING

WHAT THIS COULD RESULT FROM (ROOT CAUSES):

1.   I have never expressed an interest in the periodical.

2.   There are too few copies to go around in the office.

3.   My boss doesn't want me reading "unnecessary material" in the office.

BARRIER 2:   I DON'T LIKE TO TAKE WORK HOME

WHAT THIS COULD RESULT FROM (ROOT CAUSES):

1.   I have no quiet place to work at home.

2.   I must help with dinner, play with the kids, and fix things around the
     house in the evenings.

3.   I get tired of sitting, and need to be physically active at night.

Here are two formats for your Root Cause analysis. Additional blank formats are provided in Appendix C.

Root Cause Analysis

BARRIER: _____

_____

WHAT THIS COULD RESULT FROM (ROOT CAUSES):

1.

2.

3.

4.

5.

BARRIER: _____

_____

WHAT THIS COULD RESULT FROM (ROOT CAUSES):

1.

2.

3.

4.

5.

As people go through this process, they often discover that the majority of the "root" causes" they have listed either involve others or, more specifically, lay blame on others. A cursory glance at the sample root causes list would indicate that the "problem" in the situation is partially the spouse, the kids, and the boss. It is so easy and so very tempting to play the psychological game, "If It Weren't For Them," and to avoid taking responsibility for our own lives. If too many of your root causes lay blame or implicate others, then stop for a minute and try to expand your list to indicate the problems you are creating for yourself.

After doing a thorough Barriers Analysis, it is a relatively simple matter to find answers to the next question, "What can I do about this, and in the process diminish or remove the barrier?" Again make your list of solution possibilities as extensive and realistic as possible. In other words, identify all your real behavioral options …

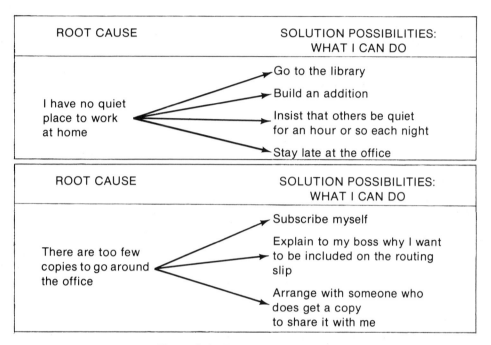

Figure 2.1   Removing Barriers

Here and on the following page are formats for your use:

Managing Root Causes

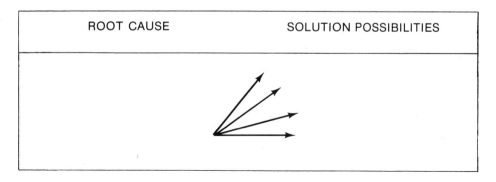

Managing Root Causes

ROOT CAUSE	SOLUTION POSSIBILITIES
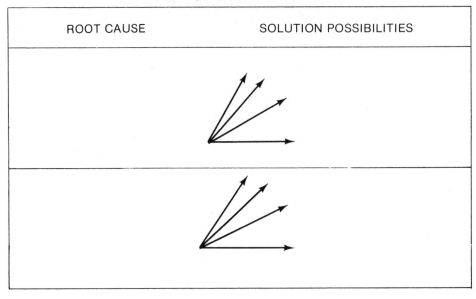	

By focusing on what you can do to manage the root causes you are likely to find that, with little or no assistance from others, you can do much to increase your level of Goal Control. Occasionally, the options you generate will be so numerous that you will need to establish priorities. One useful way to do this is to apply the following criteria to your options, or "solution possibilities":

- **Cost:** the input in terms of resources (time, energy, money, etc.) you will have to provide.

- **Contribution:** the extent to which the solution will, in fact, lead to removal of the barrier.

- **Feasibility:** how realistic is implementation of the solution alternative?

To apply these criteria, first record all your options in the left column of the chart on page 54 . Then, put an "H", "M", or "L" under each criterion, beside each solution option to indicate:

H: High Feasibility, High Cost, or High Contribution/Impact

M: Moderate Feasibility, Moderate Cost, or Moderate Contribution/Impact

L: Low Feasibility, Low Cost, or Low Contribution/Impact

OPTION/SOLUTION	COST	CONTRIBUTION	FEASIBILITY
Go to the library	L	H	M
Build an addition	H	H	L
Insist that others be quiet	L	H	M
Stay late at the office	L	H	L

This process will be most useful to you if you first consider "cost" for all your options, then "contribution," then "feasibility."

By scanning the scores, you can narrow the range of options and begin to put your plan into action. In assessing your options, apply this frame of reference:

Option Values

OPTION	COST	CONTRIBUTION	FEASIBILITY
DO IT	L	H	H
SERIOUSLY CONSIDER	L	M	H
	L	H	M
BACK-UP IDEA	M	M	M
	H	H	H
FORGET IT	H	L	L
	H	M	L

Turn the page to find a blank format for your use.

Appraising My Options

OPTION	COST	CONTRIBUTION	FEASIBILITY

Occasionally, the product of the feasibility assessment is a preponderance of "L's." This happens when people feel they don't have the resources or the power to implement their solution ideas.

More often than not, it is possible for these people to acquire the power or resources necessary for action. In the next chapter, you'll have a chance to consider ways to increase your power—your ability to influence the events that appear to restrict Goal Control.

3

Six Kinds of Power, and How To Acquire More of Each

You've established an objective, a goal, and are determined to achieve it. Then something happens, and you find yourself in a position where others are using their power to thwart your efforts:

- As manager of new products development, you've decided to build a prototype of Product "X." You're certain Product "X" has a ready market, and that the dramatic sales potential will boost corporate profits and land you a much desired promotion. The executive committee rules that no funds will be made available for prototype development and testing.

- As manager of employee relations, you set as your objective the implementation of a massive employee attitude survey. After months of research, you have selected the consulting firm you feel is best qualified to do the job. The director of personnel decides to okay the project, but only if you use the services of his consultant friend.

- As director of financial planning, you determine that you need certain information from the field regarding cost increases. Managers refuse to cooperate. Since you have no power to insist that they do, your efforts to introduce a systematic cost-reduction program are stymied.

In each of the above examples, the **Formal Power** of others was used to thwart the efforts of the new products development manager, the manager of employee relations, and the financial planner. The executive committee had more formal power than the new products manager. Similarly, hierarchy was on the side of the director of personnel. Likewise, the field had the "legitimate" right to refuse the information. In no case did our managers have the power to insist upon reversal of the decisions.

They each had some options, however. The nature and potential effectiveness of those options depended upon the **power base** they had managed to establish.

There are six distinct forms of power. Before considering them, take a few minutes to assess the nature and extent of your current power bases.

To begin, identify a goal you want to accomplish that can only be accomplished if you influence the behavior of others. Let's call these others "**key actors**": they are "key" because they can significantly hinder or help you in your efforts to achieve your goal; they are "actors" because goal achievement is dependent on their willingness to actually do something. The actions you need key actors to take are called "key actions."

Sample Actor/Action Identification

GOAL	KEY ACTORS	KEY ACTIONS
To write and publish a book	1. Publisher	1. To agree to publish, produce, and market the text
	2. Spouse	2. To help provide quiet writing time
	3. Boss	3. To provide extra time off to do research, etc.
To sell 40,000 units this year	1. Customer	1. To buy
	2. Manufacturer	2. To provide the product on time
	3. Sales Manager	3. To provide leads and a desirable territory

Using the following format, record one of your goals. Then, identify three key actors, and specifically what you want them to do (i.e., the key actions).

Identify Key Actors and Actions

GOAL	KEY ACTORS	KEY ACTIONS
	1.	1.
	2.	2.
	3.	3.

Now, bearing this goal and set of key actors in mind, read each of the following statements. Next to each statement, and for each key actor, record a 0, 1, 2, or 3 to indicate:

0 = Completely false
1 = More false than true
2 = More true than false
3 = Totally true

Here's an example:

	KEY ACTOR I (CUSTOMER)	KEY ACTOR II (MANUFAC-TURER)	KEY ACTOR III (SALES MANAGER)
1. I have something the key actor wants or values and can make it available to him or her.	3	1	2
2. I can hurt the key actor.	0	1	2

As you complete the profile, keep the same goal in mind. I suggest you consider one key actor at a time, completing all items on that actor, before beginning again with the first item with regard to your second key actor.

Determining Your Power Bases

THE GOAL I HAVE IN MIND IS: _____

	KEY ACTOR I (_____)	KEY ACTOR II (_____)	KEY ACTOR III (_____)
1. I have something my key actor wants or values and can make it available to him or her.	_____	_____	_____
2. I can hurt my key actor.	_____	_____	_____
3. The organization has granted me the authority to ask for what I want.	_____	_____	_____
4. I can help my key actor achieve his or her goals or satisfy his or her wants.	_____	_____	_____

KEY:

0 = Completely false
1 = More false than true
2 = More true than false
3 = Totally true

	KEY ACTOR I (_____)	KEY ACTOR II (_____)	KEY ACTOR III (_____)
5. I am in a position to get someone whose credentials my key actor respects to act on my behalf.	_____	_____	_____
6. I can convince someone else to hurt, punish, or deprive my key actor if I so choose.	_____	_____	_____
7. My key actor believes we have a lot in common.	_____	_____	_____
8. I know what names to drop to impress my key actor.	_____	_____	_____
9. My key actor respects the knowledge I have in areas related to my goal.	_____	_____	_____
10. I can hinder my key actor from achieving his or her goals or satisfying his or her wants.	_____	_____	_____
11. I can get someone else to give my key actor what he or she wants if I so choose.	_____	_____	_____
12. My key actor regards me as a friend.	_____	_____	_____
13. I know people who impress my key actor.	_____	_____	_____
14. I am in a position to get a friend of my key actor to act on my behalf.	_____	_____	_____
15. I am in a position to get someone else who is well connected to influence my key actor if I so choose.	_____	_____	_____
16. My key actor respects my credentials as they relate to my goal.	_____	_____	_____

	KEY ACTOR I (_____)	KEY ACTOR II (_____)	KEY ACTOR III (_____)

17. If I asked directly for what I want, my key actor would feel my making the request was appropriate.   _____   _____   _____

18. I can get someone else who has a legitimate "right" to do so to request what I need from my key actor.   _____   _____   _____

KEY:

0 = Completely false
1 = More false than true
2 = More true than false
3 = Totally true

To score your power base assessment, complete the following chart:

Power Base Scoresheet

			KEY ACTOR I	KEY ACTOR II	KEY ACTOR III
F O R M A L P O W E R	REWARD	ITEM 1			
		ITEM 4			
		ITEM 11			
		SUBTOTAL (1)			
	COERCIVE	ITEM 2			
		ITEM 6			
		ITEM 10			
		SUBTOTAL (2)			
	LEGITIMATE	ITEM 3			
		ITEM 17			
		ITEM 18			
		SUBTOTAL (3)			

Power Base Scoresheet (cont'd.)

			KEY ACTOR I	KEY ACTOR II	KEY ACTOR III
I N F O R M A L P O W E R	EXPERT	ITEM 5			
		ITEM 9			
		ITEM 16			
		SUBTOTAL (4)			
	REFERENT	ITEM 7			
		ITEM 12			
		ITEM 14			
		SUBTOTAL (5)			
	ASSOCIATIVE	ITEM 8			
		ITEM 13			
		ITEM 15			
		SUBTOTAL (6)			

The totals under each Key Actor column indicate how much power you have with each key actor as you begin to attempt to influence him or her to achieve your goal. **Absolute totals, however, may be misleading; it is possible that the kind of power you have over your key actor is inappropriate, or even counter-productive, given your goal and the type of support or behavior you are seeking to obtain.**

The eighteen items in the power profile reflect six distinct types of power. Three of these power bases can be categorized as **Formal Power,** another three as informal. In the pages that follow, each of the types will be discussed. I suggest you record your scores as we discuss each type of power.

Formal vs. Informal Power

	Actor I	Actor II	Actor III
My total Formal Power scores (total of first 3 subtotals) are:	☐	☐	☐
My total Informal Power scores (total of last 3 subtotals) are:	☐	☐	☐
Possible Score Range: 0-27			

When an organization promotes someone to manager, the promotion generally involves a change in Formal Power. Formal Power is conferred on a person; it is not necessarily earned. In other words, Formal Power is a function of position, not necessarily ability. Generally, when people think of power, they think only of formal power, and more particularly, of the power to reward others for compliance or to punish others for noncompliance: "Do it or you'll lose your job," or "Get it done early and I'll recommend a raise." Two types of Formal Power are the power to **reward** and the power to **punish.**

The Power to Reward and to Punish

	Actor I	Actor II	Actor III
My Reward Power scores are: (1st subtotals, page 59)	☐	☐	☐
My Coercive Power scores are: (2nd subtotals, page 59)	☐	☐	☐
Possible Score Range: 0-9			

When someone can exercise **Reward Power** over another, he or she is in a position to **provide** something the other wants or values. A prospective client has Reward Power over a consultant who wants to obtain a contract. A bank has Reward Power over the prospective home owner who wishes to secure a mortgage.

Coercive Power is the opposite of Reward Power. To say that someone has Coercive Power over another is to say that he or she is in a position to **take away** something the other possesses and desires to keep. A manager's power to demote (to take away an existing title) is Coercive. Conversely, the power to promote (to provide a better position) is Reward. A parent's power to loan the car is Reward; his or her power to impose a curfew is perceived as Coercive.

---

[1]For a further discussion of types of power, see J. French and B. Raven, "The Bases of Social Power." *Studies in Social Power,* ed. D. Cartright (Ann Arbor, MI: University of Michigan Press, 1959), pp. 118-149.

Many roles come with both Reward and Coercive Power. Organization charts and job descriptions generally distinguish one managerial level from another by providing precise descriptions of managerial clout. This clout or "span or control" describes how many others in the organization are subject to the manager's defined power to reward and to punish. The director of training can fire or promote a training specialist, but he or she cannot fire the president. The president, on the other hand, can presumably reward or punish everyone in the organization.

As hierarchical level increases, so does the power to reward and to punish. That may be one of the reasons many chief executive officers report a strong sense of resistance on the part of organization members to "level," to openly speak their minds, and to function other than as organizational "yes men." While seeking Rewards the "top man" can provide, employees are often more afraid of his or her equally persuasive ability to punish.

Should managers rely on Reward and Coercive Power as a primary influence device? Heavy use of Coercive Power (threatening punishment for noncompliance) can lead to dislike and mistrust. This negative reaction, in turn, may increase the likelihood that nonproductive behavior will occur. The surveillance required by use of Coercive Power can also make it less desirable. Because people tend to remain uncommitted (or antagonistic) to whatever they are forced to do, influence stemming from a Coercive Power Base will usually continue only as long as surveillance continues.[2]

Surveillance is also a potential problem when a manager relies heavily and consistently on Reward Power, or on the ability to give another person something valued in exchange for compliance. Reward Power is less effective when the manager misjudges what is valued or desired by the person he or she is attempting to influence; the increasing use of variable or "cafeteria" benefit plans whereby employees elect a combination of benefits (such as insurance, retirement, vacation) to best suit their unique needs may reflect an awareness of variations in what people perceive as rewarding. Another disadvantage inherent in relying on Reward Power is the human tendency to begin to regard rewards as "rights." Give a 5 percent merit raise three years in a row and try withholding it the next year—chances are the employee will feel deprived of a basic "right."

If your organization has given you a large measure of Reward or Coercive Power over others, you might be wise to step back and consider how heavily you tend to rely on this organizational gift. Reward and Coercive Power must be used with caution. **Avoid the consistent use of the "stick" unless you can be around all the time to make sure others are doing what you have directed them to do. Be careful of "buying" work with the promise of a "carrot"—you may run out of carrots, or they may grow stale.**

If managers are granted Reward and Coercive Power, must they use it? There are a number of choices available. Joint performance appraisals in which the subordinate evaluates the superior's contribution as well as vice versa help equalize Reward

---

[2]For a discussion of Coercive Power's negative effects, see Bernard Bass, *Organizational Psychology* (Boston: Allyn and Bacon, Inc., 1965), pp. 171-174; also see B. Raven and J. French, "Legitimate Power, Coercive Power and Observability in Social Influence." *Sociometry* 21 (1958): pp. 83-97.

and Coercive Power. The emergence of the "nonsupervisory shop," in which, among other things, everyone helps determine everyone else's salary, represents another attempt to diffuse the power to reward and to punish.

While a few managers have attempted to reduce Reward and Coercive Power differentials, they are slower to alter their reliance on a third kind of power—Legitimate or Position Power.

The Power of Your Position

	Actor I	Actor II	Actor III
My Legitimate Power scores (3rd subtotals, page 59) are:	☐	☐	☐
Possible Score Range: 0-9			

Legitimate Power is based on a definition of the rights and privileges that adhere to persons because of the roles they fulfill, such as presidents, generals, and executives. Presidents have Legitimate Power over nations as long as the people respect their right to rule. Since Legitimate Power, by definition, exists only when both parties to a relationship accept a certain set of role expectations, Legitimate Power does *not* precipitate the rebellion and resentment that characterize the common response to Coercive Power. This may explain why, after a military coup, the new regime seeks to replace Coercive Power with Legitimate Power by proving "right to rule," rigging elections, etc.

It can be argued that Legitimate Power is critical to the smooth functioning of any group, whether that group be a family, an organization, or an entire nation. If no one had the "right" to issue combat orders, there would be no success on the battlefield. If all business decisions were made by committees, the time lag between opportunity and action would be so great as to cripple the organization. If parents did not have the "right" to guide their children's activities, the socialization process would be severely hampered.

People seem to need a sense of predictability about their world. Part of that predictability is provided by a social structure of clearly defined roles. A group of strangers who come together for a purpose will in short order create a leader, a recorder, a summarizer or "devil's advocate," and so on. This happens in training sessions, task forces, and ad hoc discussion groups of all types. Once these roles are clarified, incumbents begin to enjoy exclusive "rights" due to their position. The group expects its leader to recommend (or even insist on) a certain procedure for approaching a task. If the "summarizer" does so, he or she is often ignored or resented for "usurping the leader's rights."

The emergence of cults and cult leaders provides another opportunity to observe the acting out of the need for role definition, structure, and the conferring of Legitimate Power on certain members of the community. Occasionally, the extent to which people willingly confer such power on another is disturbing to those of us who do not share their values. Parents are both astounded and disturbed when their formerly rebellious children grant control of their actions, dress, and, in many cases, thoughts, to modern-day religious leaders.

Legitimate Power, then, can be an extremely powerful force if it is supplemented by other forms of power. It is unlikely that the children who join religious communities would willingly sacrifice family and material possessions if they did not simultaneously think their new leader could offer something critically needed in exchange. It is unlikely that soldiers follow the commanding officer's orders simply because he is of higher rank. The threat of court-martial or the desire for a promotion increases the likelihood that the exercise of Legitimate Power will work as intended.

We have seen that people who rely on Formal Power back up their influence attempts with messages like these:

- Do it because of who I am: Legitimate Power.

- Do it because I can hurt you if you don't comply: Coercive Power.

- Do it because I can help you if you comply: Reward Power.

Organizational charts depict the ability of its members to deliver these kinds of messages. These charts, however, do not explain adequately who really makes things happen in an organization. The uncharted hierarchy—the influence strata based on Informal Power—can be just as critical to organizational health as the announced managerial structure. **Informal Power includes expert, referent, and associative forms of leverage.** These kinds of power must be earned and maintained. Unlike Formal Power bases, they can not be conferred.

The Power of the Expert

	Actor I	Actor II	Actor III
My Expert Power scores (4th subtotals) are: (page 60) Possible Score Range: 0-9	☐	☐	☐

Expert Power is the capacity to influence because of the knowledge or skills a person has or is presumed to have. I have Expert Power when you are willing to do as I suggest because you respect my expertise or ability.

Expert Power is a key factor in the influence attempts made by corporate planners, personnel managers, and other staff persons who typically have little or no Formal Power to direct the activities of their internal clients. It is also the primary power base of professionals who offer advice, guidance, and counsel.

And yet, having expertise does not guarantee that an individual can exercise Expert Power. **People can only exercise Expert Power if others recognize their expertise.** Expert Power cannot be conferred on a person; it must be earned. Universities and graduate schools confer degrees, but only rarely, however, can the degree or the credential by itself provide an Expert Power base. **If your expert base is to be useful, it must be possible not only for you to produce expert results, but first to convince others that you deserve their attention. You are only an expert if others give you the opportunity to be one.**

The Power of Trust and Affection

	Actor I	Actor II	Actor III
My Referent Power scores (5th subtotals) are: (page 60)	☐	☐	☐
Possible Score Range: 0-9			

Expert Power can be strengthened by a second kind of nonconferrable or Informal Power—**Referent Power.** Referent Power is based on one person's or group's affection for, or identification with, another person or group. If I like you and I perceive many similarities between our situations or needs, I will be open to your influence. The staff person who learns to use the jargon common to an operating division may be attempting to use Referent Power.

Referent Power is frequently the primary energizer of good interdepartmental relationships, and its absence can become the primary block. In one large insurance company, the underwriter's Referent Power was the major determinant of whether or not the underwriter got comprehensive or inadequate risk inspection reports from the survey people. Inadequate inspection reports could lead an underwriter to accept a "bad" risk (one that could produce a high ratio of losses to premiums). Since underwriters' salaries were based on their loss ratios, the survey people exercised a real measure of Coercive Power over the underwriters.

Further, because underwriters saw the survey department as staffed by individuals who couldn't quite make the grade in underwriting, survey personnel were antagonistic toward them. The underwriters had no Formal Power whatsoever over the survey people. The only way for an underwriter to insure adequate inspection reports was to spend time with the survey people, building good working relationships and learning to speak their language (Referent Power).

People who "speak the same language" as others, then, can often exercise Referent Power. Similarly, persons who are part of a defined voluntary group can generally exercise Referent Power over other members of that group, given the assumption, "Since we both chose to join, we must have something in common." It is thus not unusual to find that managers who usually support one another on the job belong to the same social or sports club.

In its purest sense, Referent Power is the power of **friendship,** of mutual affection and trust. Think of the people you know who would do as you ask simply because they like you and trust you. You have Referent Power over these persons.

Perhaps the most visible examples of Referent Power are provided by early adolescents.[3] Children between the ages of eleven and thirteen frequently tend to establish tightly knit peer groups, and to then define the boundaries of the group with a "club" label, similar clothing styles, and other signs of "membership." Children who are not fortunate enough to be part of the group have a difficult time convincing any member of the "in-group" to do anything without the express approval of the group as a whole:

> "If you go shopping with Elizabeth, we won't be your friends."

> "Tomorrow, we're all wearing yellow shirts and blue jeans. Make sure you don't tell Jim."

The degree of Referent Power that can be exercised by such a group over its members can be a source of great frustration to the parents when they find the peers persuading the child to do things that are inconvenient, or even antithetical, to their own values:

> "What do you mean, you absolutely have to have your yellow shirt? It's in the laundry. You've got ten other shirts to choose from!"

Expert and referent types of Informal Power can provide a significant basis for influence. If you lack Formal (Coercive, Reward, and Legitimate) Power, you can still shape the behavior of others. But what if you are not in a position to influence through friendship or expertise? There is an additional kind of Informal Power that may be available to you—**Associative Power.**

It's Not What You Know, But Who You Know

	Actor I	Actor II	Actor III
My Associate Power scores (6th subtotals) are: (page 60)	☐	☐	☐

People use Associative Power when they influence others on the basis of who they know, rather than what they know or what they can do. These people often drop names:

> "Last year, while I was working with John Kenneth Galbraith . . ."

> "It might interest you to know that my father-in-law is related to the Rockefellers."

Why do people drop names? Presumably, to increase their ability to influence your judgment or behavior. And sometimes, it works. Why? One explanation is an unstated,

---

[3]For a further discussion of the power of the adolescent peer group, see John E. Horrocks, *The Psychology of Adolescence: Behavior and Development* (Boston: Houghton Mifflin Co., 1962), pp. 219-247.

general feeling that "If this person is sifficiently worthy, important, and significant to know, and implicitly to be respected by those other people, I'd better listen to him or her."

Associative Power needs to be exercised with great caution and discretion if it is to be effective; name droppers are not generally respected. The primary difference between name droppers who get nowhere and persons who use Associative Power effectively is **relevance** and **timeliness.** If my friendship with an industry leader is **relevant** to a problem or objective that you have or that we share, then you are likely to be interested in hearing of that friendship. If the association is of no concern or help to you, then you are likely to perceive my mention of the friendship as an offensive attempt to blow my own horn.

Generally my merely knowing someone important provides little leverage by itself. The leverage increases as people I name have themselves power over you:

> "I am a good friend of John James. I'm sure that if he were aware of our intentions, he would want to help."

While, on the surface, this example may appear to involve the use of Associative Power, on closer inspection we find it is really an **indirect use of the power of another.** It's not really who I know that impresses you, but my ability to gain access to that person's resources.

THE DIRECT AND INDIRECT USE OF POWER

Any of the six kinds of power can be exercised directly or indirectly. **The direct use of power is reliance on one's own ability** to deliver rewards, to mete out punishments, to give advice, etc.

The indirect use of power occurs when one person relies on the power of a second person to influence a third. I may have no power base in my relationship with you, but if I know someone you like, respect, or value, I may be able to get that person to influence you for me:

> **Using Referent Power Indirectly:** "If we're going to get the appropriations committee to approve this one, we'd better seek John's endorsement. The committee really trusts John's judgment in these areas."

> **Using Expert Power Indirectly:** "If we're going to get that specialist to consider your case, we'll have to convince Dr. James to call him on your behalf."

> **Using Referent Power Indirectly:** "If we're going to get the appropriate committee to approve this one, we'd better seek John's endorsement. The committee really trusts John's judgment in these areas."

While the use of the power of others can be effective, it is a highly risky option. There is always the possibility that the intermediary you select will, intentionally or unintentionally, distort your intent or misrepresent your objectives. Further, you risk incurring the intermediary's resentment as you ask one favor too many. Finally, the person whom you are attempting to influence may begin to lose respect for you or your cause as you persist in getting others to speak or act for you.

Most people can find a way to build a power base even if they have not been endowed with formal sources of leverage. Occasionally, not having Coercive and Reward Power can be an advantage, since it provides an incentive to earn Expert and Referent Power, and thus to build and maintain trusting relationships with others.

Now, let's return to the questionnaire you completed earlier, (see pp. 57-59) and begin to take stock of the kinds of leverage you have at your disposal. We'll begin by assessing your ability to reflect on direct rather than indirect forms of leverage. Complete the following chart by referring to the scores you recorded on pages 59–60.

TYPE OF POWER	DIRECT LEVERAGE		Key Actor I			Key Actor II			Key Actor III			INDIRECT LEVERAGE	
	ITEMS	SCORES	D	D÷2	I	D	D÷2	I	D	D÷2	I	ITEMS	SCORES
REWARD	1 + 4											11	
COERCIVE	2 + 10											6	
LEGITIMATE	3 + 17											18	
EXPERT	9 + 16											5	
REFERENT	7 + 12											14	
ASSOCIATIVE	8 + 13											15	
TOTALS													

For example, if your scores for items 1, 4, and 11 for your key actors were:

ITEM	SCORES
1	3
4	3
11	1

You would complete the first line on the chart as follows . . .

NOTE: "D" stands for "Direct," and "I" stands for "Indirect."

TYPE OF POWER	DIRECT LEVERAGE		KEY ACTOR I			INDIRECT LEVERAGE	
	ITEMS	SCORES	D	D÷2	I	ITEMS	SCORES
REWARD	1 + 4	3 + 3	6	3	1	11	1

Note that, comparing the direct and indirect forms of leverage totals for each key actor, we divide the D (Direct) score by two because there were twice as many direct leverage items as indirect.

To interpret the profile, find your two highest scores for each key actor. As you look at your scores, consider only the scores in the columns "D÷2" and "I." Note the highest score as your primary power base and the second highest score as your secondary power base. Then, check the "D" or "I" to show whether the power is direct (falling in the "D÷2" column) or indirect (falling in the "I" column).

KEY ACTOR	PRIMARY POWER BASE	SECONDARY POWER BASE
I _____	_____ D □ I □	_____ D □ I □
II _____	_____ D □ I □	_____ D □ I □
III _____	_____ D □ I □	_____ D □ I □

How appropriate and effective are your primary and secondary power bases? To answer this question, you'll need to consider both the advantages and disadvantages associated with the use of each type of power. The outcomes of each can be dramatically different. For example, the use of Reward and Coercive Power can stimulate rapid action. It does not tend to inspire the ongoing levels of commitment that the effective use of Expert or Referent Power can stimulate. Conversely, if you elect to rely on Referent or Expert Power, you risk rejection of your request.

The outcomes (both positive and negative) that tend to occur as we exercise each type of power are summarized on the chart on the following pages. Considering each of your key actors one at a time, place a checkmark (✔) beside each outcome you need or want in the first column, and beside each outcome you can tolerate or accept in the second column.

Primary and Secondary Power Bases

EXERCISE	KEY ACTORS I II III	I WANT/NEED	KEY ACTORS I II III	AND CAN TOLERATE/ACCEPT
REWARD POWER	☐ ☐	rapid action.	☐ ☐ ☐	desire on the part of the other person to do the minimum required to get the reward.
	☐ ☐	some form of give-and-take with the other person as to "how many rewards" are warranted by "how much work."	☐ ☐ ☐	diminishing ability to influence as reward begins to lose its appeal; as it begins to be assumed to be a "right."
			☐ ☐ ☐	the need to keep making the reward more attractive.
COERCIVE POWER	☐ ☐	rapid action.	☐ ☐ ☐	resentment toward me.
	☐ ☐	absolute compliance (or that the other person do things "my way").	☐ ☐ ☐	fear of me.
			☐ ☐ ☐	desire on the part of the other person to withdraw from the situation as soon as possible.
			☐ ☐ ☐	diminishing ability to influence as coercion begins to lose its ability to provoke fear (and action).
			☐ ☐ ☐	need for constant surveillance lest the other "stop performing."

Power	☐☐☐	☐☐☐
LEGITIMATE POWER	compliance with my wishes, without resentment.	lack of certainty that desired action will occur, as the other person questions whether I do, in fact, have a certain set of "rights."
ASSOCIATIVE POWER	the other person to know I am acquainted with "impressive" persons who value me and my beliefs.	rejection of my request if the other person is not impressed.
REFERENT POWER	to inspire commitment to *me*, as opposed to a specific task. a give-and-take as to what's best for both of us.	being "open" or vulnerable to the other person, risking rejection of my request. need to *work* to maintain trust levels, as trust is difficult to build and easy to destroy.
EXPERT POWER	commitment to the project or program, to what I want the other to do.	need to work to *maintain* respect of the other. challenge of my methods when the other person discovers another "expert" who has a different opinion.
INDIRECT POWER	action on the part of someone I can't influence or with whom I don't want to interact.	using up a favor. refusal on the part of the influencer to do as I ask. chance that the primary influencer will misinterpret my wishes. the negative outcomes associated with the type of leverage the third party will use.

After completing the chart for each of your three key actors, go back and consider the pattern of your checkmarks. **Reliance on a particular power base is probably not appropriate if you can't tolerate or accept any of the possible negative outcomes.** In other words, if you have no checkmarks in Column II for a particular power base, then you should probably strive to find another way to influence your key actor.

After going through this process for each of your key actors, it is possible that you will find that the power bases currently available to you are not appropriate; perhaps they are not compatible with what you are trying to achieve or willing to accept in terms of the relationship. What then? The next step is to consider what you can do to establish the kind of power base you need to succeed in the way you want to succeed.

STRATEGIES FOR GETTING POWER

When people feel they lack the power to accomplish their goals, they do one of two things: they give up, or they attempt to increase or diversify their power bases. Most of us are continually involved in attempts to get in a position of influence (to enhance our power base) or to actually influence others. The most effective influence attempts involve effecting outcomes while simultaneously enhancing our power base—our ability to influence future outcomes. The author who writes a book is (ideally) influencing the behavior of readers while simultaneously building Expert Power. The salesman who "rewards" a prospect with a valued commodity generally attempts to do so in such a way that a Referent base begins to emerge that, in turn, will make future calls both more pleasant and more profitable. The friend who caringly offers counsel and advice is attempting to influence the behavior of the other person and is, at the same time, whether wittingly or unwittingly, intensifying the Referent base.

Seven distinct power-getting strategies are available to you. If you determined that you are not in a position to influence your key actors with the most appropriate power base, then keep these key actors in mind as you complete the following profile. If you already have the required leverage, then identify another goal you wish to accomplish and the key actors whose support you will need. Scan the chart on pages 70 and 71 to identify the kind or kinds of power that would be most appropriate or effective with each key actor. Make your notes here:

My goal is to: _____

KEY ACTOR I	KEY ACTOR II	KEY ACTOR III
Indicated Power Base	Indicated Power Base	Indicated Power Base
Primary:	Primary:	Primary:
_____	_____	_____
_____	_____	_____

KEY ACTOR I	KEY ACTOR II	KEY ACTOR III
Indicated Power Base	Indicated Power Base	Indicated Power Base
Back-up:	Back-up:	Back-up:
_____	_____	_____
_____	_____	_____

Keeping each of these key actors in mind, read each of the following item sets. Spread seven points across each set for each key actor to indicate the degree to which you are currently using this strategy in your relationship with the key actor. For example, if you rely heavily on Item 1 in Set I and Items 2 and 3 don't describe your behavior, you might spread your seven points this way:

SET I:	KEY ACTOR I
1. I am getting in a better position to provide things of value to others who, in turn, can influence this person.	6
2. I am getting in a better position to be able to provide this person with the things he or she wants.	1
3. I am doing nothing to get in a position to influence this person.	0

Remember to spread **seven** points across **each** set for **each** key actor. Use whole numbers only.

Power-Getting Profile

	KEY ACTOR I	KEY ACTOR II	KEY ACTOR III
SET I:			
1. I am getting in a better position to be able to provide things of value to others who, in turn, can influence this person.	☐	☐	☐
2. I am getting in a better position to be able to provide this person with the things (s)he wants.	☐	☐	☐
3. I am doing nothing to get in a position to influence this person.	☐	☐	☐

Power-Getting Profile (cont'd.)

	KEY ACTOR I	KEY ACTOR II	KEY ACTOR III
SET II:			
1. I am getting in a better position to cause this person difficulty or pain when and if I so choose.	☐	☐	☐
2. I am gaining this person's friendship or convincing him or her that we have much in common.	☐	☐	☐
3. I am doing nothing to get in a better position to influence this person.	☐	☐	☐
SET III:			
1. I am changing the role I fill, or this person's perceptions of my "rights" and "privileges."	☐	☐	☐
2. I am changing others' perceptions (who, in turn, can influence this person) of my "rights" and "privileges."	☐	☐	☐
3. I am doing nothing to get in a better position to influence this person.	☐	☐	☐
SET IV:			
1. I am mastering subjects or skills or undergoing experiences that this person respects.	☐	☐	☐
2. I am gaining this person's friendship or convincing him or her that we have much in common.	☐	☐	☐
3. I am doing nothing to get in a better position to influence this person.	☐	☐	☐
SET V:			
1. I am building or strengthening a friendship with this person or convincing him or her that we have much in common.	☐	☐	☐

Power-Getting Profile (cont'd.)

	KEY ACTOR I	KEY ACTOR II	KEY ACTOR III
2. I am getting to know or to meet people whom this person regards as famous, impressive, or awesome.	☐	☐	☐
3. I am doing nothing to get in a better position to influence this person.	☐	☐	☐

SET VI:

	KEY ACTOR I	KEY ACTOR II	KEY ACTOR III
1. I am getting in a better position to cause this person difficulty or pain when and if I so choose.	☐	☐	☐
2. I am getting in a better position to cause difficulty or pain for others who, in turn, can influence this person.	☐	☐	☐
3. I am doing nothing to get in a better position to influence this person.	☐	☐	☐

SET VII:

	KEY ACTOR I	KEY ACTOR II	KEY ACTOR III
1. I am getting in a better position to be able to provide this person with the things (s)he wants.	☐	☐	☐
2. I am mastering subjects or skills or undergoing experiences that this person respects.	☐	☐	☐
3. I am doing nothing to get in a position to influence this person.	☐	☐	☐

SET VIII:

	KEY ACTOR I	KEY ACTOR II	KEY ACTOR III
1. I am getting in a better position to cause this person difficulty or pain when and if I so choose.	☐	☐	☐
2. I am mastering subjects or skills or undergoing experiences that this person respects.	☐	☐	☐
3. I am doing nothing to get in a position to influence this person.	☐	☐	☐

Power-Getting Profile (cont'd.)

	KEY ACTOR I	KEY ACTOR II	KEY ACTOR III
SET IX:			
1. I am getting in a better position to be able to provide this person with the things (s)he wants.	☐	☐	☐
2. I am getting in a better position to cause this person difficulty or pain when and if I so choose.	☐	☐	☐
3. I am doing nothing to get in a position to influence this person.	☐	☐	☐
SET X:			
1. I am getting to know or meet people whom this person regards as famous, impressive, or awesome.	☐	☐	☐
2. I am getting to know or meet people regarded as famous by others who, in turn, can influence this person.	☐	☐	☐
3. I am doing nothing to get in a better position to influence this person.	☐	☐	☐
SET XI:			
1. I am getting in a better position to be able to provide this person with the things (s)he wants.	☐	☐	☐
2. I am getting to know or meet people whom this person regards as famous, impressive, or awesome.	☐	☐	☐
3. I am doing nothing to get in a better position to influence this person.	☐	☐	☐
SET XII:			
1. I am building or strengthening a friendship with this person, or convincing him or her we have much in common.	☐	☐	☐

Power-Getting Profile (cont'd.)

	KEY ACTOR I	KEY ACTOR II	KEY ACTOR III
2. I am changing the role I fill, or this person's perceptions of my "rights" and "privileges."	☐	☐	☐
3. I am doing nothing to get in a better position to influence this person.	☐	☐	☐

SET XIII:

	KEY ACTOR I	KEY ACTOR II	KEY ACTOR III
1. I am mastering subjects or skills or undergoing experiences that this person respects.	☐	☐	☐
2. I am mastering subjects or skills or undergoing experiences that inspire the respect of others who, in turn, can influence this person.	☐	☐	☐
3. I am doing nothing to get in a better position to influence this person.	☐	☐	☐

SET XIV:

	KEY ACTOR I	KEY ACTOR II	KEY ACTOR III
1. I am building or strengthening a friendship with this person, or convincing him or her that we have much in common.	☐	☐	☐
2. I am getting in a better position to be able to provide this person with the things (s)he wants.	☐	☐	☐
3. I am doing nothing to get in a better position to influence this person.	☐	☐	☐

SET XV:

	KEY ACTOR I	KEY ACTOR II	KEY ACTOR III
1. I am getting to know or meet people whom this person regards as famous, impressive, or awesome.	☐	☐	☐
2. I am mastering subjects or skills or undergoing experiences that this person respects.	☐	☐	☐
3. I am doing nothing to get in a better position to influence this person.	☐	☐	☐

Power-Getting Profile (cont'd.)

	KEY ACTOR I	KEY ACTOR II	KEY ACTOR III

SET XVI:

1. I am getting in a better position to cause this person difficulty or pain if and when I so choose. □ □ □

2. I am changing the role I fill, or this person's perceptions of my "rights" and "privileges." □ □ □

3. I am doing nothing to get in a better position to influence this person. □ □ □

SET XVII:

1. I am building or strengthening a friendship with this person, or convincing him or her that we have much in common. □ □ □

2. I am building or strengthening a friendship with others who can influence this person. □ □ □

3. I am doing nothing to get in a better position to influence this person. □ □ □

SET XVIII:

1. I am changing the role I fill, or this person's perceptions of my "rights" and "privileges." □ □ □

2. I am getting to know or meet people whom this person regards as famous, impressive, or awesome. □ □ □

3. I am doing nothing to get in a better position to influence this person. □ □ □

SET XIX:

1. I am changing the role I fill, or this person's perceptions of my "rights" and "privileges." □ □ □

Power-Getting Profile (cont'd.)

	KEY ACTOR I	KEY ACTOR II	KEY ACTOR III
2. I am getting in a better position to be able to provide this person with the things (s)he wants.	☐	☐	☐
3. I am doing nothing to get in a better position to influence this person.	☐	☐	☐

SET XX:

	KEY ACTOR I	KEY ACTOR II	KEY ACTOR III
1. I am getting to know or to meet people whom this person regards as famous, impressive, or awesome.	☐	☐	☐
2. I am getting in a better position to cause this person pain or difficulty when and if I so choose.	☐	☐	☐
3. I am doing nothing to get in a better position to influence this person.	☐	☐	☐

SET XXI:

	KEY ACTOR I	KEY ACTOR II	KEY ACTOR III
1. I am changing the role I fill, or this person's perceptions of my "rights" and "privileges."	☐	☐	☐
2. I am mastering subjects or skills or undergoing experiences that this person respects.	☐	☐	☐
3. I am doing nothing to get in a better position to influence this person.	☐	☐	☐

Now, look back over the points you assigned, and complete the following scoring format.

STRATEGY	SET-ITEM	KEY ACTOR I	KEY ACTOR II	KEY ACTOR III
CANDY STORE	1–2 VII–1 IX–1 XI–1 XIV–2 XIX–2			
TOTALS				

STRATEGY	SET-ITEM	KEY ACTOR I	KEY ACTOR II	KEY ACTOR III
ARSENAL	II-1 VI-1 VIII-1 IX-2 XVI-1 XX-2			
TOTALS				
CROWN PRINCE	III-1 XII-2 XVI-2 XVIII-1 XIX-1 XXI-1			
TOTALS				
LOOK WHAT I'VE DONE	IV-1 VII-2 VIII-2 XIII-1 XV-2 XXI-2			
TOTALS				
FRATERNITY	II-2 IV-2 V-1 XII-1 XIV-1 XVII-1			
TOTALS				
PERSON COLLECTOR	V-2 X-1 XI-2 XV-1 XVIII-2 XX-1			
TOTALS				

STRATEGY	SET-ITEM	KEY ACTOR I	KEY ACTOR II	KEY ACTOR III
NETWORK	I-1			
	III-2			
	VI-2			
	X-2			
	XIII-2			
	XVII-2			
TOTALS				
NO INFLUENCE	I-3			
	II-3			
	III-3			
	IV-3			
	V-3			
	VI-3			
	VII-3			
	VIII-3			
	IX-3			
	X-3			
	XI-3			
	XII-3			
	XIII-3			
	XIV-3			
	XV-3			
	XVI-3			
	XVII-3			
	XVIII-3			
	XIX-3			
	XX-3			
	XXI-3			
TOTALS ÷ 3.5				

Note: You are asked to divide the "No Influence" totals by 3.5 because there are three and one-half times as many "No Influence" items as there are items for any other single strategy.

The Candy Store Strategy—Increasing Reward Power

My Candy Store score is (see p. 79):

I: ☐   II: ☐   III: ☐

Score Key:

        0-10:   Minimal Use of Strategy
     11-31:   Moderate Use of Strategy
     32-42:   Substantial Use of Strategy

As its name implies, this strategy involves cornering the market on all available goodies (rewards). If I were to use this strategy to increase my Reward Power over you, I would find out what you prize, and then try to obtain ample quantities of those items. To the extent that I could eliminate your options by cornering the market, I would further increase my potential to influence you. Unions often use the Candy Store Strategy to increase their capacity to influence people to join: "The only way to get good working conditions and raises is to join the union."

Sometimes, the Candy Store Strategy involves the accumulation of tangible items of value to the other person. The teenager who amasses the best record collection in town is often in a better position to influence who comes to parties and where and when they are held than is the teenager whose collection is less impressive. Some adults use their discretionary income to gather objects that will enhance their level of social influence or indispensability. One couple who had found it extremely difficult to develop friendships would ask people to dinner, and then wait for the return invitation that rarely came. Realizing that many of the people they most enjoyed shared an interest in tennis, and realizing that public and even private courts were overbooked, they determined to build a court and take up the game themselves. Their Candy Store was an instant success, and our tennis couple found they had the power to initiate social events with little fear of refusal. Recognizing a good idea, they elaborated upon the concept the next year, and installed a swimming pool and a gas barbecue.

But you needn't be wealthy to build your Candy Store; you can also amass intangible things, valuable to someone else. Information often constitutes the rewards that stock the Candy Store. One consulting firm gathered data on the unit costs to produce all products in all client plants and stored that data in its computers. There was then very little likelihood that the client, who very much appreciated the value of being able to access this data, would sever its relationship with the consulting company.

In another case, a personnel manager finally tired of being the unempowered staff person whom nobody feared or respected. He instituted a manpower planning and skills inventory system and, before long, was the only one in the organization who could match job openings with talent on an organization-wide basis. People quickly learned that the personnel manager's recommendations were crucial to getting a promotion. Information was, again, the basis for building a Reward Power base.

The Candy Store is an accumulation strategy. In this sense, it has much in common with the Arsenal Strategy.

The Arsenal Strategy—Increasing Coercive Power

My Arsenal Strategy score is (see p. 80):

I: ☐   II: ☐   III: ☐

Score Key:

0–10:   Minimal Use of Strategy
11–31:   Moderate Use of Strategy
32–42:   Substantial Use of Strategy

This approach is taken by people who seek to enhance their Coercive Power base. Very simply stated, the Arsenal approach is to collect as broad a range of weapons as is possible. The well-stocked arsenal is capable of yielding an appropriate weapon for every occasion.

Consider the auto repairman who accepts a transmission in order to make a minor adjustment at a modest price. When the customer returns, the mechanic claims that a total rebuilding is necessary, at a high cost. Anticipating the customer's resistance, the mechanic takes the transmission apart, thereby putting himself in a position to demand the job or have the customer pay for his labor. (Chances are, he also guarantees that the customer will go elsewhere for service the next time!) Or, consider the employee who stimulates the formation of a women's action group. As she does so, she builds an arsenal by getting herself in a position to institute a class action suit if management ignores the rights of women workers. (At the same time, she is risking the loss of her job if such a suit is brought, and management reacts vindictively.)

Information is often the weapon that stocks the Arsenal. At its extreme, information is sought for the express purpose of influencing another through blackmail. A legal form of the same dynamic occurs when people hire a detective to determine the whereabouts or comings and goings of another person.

Consultants in the business of personnel testing are in a frighteningly powerful position to act on the Arsenal Strategy if they so choose. They are paid to gather information about the lives, thought patterns, behavior patterns, ambitions, and fears of promotable candidates or prospective employees. Whether or not they actually make use of "negative" findings to further their own self-interest is beside the point; the Arsenal is stocked, ready to yield its weapons if (s)he who holds the key so desires. Sometimes, organizations find it necessary to gather negative information about a competitor. They are then in a position to use that information to draw customers away from the competitor. Is this unfair or immoral? Probably not: if the information is valid, the customer truly benefits from switching suppliers, while the competitor may be forced to invest resources towards improvement of its methods.

People who are attempting to build extremely strong leverage positions, and for whom reliance on Formal Power has a strong appeal, will often stock both the Candy Store and the Arsenal. They thus reach a position to provide what is valued by the other person, and to deliver punishments that are feared by the other person; when the "good guy" route doesn't work, they can resort to less kindly strategies. The influencee often does not choose to escape—after all, the influencer is the source of rewards. Nor is there a danger that as the "carrots" grow stale, the influencer's clout will diminish—the carrot retains its appeal by contrast to the rod.

Building the Arsenal is an extremely risky strategy, as it motivates those whom you would coerce into banding together to thwart your efforts. The outcome is often lose–lose as Arsenal meets Arsenal. Organizations that rely heavily on coercive tactics to stimulate productivity are the most likely to inspire the formation of suspicious unions.[4]

The Crown Prince Strategy—Increasing Legitimate Power

My Crown Prince score is (see p. 80):

I: ☐   II: ☐   III: ☐

Score Key:

0–10:	Minimal Use of Strategy
11–31:	Moderate Use of Strategy
32–42:	Substantial Use of Strategy

The Crown Prince Strategy includes two key tactics: change your role, or change other people's expectations. You can try to get yourself promoted, elected, or appointed to a position that carries greater authority, or you can try to change the role expectations people hold about the rights and privileges attached to your present role or position.

For example, a sales representative asks for a title change in order to impress prospects. The new title ends up impressing customers who show more deference to the "sales director" than they did to the "sales representative." Or consider the manager who used a very simple Crown Prince tactic that made an enormous difference in his overall impact on the organization. Hired by the personnel manager as a "training specialists," this individual quickly realized that the personnel department lacked credibility in the organization. Rather than fight what appeared to be a losing battle to enhance the department's reputation, our "training specialist" decided to become known as the "head of human resource development." At about this time, the blank formats for the new corporate directory landed on his desk. He listed his name and then his function as "human resource development." The new functional title began, in this way, to assume a legitimacy of its own.

Women today are trying to gain Legitimate Power by changing the role expectations associated with femaleness. They are attempting to erase the expectations that women are or should be emotional, passive, physically weak, and content in the home. They are trying to prove that women have rights to pursue careers, to be assertive without losing their "femininity"; that they are physically strong enough to drive trucks, to work in coal mines, etc. And, in many ways, they have succeeded. Legislation now

---

[4]Hjalmar Rosen, "Union Organizations: A Challenge to the Unity of Organizational Humanizing Attempts." *Humanizing Organizational Behavior,* ed. H. Miltzer and Frederic Wickert (Springfield, IL: Charles C. Thomas Publisher, 1976), pp. 47-67.

exists to insure that women as well as men have opportunities to become the Crown Prince.

While women, as a group, are increasing their Legitimate Power in the working world, other groups find theirs is declining. Within the last few years, a new social norm has emerged—no longer are those in positions of authority assumed to be "right"; increasingly, they are assumed to be "wrong," or at least suspect. Key government officials, for example, used to enjoy the Legitimate Power to decide and then inform the public. Today, their Legitimate Power seems to be limited to finding out and then expressing the public's opinion. There is an increasingly popular view that people must earn power; power is no longer simply a matter of getting into the right role or position. The more prevalent this view becomes, the less productive will be the Crown Prince Strategy. Attempts to build Expert Power as opposed to Legitimate Power now characterize the power-building attempts of our emerging leaders. The Look What I've Done Strategy, if well applied, can be extremely effective.

The Look What I've Done Strategy—Increasing Expert Power

My Look What I've Done Strategy score is (see p. 80):

I: ☐   II: ☐   III: ☐

Score Key:

0–10:   Minimal Use of Strategy
11–31:   Moderate Use of Strategy
32–42:   Substantial Use of Strategy

A basic tactic of this strategy is to find out what credentials or experiences prompt respect and to then go about acquiring these credentials or these experiences. Several corporate staff personnel have reported that they rely heavily on the Look What I've Done Strategy for getting power: "I'm always letting them know what I did in former jobs"; "The whole company knows that I have my Ph.D."

There are three keys to the effective use of the Look What I've Done Strategy: one is **competent performance;** the second is **visibility;** and the third is **relevance to a pressing problem.** There are legions of competent performers in organizations who don't enjoy much Expert Power. Why not? Because in performing competently, they are simply doing as expected. Competent performance, in and of itself, may bring predictable promotions and compensation increases. Alone, however, it will not guarantee that the performer can exercise any more leverage in the system than any other competent performer.

Competence blended with visibility is likely to generate more power. How do some people in organizations manage to become more visible than others? One way is by being the first to head up a new function. New functions are carefully watched, so, while this carries some risk, it also insures visibility. Functions that have been operating effectively for years are taken for granted; the manager isn't watched, nor is he noticed, unless the performance of the function starts to slip.

Another way to insure visibility in an organization is to stimulate changes, and, in the process, to take risks. For example, the head of marketing decides to invest substantial resources in a campaign that represents a major depature from the company's traditional way of doing things. The top executives go along, but nervously. The head is watched; the campaign is watched. When it succeeds, and sales volume goes up, she is a hero. There is no need for her to point out what she has done; everyone already knows about it. Or consider the area manager who decides to test market a product that other area managers have refused to touch. The product dramatically increases the area's sales volume. As the profitability levels of his division outstrip the other divisions, he gains dramatically in power.

Competence needs to be blended with visibility in order for the Look What I've Done Strategy to work. But what happens if a highly competent individual introduces a highly visible change that doesn't much matter to the organization as a whole? Nothing, at best. At worst, the Expert Power of the innovator is diminished as (s)he is accused of inappropriate priorities and of dabbling in irrelevancies. Thus the third key to successful implementation of the Look What I've Done Strategy is relevance to key organizational concerns. The individual who introduces a new product when the major problem is quality control around existing products is not likely to increase his or her Expert Power. The personnel manager who introduces job enrichment to increase employee morale will not increase his or her leverage unless tardiness, absenteeism, sabotage, and low productivity levels are a problem. One executive I know worked mightily to introduce a cost-effectiveness program in a company that produced critical fuels for the military on a cost-plus basis. He is no longer associated with the organization!

The key to effective pursuit of the Look What I've Done Strategy, then, is: (1) identifying a pressing organizational problem; (2) finding a solution that will bring with it high visibility; (3) implementing the solution in a competent fashion. This approach is comfortable for people who have a willingness to take risks and a greater need for power than for affiliation. In the process of increasing Expert Power, people often find that they must accept a certain distancing from people they formerly regarded as peers and friends.[5] Suddenly, they are perceived as being on a different level. In the process, their Referent leverage may diminish. Those who are unwilling to accept this distancing should probably consider, as an option, the Fraternity Strategy.

The Fraternity Strategy—Building Referent Power

My Fraternity Strategy score is (see p. 80):

I: ☐   II: ☐   III: ☐

Score Key:

0–10:	Minimal Use of Strategy
11–31:	Moderate Use of Strategy
32–42:	Substantial Use of Strategy

---

[5]R. Bales, "The Equilibrium Problem in Small Groups." *Working Papers in the Theory of Action*, R. Bales and E. Shils (Glencoe, IL: Free Press, 1953), pp. 111-161.

To use this approach, it is necessary to give people reasons to like you, trust you, or identify with you. Individuals attempting to use the Fraternity Strategy try to get to know others socially. These people can subsequently make things happen through the friendship network that pervades the organization.

The real key to effective implementation of the Fraternity Strategy is **trust.** Trust is terribly difficult to build, and frighteningly easy to destroy. Think of one person whom you trust, someone that you "simply know" would not do or say anything detrimental to you. Check all of the following that apply to this person:

- ☐   This person is available when I need him or her.

- ☐   I feel free to show my weaknesses as well as my strengths to this person.

- ☐   I can express my negative feelings openly to this person: when I am angry, I can say so; when I am sad, I can say so; when I am scared, I can say so.

- ☐   This person makes it easy for me to express my positive feelings: I am comfortable telling this person that I care about him or her.

- ☐   This person lets me know where I stand by openly expressing feelings (positive or negative) to me.

- ☐   This person wants to see me fulfill my potential, to succeed as I define success.

- ☐   This person defends me when others attack me or say disparaging things about me.

- ☐   This person likes being with me when I am down as well as when I am up.

- ☐   This person gives me the benefit of the doubt; when I do something that upsets him or her, (s)he assumes I had a good reason for doing so.

- ☐   This person enjoys my being different in some ways from him or her; there is no pressure to conform, to think the same, to be the same.

If building Referent Power is part of your strategy with your key actors, then consider the degree to which you are giving your key actors reasons to trust you. Are you available when your key actor needs you? Do you express your feelings openly to that person, and encourage him or her to do the same with you? Do you, or would you, defend your key actor when and if others said disparaging things? Do you really want to see your key actor fulfill his or her potential? Do you enjoy being in the company of your key actor? Do you give your key actor the benefit of the doubt, assuming the "best" rather than the "worst"? If you answered "no" to any of the above questions, then you're likely to meet with limited success as you attempt to build Referent Power based on trust. If the Fraternity Strategy is your chosen course, and if total trust does not appear possible, then consider using another Referent Power-building tactic: convincing the other person that you share an important goal.

Referent Power begins to build between people as they realize they have something in common, that they are after the same things in life, or that they face common obstacles. The degree of power increases as these persons appreciate that, through joint effort, they can increase the likelihood that they will achieve their shared objectives. An example of this approach is provided by the antidiscrimination movements of the last few years. By joining forces, women, blacks, and other minorities have managed to exert influence over legislators that perhaps no group could have done alone.

As organizational complexity increases, the need for coordination increases. Coordination by fiat becomes less and less workable as specialization intensifies, and functions and support services proliferate. Cross-functional or peer loyalties and friendships often make the difference between a manager who can make things happen and one who cannot.

If you work in an organization that emphasizes team effort across functional lines, it is especially important that you be able to build Referent Power. Managers in such organizations need to influence persons who are not directly under their control or jurisdiction if they are to get their job done.

Peer friendships are also becoming important to the nonmanager who works in an organization that utilizes the team approach to production. Under the team approach, the workers themselves assume managerial functions. Workers determine one another's raises, and assume accountability for training. Evaluation is based on team results, as opposed to "star" performance. Those who refuse to build Referent Power, who disclaim interest in team objectives or in the work and problems of the group as a whole, are regarded as "bad players" and are evaluated accordingly.

Building some degree of Referent Power appears to be less and less a matter of choice for those who want to succeed, and who are to some degree dependent on others for their goal accomplishment. Some of the tactics that can be used to implement the Fraternity Strategy are:

- Identify what you have in common with the other person. Look first at activities, then at goals, and finally at values. Remember, **there are several means to attaining the same ends. Shared values may lie behind apparently contradictory goals.**

- Having identified your "least common denominator," look for ways in which you and the other person can support one another's efforts. **Analyze your respective resources or strengths to determine what each of you can bring to bear on the situation.**

- Make a "contract" with the other person and **live up to it. The more contracts are fulfilled, the more the other will learn to trust you.**

- At all cost, avoid "winning" at the other's expense. **Work to create win-win outcomes.**

- Create "symbols" to remind yourselves and others of your common bond: uniforms, naming your newly formed group, establishing a special handshake, etc. **By giving your alliance a visible identity, you make it more difficult for either of you to act in ways which weaken the alliance.**

- Develop a shared language, or learn to use the jargon that characterizes the other person's specialty. **A shared language is extremely helpful in developing mutual understanding.**

Applying the Fraternity Strategy depends upon establishing a dialogue with the other person. Sometimes, you may have to give the other person a reason to talk with you in the first place. Relying on Formal Power to initiate a dialogue is risky; it implies a win–lose relationship from the start. Relying on Expert Power is also problematic, as it can create a social distance ("I am the expert; you are not."). Associative Power can be used to give the other person a reason to begin communicating with you.

The Person Collector Strategy—Building Associative Power

My Person Collector score is (p. 80):

   I: ☐   II: ☐   III: ☐

Score Key:

0–10:	Minimal Use of Strategy
11–31:	Moderate Use of Strategy
32–42:	Substantial Use of Strategy

Did you ever know anyone who made it a point to get to know leaders in his or her field? If so, you have seen the Person Collector Strategy in action. Whether intentionally or not, these people are getting in a position to exercise Associative Power—to influence others on the basis of who they know.

Sometimes, life's events simply put us in a position to meet famous people; at other times, a concerted effort is required. People often shy away from building Associative Power because they assume that the "celebrity" doesn't want to be bothered with "insignificant me." Those who effectively implement the Person Collector Strategy assume that there is no harm in trying. One ten-year-old girl discovered that a top musician was visiting some people in her home town. She knew that her mother was acquainted with the host and hostess, so she asked her mother to call and try to arrange a meeting with the musician for her. The mother refused, feeling that to do so would be impolite and unfair to the musician. The child then took matters into her own hands. She called the hostess, introduced herself, and asked for an audience with the musician. Much to the mother's surprise, the musician decided he'd like to meet the girl who overcame shyness and protocol in order to meet him. The little girl spent an entire afternoon with the musician, and from that time on has been able to exercise significantly more influence in her peer group.

Getting to know important people can be useful. Alone, however, it is unlikely to greatly intensify the leverage base, unless the expertise or resources possessed by these others are relevant to what you want to accomplish.

The Network Strategy—Getting in a Position to Indirectly Influence Others

> My Network Strategy score is (p. 81):
>
> I: ☐   II: ☐   III: ☐
>
> Score Key:
>
> 0-10:   Minimal Use of Strategy
> 11-31:   Moderate Use of Strategy
> 32-42:   Substantial Use of Strategy

The objective of Networking is to get in a position to influence, through an intermediary, the person you really want to affect. All the other power-getting strategies may come into play in this process. However, because the third party might distort the original intent, it is probably advisable to attempt to affect the intermediary through Referent or Expert Power. (The use of Coercive Power is likely to inspire your "agent" to sabotage your efforts.)

One university lecturer used the Network Strategy in a global way to affect a mutually productive outcome for everyone involved. Under the auspices of his university, he had invented a device that represented a major technological breakthrough for the machine tool industry; one of his stated objectives for an impending sabbatical was to establish a consortium of universities and industrial concerns interested in further refinement and utilization of the device and its related technology. But given his status as lecturer (as opposed to a higher-status "professor"), he suspected he would have a difficult time getting an audience with the academic and industrial leaders whom he hoped to see. So he carefully researched both the academic and industrial network, finding out who was doing what and who was talking with whom about what. He visited thirty countries over a period of twelve months, talking with persons who not only wanted to listen, but who were in a position to open the door to others of yet greater status. In effect, he used a combination of Indirect Expert, Referent and Legitimate Power to bolster his own Expert Power. His objectives were fully realized.

One young woman I know was made responsible for enhancing the career mobility of civilian women within one branch of the federal government. With the exception of a half-time secretary, she had no Formal Power whatsoever over the people she needed to influence in order to accomplish her objectives. She quickly realized that she would achieve nothing by relying exclusively on the Legitimate Power granted by law to her position, so she embarked on a networking effort, getting to know a wide variety of people throughout the system. In effect, she built a network of people who respected and trusted her. Later, when she had to make a direct request of individuals not affected by her jurisdictional powers, she was able to summon the help of "friends in court" who acted on her behalf.

The Network Strategy takes a long time to implement, and there is a danger that those who are "networked" might feel manipulated. Manipulation is not necessarily a

Power Summary

KINDS OF POWER	OUTCOMES	GETTING POWER STRATEGY	TACTICS
REWARD	• Rapid action • Desire to get maximum reward for minimum work	CANDY STORE	• Accumulate things of value to other or information of use to other
COERCIVE	• Rapid action • Compliance • Resentment • Fear • Need for surveillance	ARSENAL	• Accumulate punishments which could be levied on other or accumulate damaging information
LEGITIMATE	• Compliance uncertain as "right to rule" is questioned	CROWN PRINCE	• Change role • Change role expectations
REFERENT	• Commitment to person	FRATERNITY	• Build trust • Build commonality of group affiliation or of interest
EXPERT	• Commitment to task	LOOK WHAT I'VE DONE	• Obtain credentials or undergo experiences that other respects
ASSOCIATIVE	• Compliance and commitment uncertain if other person not impressed	PERSON COLLECTOR	• Get to know "famous others"
INDIRECT	• Intermediary must be willing to influence others on your behalf • Loss of control if intermediary distorts your intent • Sphere of influence increases • Any of above outcomes, depending on power used by the intermediary	NETWORK	• Get to know others who have power over person you really want to influence

characteristic of networking, however. The most effective networking efforts, when viewed over the long run, are markedly nonmanipulative: participants in the network understand from the beginning why they are involved.

Just as each power base presents advantages and disadvantages, so each power-getting strategy is beneficial in some circumstances and detrimental in others.

POWER-GETTING ATTEMPTS: AN OVERVIEW

Each of us is surrounded by, and is a participant in, power-getting attempts; to deny or ignore these attempts can be destructive. Consider the case of the sudden resignation of a corporate chief executive officer in a Fortune 500 industrial organization where the lines of succession were not clear. During the months required to appoint a successor, power-getting strategies effectively counterbalanced each other and immobilized the corporation. Decisions were deferred or made on the basis of political concerns (who will it please, and who will it displease), rather than on the basis of contribution to long-term corporate health. Not surprisingly, the choice of the successor was the result of a power play among members of the top echelon of the company, competing for the top spot. Rather than permit the appointment of a person from the "enemy camp," they urged the appointment of a less threatening, unempowered, neutral third party. The organization now faces a dramatic profit reduction and lack of unified effort among the divisions.

Even though power-getting strategies can be disruptive, they should not be disclaimed or ignored. Talking with a few managers who have chosen or been forced to leave their jobs would rapidly convince anyone of the need to "tune into" the power-getting strategies of others, and to exercise judgment in selecting the most effective strategy for oneself:

> "I was fired because I found out the company was facing a much greater financial loss due to compliance suits than my boss, the head of EEO, was admitting to top management."

> "The more of an expert I became, the more I threatened the others. Instead of trying to learn from me, they spent all their energies competing with me."

> "I left because advancement in that place is totally dependent upon political savvy and has nothing whatever to do with ability to contribute to results."

These managers left, or were forced to leave, their respective organizations because they did not choose to (or, perhaps, were unable to) utilize the appropriate power-getting strategies in key situations. Because we all have multiple organizational affiliations, and daily find ourselves in a wide variety of situations when we need to influence others to accomplish our goals, flexibility in the use of power-getting strategies is important. Consider Mr. X.

Mr. X was ambitious when he joined the ABC Company at age twenty-five. For a year and a half, he took pains to get to know others. He and his wife entertained coworkers frequently at their home. Within a few months, he had friends throughout the organization, at every level, performing every type of function. People liked him, trusted him, and sought his company.

At the same time he was building up his Referent Power on a wide scale, he was working to build Expert Power. He read every industry periodical he could get his hands on, and took industry-related courses most evenings at local universities. He took risks, recommended changes, and "broadcast" his increasing technical competence in ways which impressed (but did not offend) others. Within a year and a half of joining the company, he knew he was being groomed for a top job in the company. Within two years, he was named as one of three vice presidents. The other two vice presidents were twice his age, but did not enjoy the Expert and Referent Power he enjoyed. Their power base was primarily Legitimate.

But a popular quotation unfortunately began to apply to our Mr. X: "Power tends to corrupt, and absolute power corrupts absolutely." Mr. X realized that he had a good thing but became quickly impatient for more. He used his Legitimate Power as vice president to bring more sections under his control. As more and more people reported directly to him, he was unable to spend the amount of time he previously had with individuals. These individuals began to resent the unavailability and inaccessibility of someone they had previously regarded as a friend. Sensing their hostility, our Mr. X began to avoid one-on-one meetings, preferring to do business in group situations.

While in groups, Mr. X began to erode his Expert Power—he stopped listening, and started mandating. He began behaving as though he were the only expert in the room on everything. Within a short period of time, others began to question that he was, in fact, an expert on anything. He had effectively undone his Expert and Referent bases, and replaced them with Reward and Coercive Power. He became the "boss," not the "friend" or "expert." In stocking the Arsenal, he endangered the Fraternity. In expanding his Candy Store, he encouraged people to look not at what he had accomplished (Expert Power), but at what he had not accomplished. Subsequent networking attempts were seen as manipulations, and people began to resist involvement with him. Mr. X was not content to rely on his own resources—his Expert and Referent Power. He was determined to bolster his position with more tangible forms of clout; in the process, he lost the leverage of trust and respect."

It is not the accumulation of Reward or Coercive Power that is damaging, but the simultaneous attempt to build Formal and Informal Power. Such simultaneous attempts carry a double message that breeds caution rather than commitment or ready compliance:

> "I want you to take care of your sisters and brothers tonight. It will be good for you to develop a sense of responsibility. On top of that, if you refuse, you'll lose your right to use the car on Saturday night."

> "I want you to try your best to get the report typed by noon tomorrow. I know you've been working extremely hard lately, and that you need a night off. I don't like seeing you get run down. However, those who make it here are willing to do that extra bit when the need arises."

In the first example, the older sibling is unlikely to believe his parents really are concerned about his or her "sense of responsibility." In the second example, the reference to the Reward System effectively overshadows the manager's concern for the physical well being of the subordinate. In both cases, the Informal Power base would have remained intact, though not utilized, if the messages had been limited to the true reward and coercive consequences:

> "In exchange for using the car this weekend, we'd like you to sit tonight."

> "If you really want to succeed here, you'll have to put in the extra effort now, when it is most needed."

Are Your Power-Getting Strategies Appropriate: Will They Work?

Are you, like Mr. X, pursuing power-getting strategies that undermine one another? Look back at the scoring chart you filled in on pages 80-81. Consider each of your key actors in turn. Transpose your total scores onto this chart for ease of reference.

KEY ACTOR	CANDY STORE (A)	ARSENAL (B)	CROWN PRINCE (C)	LOOK WHAT I'VE DONE (D)	FRATERNITY (E)	PERSON COLLECTOR (F)	NETWORK (G)
I							
II							
III							

The highest possible score for any of the strategies is 42. As you analyze your scores, consider:

- How much of your energy is spent in building *Formal* as opposed to *Informal* Power with each of your key actors? To find out, compare the total of A+B+C with the total of D+E+F.

My A+B+C total is: I: ☐   II: ☐   III: ☐

My D+E+F total is: I: ☐   II: ☐   III: ☐

If the scores are in range of one another, then be careful. Chances are you are negating your own efforts to build an informal base as you build formal leverage over that key actor.

- How much of your energy is spent in building *indirect* as opposed to *direct* forms of leverage? To find out, for each of your key actors add the A+B+C+D+E+F scores, and divide the total by 6. Compare this result with your G score for each key actor.

(A+B+C+D+E+F) ÷ 6:	I: ☐	II: ☐	III: ☐
My "G" score is:	I: ☐	II: ☐	III: ☐

If your G score is close to or greater than the other score, then you may be pursuing indirect forms of leverage when your energies could be more productively devoted to building a direct power base.

- Are you trying hard enough to get in a position to influence your key actor? Or are you spending time and energy just wishing you could have your way? To find out, add your A+B+C+D+E+F+G scores for each key actor. Then, divide this total by two. Compare this total with the H score (divided in half) for each key actor.

(A+B+C+D+E+F+G) ÷ 2:	I: ☐	II: ☐	III: ☐
My "H" score is:	I: ☐	II: ☐	III: ☐

If your "H" score is 25 percent or more of the total, then you are probably not doing as much as you should to get in a position to influence your key actor.

If you retain flexibility and exercise judgment as you maneuver to influence those whose support or cooperation you need to achieve your goals, then chances are very great that you will succeed. Establishing the appropriate power base is the first step. Using that power base in an effective manner is the next step. In the next chapter, you'll be given an opportunity to consider the options you have as you actually attempt to influence others.

4

Your Influence Options

Getting the power to influence others in support of your goals is critical to a-chieving success. Equally critical is the appropriate use of that power through selection of the most effective Influence Style.

There are four distinct Influence Styles. Which do you prefer to use? To get one indication, think of a specific person or group of persons with whom you spend a great deal of time. Then, read each of the items that follow and, in the box to the right of each item, place a number from 0 to 5 to indicate the extent to which the behavior describes you. Use this scale:

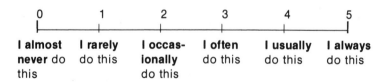

0	1	2	3	4	5
I almost never do this	I rarely do this	I occasionally do this	I often do this	I usually do this	I always do this

Your Influence Styles

1. I take only when I can give in return, and when I give, I expect to get something back. ☐

2. I tell people not only what to do but how to do it, and assume I have a right to do so. ☐

3. I ask people to do things for me to make my life easier because they care for me. ☐

4. I try to understand how others view a problem and work with them to discover "best" solutions. ☐

5. I compromise and ask others to do the same in order to resolve conflicts. ☐

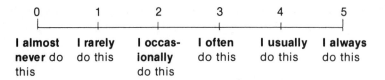

6. I let people know that if they value what I can do for them, they'll follow my lead or do as I say. ☐

7. I convince people that my ideas are sound and that they therefore should listen to me. ☐

8. I accept the ideas of others and then build upon them to find "best" approaches. ☐

9. I set up "games" or "contests" in which the wishes of the best player prevail. ☐

10. I let people know that I can make things difficult for them if they don't do as I say. ☐

11. I impress people on the basis of the people I know. ☐

12. I get involved by making it possible for others to do what they want to do and, in the process, I affect the decisions they make. ☐

Now, to begin to understand your influence style preferences, make these additions:

ITEM	YOUR SCORE	ITEM	YOUR SCORE	ITEM	YOUR SCORE	=	INFLUENCE STYLE
1		+ 5		+ 9		=	NEGOTIATION
2		+ 6		+ 10		=	DIRECTION
3		+ 7		+ 11		=	ENLISTMENT
4		+ 8		+ 12		=	INVOLVEMENT

Fairly balanced scores indicate either that you have some degree of comfort with all the approaches or that this test is too brief to reveal your preferences in specific situations. If you would like to have a more precise indication of the influence styles you tend to use, then spend twenty to thirty minutes completing the more elaborate "Influence Styles Profile" in Appendix D. **If you do plan to complete the profile,**

please do so before continuing with this chapter. Familiarity with the model we will be discussing tends to skew the profile results.

THE INFLUENCE MODEL

Whenever you attempt to influence your subordinates, your peers, or your boss, you consciously or unconsciously select one of four influence strategies—**Involvement, Enlistment, Negotiation, or Direction.**

The essential differences between these four strategies lie in the kind of power used, and the extent to which you will accept a range of responses rather than fixed or predetermined responses from the person you are attempting to influence.

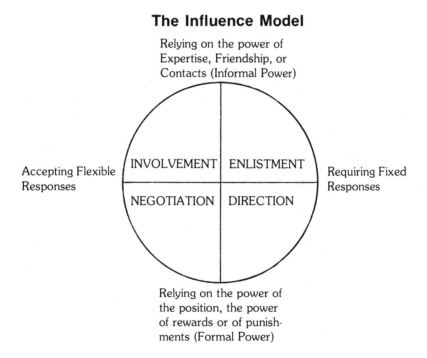

The Influence Model

Relying on the power of
Expertise, Friendship, or
Contacts (Informal Power)

Accepting Flexible
Responses

INVOLVEMENT   ENLISTMENT

NEGOTIATION   DIRECTION

Requiring Fixed
Responses

Relying on the power of
the position, the power
of rewards or of punish-
ments (Formal Power)

The use of Negotiation and Involvement Strategies requires that the influencer be willing to accept a range of responses (procedures, plans, methods) from those (s)he is attempting to influence. Direction and Enlistment Strategies give others almost no latitude, as they spell out not only what to do, but *how* to do it.

Persons using the Involvement Strategy look to others to contribute as much as they can, to hold themselves accountable for results, and to openly influence events.

The Involvement approach requires that people work together to enrich one another's resources and to decide how shared resources are to be used. Task force members often involve others as they seek best solutions to shared problems. Vested interest and hierarchy are laid aside in an attempt to confront and openly resolve differences of opinion.

People who favor Negotiation Strategies require that others do only what they formally agree to do, show initiative only in prescribed areas, and hold themselves accountable only for the terms of the contract, not overall results. The manager who negotiates is usually prepared to give a little to get a little: "I'll give you a raise (which you value) if you'll work harder (which I value)." Labor-management disputes often involve heavy use of the negotiation strategy: "We'll lower our wage demands (which we don't want to do) if you'll give us flexible working hours (which you don't want to do)." Negotiations can also take the form of a contest: "We'll do it your way if you can get the Appropriations Committee to approve; otherwise, we'll do it my way."

Persons relying on the Direction Strategy require that others do what they are specifically told to do, neither taking initiative nor attempting to influence outcomes. The Directing manager attempts to overcome anticipated resistance by purchasing compliance through rewards, or demanding compliance through threats and sanctions. This individual knows exactly what behavior is wanted from the other person (fixed response), and will use whatever measures are available to insure compliance.

While enlisting, people seek a specific kind of limited assistance, generally discouraging a give-and-take of ideas or a mutual influencing of events. Enlistments are often based on **need**: "Please give me a larger office; I need more space." Or, the basis can be **information**: "A larger office will make it easier for me to impress customers." Finally, the basis of the appeal can be **emotion**: "You know me well enough to appreciate how I hate confined spaces."

The difference between the four kinds of strategies are reflected in specific behaviors. The list of behaviors that follows indicates the specific approaches that are taken by people who try to implement each of the influence styles.

Involvement

SHARING   Getting involved by building on others' ideas (I suggest we pool our resources, exchange ideas, contacts—and in the process come up with something neither of us could have managed alone.)

ENABLING   Getting involved by offering information (I'm going to give you something—information, contacts, emotional support—and leave it to you to decide what to do with it.)

COOPERATING   Getting involved by supporting or accepting the suggestions of others (I'll do as you ask and, in the process, I expect that I'll be able to affect the final outcome.)

Enlistment

SOLICITING   Asking for support because of need (Do as I ask because I need your help, and my cause is worthwhile.)
ADVISING   Asking for support on the basis of information (Do as I ask because I have given you good and sufficient reason.)
COURTING   Asking for support on the basis of friendship (Do as I ask because I am charming, or because you like me.)

Direction

ORDERING   Giving instructions without options (Do as I say because I have the "right" and the clout to tell you what to do.)
FORCING   Making demands while discouraging refusal (Do as I say if you want to avoid injury, or because you want to get what you want.)
BLOCKING   The opposite of forcing; preventing others from taking action due to their desire to get something of value or to avoid punishment (Don't do it; if you do, I'll make you sorry you did; if you don't, I'll reward you.)

Negotiation

TRADING   Exchanging value for value (I'll give you something you want if you'll give me what I want.)
COMPROMISING   Giving in to get closure—lose-lose concession (I'll give in on that one if you'll give in and do as I ask.) Sometimes used to minimize the extent of loss that could occur if the contest continued.
CONTESTING   Setting up win-lose situations (There's one way to resolve this—if I win, you'll do it my way; if you win, I'll do it your way.)

As the list of behaviors indicates, both the Negotiation and Direction Strategies incorporate a reliance on Formal Power—the power to reward or to punish, or the power of rank or position. Use of the Enlistment and Involvement Strategies involves reliance on informal kinds of leverage—the power of friendship, contacts, or expertise. **None of the strategies is inherently "good" or "bad." Each can be appropriate or inappropriate, depending on the situation.**

USING POWER EFFECTIVELY: IS YOUR INFLUENCE STRATEGY APPROPRIATE?

The Influence Strategy you choose can have a significant impact on others' commitment to your goals and appreciation of the relationship, and on the speed with which action is taken. Direction used appropriately (when you have the power to make demands), will lead to rapid compliance; rarely will it generate commitment. Involvement may generate commitment, but the time required to work through differences, and define shared goals may make this strategy less effective. Negotiation tends to build commitment, either to the terms of the contract or to the rules of the game. Enlistment is risky—the other person is free to deny your request.

The difference in impact between Direction and Involvement Strategies was dramatically illustrated by a series of events which occurred in the marketing and sales division of a major pharmaceutical company. For years, the division had been managed by an individual who used the Involvement Strategy whenever possible. Divisional goals were formulated by those persons who had to implement the plans. Employees in the field were encouraged to make suggestions and to join problem-solving sessions. Then, the president of the company retired. His successor brought in a new vice president of marketing who believed in "telling the troops what to do." Believing their ideas were no longer desired or respected, many division managers left to join competing organizations. Within months, the division's results showed a sharp decline.

In selecting an effective influence strategy, it is important that you consider your **goals,** the **urgency** of your task, and the **commitment** or the **contribution** from others that you are seeking.

What is the Nature of Your Goals?

In considering any two persons and any two of their goals, it is possible to classify these goals as **interdependent** (the realization of one is dependent on the realization of the other, and vice versa); **independent** (to realize one is neither to help nor to hinder efforts to realize the other); **counterdependent** (to realize one is to make it more difficult to realize the other); or **one-way dependent** (one person's goal depends on getting help from another person, and the dependency is not reciprocal).

Involving others is most effective when there is an interdependency of goals— when your goals and the goals of others are the same or mutually dependent for their achievement.[1] By definition of a partnership, one partner cannot succeed unless the other also fares well.

Sometimes, the interrelatedness of goals is not so obvious. Clarifying the superordinate (shared) goal can, in itself, begin to shift the power strategy and the nature of the relationship. Consider the diverse adversary groups in a southwestern U.S. city who were at odds over integration and busing issues. The power plays got so extreme that several people feared that, with schools opening, buses would be overturned and children would be hurt. After several days of discussion with representatives of the opposing groups, during which they were urged to continually redefine and broaden

---

[1]The importance of goal interdependence and mutuality of effort is discussed in Douglas McGregor, *The Human Side of Enterprise* (New York: McGraw-Hill, 1960).

their objectives, the groups arrived at similar-stated objectives. Once militants and conservatives both black and white, were able to speak about their shared desire to both protect children from harm and provide educational opportunity for all, it was possible to put pent-up energies into problem-solving rather than into devising ways to undermine the efforts of perceived opponents. They had, in effect, redefined their goals and, in the process, realized they were interdependent.

Sometimes, it is impossible to derive superordinate goals. When goals are essentially conflicting, or counterdependent (i.e., when achieving one necessarily prevents achieving another, or when resources are scarce and possession by one party means the other must do without), then some form of Direction may be the only workable strategy. Imagine two managers, both of whom have an immediate need to access the organization's data processing services. Further, assume that computer availability is limited, and that it is impossible to satisfy the requests of both managers. If a compromise is out of the question in the mind of either manager, and if problem-solving discussions have been fruitless, then chances are that both Manager X and Manager Y will attempt to summon all their organizational clout to direct the data processing people to favor their request.

In our society, resources are rarely so scarce that someone must go without. There is usually some room for a trade, or perhaps for compromise. When goals are independent, a trade (one form of Negotiation) may be indicated. Negotiation can result in desirable outcomes if my success is dependent neither on your success nor on your failure. For example, both our goals may be to become account executives. We could both choose to pursue a career path in different account specialties. In this case, we might negotiate a trade of information, clients, or political support.

When goals are counterdependent or conflicting, and neither party can successfully direct the outcome, then Negotiation with an intent to compromise may be most useful. Consider labor-management disputes. Labor wants higher wages; management's goal is to generate higher profits. Their goals are counterdependent, at least when viewed over the short term. Successful negotiations often involve use of compromises on both sides.

Sometimes, one person's goal depends on getting help from someone else, and the dependency is not returned. If, for example, I want to spend two years doing research and, in order to do so, I need a grant from you, then my goal achievement is dependent upon your support. Your goal (to stimulate research) does not, however, depend on me for its achievement. In such a case, I might appropriately enlist your support.

To summarize, when goals are **interdependent,** Involvement of the other person is indicated. When goals are **independent** or **counterdependent,** Negotiation may be effective. When goals are **counterdependent** (conflicting), Direction may be necessary. When there is a **one-way goal dependence,** Enlistment is a strategy worth considering.

One manager I know found this distinction between goals particularly helpful as he planned how to reach his objective—to initiate programs that would reverse some disturbingly negative employee attitudes about:

- The adequacy of supervision.

- The effectiveness of management-employee communications.

- The degree of trust in top management.

The goal of the people he was attempting to influence (employees and their managers) was higher levels of job productivity. The goals were thus entirely interdependent. Realizing this, the manager delayed introduction of change programs until he managed to build an Informal Power base. He then used surveys, interviews, and group planning sessions to involve organization members in deciding how to best reverse nonproductive attitudes. The result was a high level of commitment to the training programs, appraisal systems, and career planning procedures that were developed. While his approach consumed a great deal of time, the levels of commitment and the success of the effort justified the delay. In some cases, however, delay is unacceptable and a different approach may be necessary.

How Urgent is Your Task?

It takes time to problem-solve around the goals we want to achieve and then to work through differences of opinion regarding the best means to apply strategies. If urgency is an issue, Involvement is not indicated. When a fire is raging, it is inappropriate to sit down and discuss the pros and cons of different firefighting methods. Someone must take charge, and unilaterally direct the use of resources. Direction, then, may be indicated when even a slight delay would be detrimental. This is why military personnel are taught to honor the "legitimate" right of commanding officers to command, and why insubordination is regarded as a critical offense.

When some delay is acceptable, Negotiation is possible. Negotiations can, and frequently do, lead to deadlocks. If you can't afford a deadlock, then you probably can't afford to negotiate. If, on the other hand, you can tolerate a deadlock better than the other person, then you might consider Negotiation. Your lack of urgency can give you a competitive edge. One of our largest American corporations appears to be very aware of this dynamic. Cash flow considerations, backed by numerous large contracts, have put the corporation in a position to not only tolerate, but to benefit (in terms of cash flow improvement) from a strike in one of the divisions. The situation makes it possible during contract negotiations for management to demand that the unions permit workers to perform multiple tasks, crossing jurisdictional lines.

If the other person has time on his side, and you don't, Enlistment may be the best strategy. (This assumes that your goals are not conflicting, and that the other person has some reason for considering your plea.) Politicians often find "appeal" useful as they rely on unique blends of charisma, cause, and issues to attract campaign dollars and votes.

What Kind of Commitment Do You Need?

When people are directed to do something, they are likely to lose whatever commitment they might have had to the effort and may even become antagonistic to what you hope to accomplish. When this happens, they contribute only as much as they have to in order to avoid punishment. Levels of commitment are thus lowest when the Direction Strategy is used. Rebellion, compliance, or avoidance are predictable outcomes.[2] Direction is effective when you can precisely define the contribution you require, and want nothing more nor less from the other party.

Negotiation can generate commitment to living up to the terms of an agreement, but rarely does it produce a willingness to jeopardize one's own position for the benefit of a broader goal. Given its quid pro quo characteristics, Negotiation works only when short-term acceptance of a contract is sought. The potentially negative effects of inappropriate Negotiation, with resulting lack of commitment to overall goals, is often illustrated when employees are charged with achieving a specific rate of return or profit percentage, regardless of changes in their situation. One sales representative had negotiated a contract with his boss that called for achieving a seven percent increase in volume by the end of the year. By the middle of November, he had realized this percentage, and so had deferred reporting additional sales for the period so they could be credited to the following period. This individual's commitment was clearly to his contract, not to the overall financial goals or objectives of the department. His boss might have fared better if he had involved the sales rep in initially setting sales and market objectives, thereby generating a longer term commitment.

Long-term commitment of both parties (e.g., manager and subordinate) is most likely to occur when Involvement, with flexible outcomes and use of Informal Power, is the primary strategy.[3] The Japanese system of employment, which historically bound employer to employees, constructively used this dynamic. The influence process in that system was heavily dependent upon Informal Power, since managers had little or no Formal Power to fire (Coercive Power) or to grant raises (Reward Power). The outcome, and perhaps one key to Japanese productivity, was interdependency between boss and subordinate coupled with high levels of employee commitment to the organization and its objectives. **Only with the Involvement Strategy do you encourage the other party to share accountability for the results of your joint venture.**

Enlistment tends to work when there is some level of commitment or acceptance even before the request for assistance is made. Rarely does Enlistment generate commitment, however. It is an appropriate strategy when you seek permission, acquiescence, or support rather than commitment to and involvement in goals or programs.

In organizational life, Enlistment is indicated when you want the freedom to investigate options without, for the moment, additional inputs or constraints: "I'd like a few weeks to investigate the pros and cons of acquiring a business in the XYZ industry"; "I need some time to rearrange my work space so that I can minimize distractions due to hall noise"; "I need a few days off to deal with some personal affairs." In all these

---

[2]B. Bass et al., "Management Styles Associated with Organizational Task, Personal and Interpersonal Contingencies." *Journal of Applied Psychology* 60 (1975): pp. 720-729.

[3]The manager who relies heavily on Involvement approximates the "9-9 Manager" described in Robert R. Blake and Jane Srygley Mouton, *Building a Dynamic Corporation through Grid Organization Development* (Reading, MA: Addison-Wesley Publishing Co., 1969).

cases, there is a request for a specific kind of support along with minimal involvement of the other: "Don't give me your impressions of the XYZ industry yet"; "Don't help me rearrange my work space"; "Don't ask about my personal affairs."

What Controls Are Available To You?

As we have seen, the Involvement Strategy tends to generate the highest levels of commitment. When a person is committed to an effort, there is no need for surveillance—for controls that alert you when the other stops performing in your best interest. On the contrary, to impose surveillance in case the other person's commitment begins to wane is to hasten the loss of commitment: "He obviously doesn't trust me, so why should I bother?" Tight controls and Involvement are incompatible. When such controls are unavailable, then Involvement may be the most effective strategy.

Negotiation, too, generates a measure of commitment—at least to the terms of the contract, if not the longer term effort. Successful implementation of the Negotiation Strategy, then, requires a well-defined and mutually understood contract. A negotiation based on a poorly formulated contract created a great deal of stress in our household not long ago. My husband and I had a long-term houseguest who wanted to give up "guest privileges" and becoming a helpful member of the household as rapidly as possible. We opted for a trade—he would paint the living room and we would happily provide all his food, do his laundry, etc. He painted the living room, but over a six-week period. We resented having the room disheveled for such a long time. He, however, felt quite confident he was living up to the terms of the contract. We had failed to clarify to him the importance of getting the room back together rapidly. Despite the room's present beauty, bad feelings persist over the arguments that ensued as our unspecified expectations went unmet. In effect, the rules of the game were not clearly understood and the negotiation was less than optimally successful as a result. Negotiation is effective only if rules covering "fair play" and "foul play" can be developed and communicated.

The Direction Strategy minimizes commitment, as the other is forced into taking action or precluded from doing something (s)he wants to do because of a desire to get something of value (Reward Power) or to avoid punishment (Coercive Power). The motivation of the person being so directed is to find a way to acquire the reward or to avoid the punishment, *not* to perform in accordance with the mandate. Surveillance therefore becomes a necessity. Organizations in which "the mice play while the cat's away" are generally characterized by a directive managerial style. If you are not in a position to establish tight surveillance procedures, then Direction is probably a strategy to be avoided.

Given the one-way goal dependence inherent in the Enlistment Strategy, controls are neither possible nor necessary. We cannot control the response of those to whom we appeal; we can only make sure that all we risk is a denial of our requests, that the persons to whom we appeal would not gain by compounding rejection with other forms of punishment.

Selecting a Power Strategy

CONDITIONS	STRATEGIES			
	INVOLVING OTHERS	NEGOTIATING WITH OTHERS	DIRECTING OTHERS	ENLISTING OTHERS
GOALS	Your goals are interdependent; to reach yours is to contribute to the ability to others' reach theirs and vice versa.	Your goals are independent; not related.	Your goals are counter-dependent; if you succeed, chances are the other will fail.	You can't reach your goal without the others' help, but their goals are not dependent upon you.
CONTROLS	You rely on the on-going commitment and judgment of the other person.	"Rules" covering fair play and foul play exist and are understood by all parties to the contract.	You have ways to find out about "sabotage" before you're badly hurt; constant or frequent surveillance is possible.	The worst thing the other person can do is turn you down—they would not gain by hurting you in other ways.
URGENCY (TIME)	Time is available for exploration and problem solving. Delay would not hurt either of you.	Delay would hurt the other more than you; you can tolerate a deadlock better than the other; or, delay would hurt both of you.	Delay would be detrimental to you.	Delay would hurt you than the other person.
BALANCE OF POWER	Both parties have information or expertise the other party needs; or, both parties trust and respect each other.	Both parties can help (reward) or hurt (punish) each other.	You can reward or punish the other person more than (s)he can reward or punish you.	The other person likes you, respects you, and is not in a position to be hurt by you.
COMMITMENT REQUIRED	Long-term commitment of the others to your goals is sought.	Commitment to a contract or agreement is more important than commitment to goals.	Long-term commitment of the other person is not important; opposition or antagonism is acceptable (the other person can be "replaced").	Permission or acquiescence is more important than commitment; opposition or antagonism is not acceptable.

Our desire or capacity to implement controls or surveillance procedures is, in large part, a function of the **balance of power** that exists. Assessing the relative balance of power is critical to a selection of the most appropriate influence style.

What is the Balance of Power?

The Involvement Strategy is characterized by a give-and-take of ideas and opinions and by mutual respect. It becomes a workable strategy, then, only when both parties have information or expertise that is of interest to the other, or when mutual trust and respect exists. In short, **effective use of the Involvement Strategy requires a balance of Informal Power.**

The presence of Informal Power is also critical to effective use of the Enlistment Strategy. Only if someone likes you, respects you, and trusts you are they likely to honor your request. Effective enlistments are a product of a strong referent base.

A balance of Formal Power is key to a successful Negotiation. Trades are only satisfying if one person's power to reward is equalled by the other's power to do the same. Compromises are rarely equitable if the power to coerce is unevenly distributed. The results of contests are inconclusive or of little impact if a power imbalance exists as the "game" begins.

Like Negotiation, the Direction Strategy is based on the use of Formal Power. However, because Direction may inspire resentment and resistance, it works only when the balance of Formal Power is on your side.

In selecting an Influence Strategy, it is important to think about the relationship between your **goals** and the goals of the other, the **urgency** that exists for either of you, and the **commitment** or **contribution** you require. It is also important to consider the **controls** available to you to determine whether the other person is acting on your behalf or not, and the **balance of power** that exists in your relationship. All of these criteria are summarized in the table on page 107.

As you use this table in any given situation, you are unlikely to find a perfect match between your situation and a single strategy. While your need for the other's commitment may point to Involvement, urgency may point to Direction. Or, perhaps you depend on the other person for your goal attainment, but the dependency is not returned. You consider Enlistment, only to find that you need a greater degree of ongoing commitment than this strategy tends to promote. While the table can be helpful, it cannot substitute for good judgment.

The Importance of Flexibility and Judgment

As your situation changes, so must your Influence Strategy. The effective manager is aware of all the options, and is able to blend judgment with personal style preferences in dealing with managerial dilemmas as they occur. The importance of being able to shift strategy was illustrated by a manager in an automobile manufacturing organization as he moved through the stages of an assembly plant launch preparation and the launch itself to a more routinized plant operation.

During the months preceding the launch, the plant manager effectively enlisted the cooperation of others. He was faced with the job of enticing highly qualified people to leave their present positions to join him in a remote location in a potentially high-risk situation (launch failure). Other plant managers, reluctant to lose their best people, were using all the Reward Power at their disposal to keep their best technicians and managers. The new plant manager was not in a position to counter with the promise of rewards or with the threat of coercion. He had to rely exclusively on Informal Power, taking advantage of others' perceptions of his administrative and managerial track record (Expert Power), of the Referent Power accorded a man who had "come up through the ranks," and of the Indirect Power coming from a well-established network of friends and acquaintances throughout the corporation.

Once the manager had succeeded in getting his people on board, he continued relying on Informal Power, but began looking to his staff members to exercise more influence over plant events. In effect, the manager moved into the Involvement Strategy. He felt his primary prelaunch objective was to pool and synthesize the expertise of his newly recruited resources, and in the process to create a new concept for plant operations. Needing the input and commitment of everyone, he permitted almost total freedom as future functional heads began to structure their departments, work out interdepartmental relationships, and staff their operations. Everyone involved at prelaunch, regardless of his or her eventual role in the operation, had a voice in decisions that would affect eventual plant-wide conditions. There was little trace of hierarchy or of the use of formal kinds of leverage.

Just prior to the launch, the plant manager moved away from the "one person, one vote" practice. He began to exercise and impose more formal leverage over his department heads and their staff members. While still giving them room to exercise judgment, he made it very clear that everything had its price. In effect, he assumed the posture of a Negotiative manager. Engineering wanted authorization to establish an innovative storage and retrieval system for finished subassemblies. The manager was skeptical of the plan, but negotiated a deal—try it and if it succeeds, we'll implement it plant-wide; if it fails, we'll drop the idea for good. In response to Quality Control's request for on-line inspection stations, the manager negotiated a compromise—"I won't do that, but I will train production workers to inspect assemblies at specified points." He got lower reject and rework cost standards by trading tighter vendor specifications with higher costs as requested by Materials Handling.

The Negotiation Strategy was effective as the new operation was being debugged and fine-tuned. Once new operating policies and procedures were in place, the primary focus was on productivity. The need for predictability, routinization, and speed emerged. The plant manager responded to the need by shifting to the Direction Strategy. People were rewarded for following the rules, and punished for failure to cooperate. Production quality and cost objectives were firmly upheld by the manager.

That the manager used his influence options appropriately is demonstrated by the results of the launch. Full production was achieved in less than three months, at which time the plant was outperforming 80 percent of other on-line assembly plants in the corporation.

Flexibility in Strategy Implementation

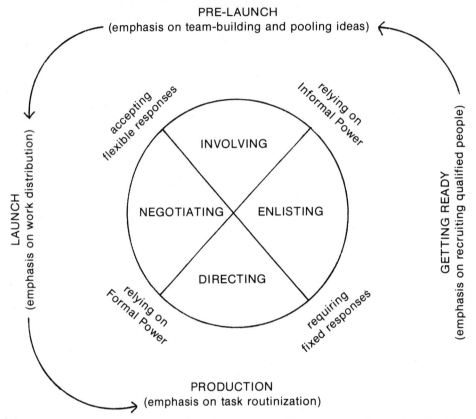

PRE-LAUNCH
(emphasis on team-building and pooling ideas)

LAUNCH
(emphasis on work distribution)

GETTING READY
(emphasis on recruiting qualified people)

accepting flexible responses

relying on Informal Power

INVOLVING

NEGOTIATING   ENLISTING

DIRECTING

relying on Formal Power

requiring fixed responses

PRODUCTION
(emphasis on task routinization)

After nine months, new product lines were added and both day and night shifts became necessary. In response to these new kinds of problems, his influencing strategy returned to drawing upon the resources of his staff. The plant manager, recognizing and responding to the changed situation, again moved into the Involvement and Negotiation modes.

As the plant manager experienced, the individual who seeks to be effective in the complex and rapidly changing organizations of today will probably have to function with some degree of comfort with all influence strategies. **Flexibility is the key to the effective management of power.**

Flexibility may require a shift in the power base or the acquisition of more of a certain kind of leverage. The subordinate with an innovative idea who can't get his or her boss to risk endorsement needs to acquire power of some kind if (s)he is to contribute ideas to the organization.

Maintaining a success syndrome depends on your ability to generate the kind and degree of leverage that you need to put your selected influence strategy into operation. Increasing Formal Power is not conducive to involving others or enlisting their support. Increasing Informal Power rarely puts you in a position to be directive. Kinds of power and power-getting strategies were discussed in the last chapter. The following chart summarizes the relationship between power and influence style.

Power Dynamics

KINDS OF POWER	GETTING POWER	STRATEGIES FOR USING POWER
FORMAL • Reward ⟶	Candy Store Strategy	DIRECTING • forcing • ordering • blocking
• Coercive ⟶	Arsenal Strategy	
• Legitimate ⟶	Crown Prince Strategy	NEGOTIATION • trading • compromising • contesting
INFORMAL • Expert ⟶	Look What I've Done Strategy	INVOLVEMENT • sharing • enabling • cooperating
• Referent ⟶	Fraternity Strategy	ENLISTING • soliciting • advising • courting
• Associative ⟶	Person Collector Strategy	
INDIRECT ⟶	NETWORKING ⟶	ALL OF THE ABOVE

AN EXERCISE: IDENTIFYING AND SELECTING INFLUENCE STRATEGIES

The plant manager in the example was able to select the most effective Influence Strategy in a variety of different situations. Can you do the same? To get one indication, complete the exercise on the next few pages.

To begin, read the three situations and alternative responses that follow. Then, list in Column I the Influence Strategy you think is being used by the character in the incident. Then, choose the response you think would be most effective, and put a "1" in Column II beside the response. Next, decide which response you would make if your first response choice were not available, and put a "2" beside that response. Finally, mark the response you feel should be a last resort with an "X." (The table on page 107 can help guide you as you decide which influence style would be most effective.)

Use these symbols as you identify the kinds of Influence Style used:

Inv. — Involvement
Neg. — Negotiation
Dir. — Direction
Enl. — Enlistment

Influence Strategy Profile

SITUATION I

You are the manager of a unit. For months, you have been widely regarded as one of the best managers in the company. Your unit has consistently met its quality and quantity standards; turnover and absenteeism rates have been the lowest of any unit. You have reason to believe you're being seriously considered for a promotion that you want very much. In short, everything had been going along fine—until two weeks ago. At that point, you got a new boss who seems intent on ruining your unit's record. The more work your people do, the more he shovels out. Your people have begun to make comments like, "All we get for doing good work is more work." Some of your people are even saying, "It's all your fault—you're riding us to make sure you get your promotion." Absenteeism and tardiness are increasing, and so are error rates. You want to influence the boss so that he changes his ways.

What kinds of influence options do the following responses represent? (Column I) Which would you try first? Second? Last? (Column II)

Col. I	Col. II		
		A.	Go to the boss and suggest you both sit down and specify the results that your unit will be expected to achieve over a certain period of time.
		B.	Go to the boss and explain how his behavior has been affecting the morale in your department, asking him to use the methods used by his predecessor.
		C.	Go to your boss's boss, and explain the situation to him, asking him to insist the new boss change his ways. (Hint: remember the focus of your influence is your boss.)
		D.	Tell your new boss if he'll let you run your unit as you see fit, you'll guarantee a return to high-level, high-quality production.
		E.	Mention to your new boss that the other day you played tennis with a known expert on performance effectiveness and had told him something of your dilemma. Then, suggest the new boss reconsider the way he behaves and the impact his behavior is likely to have. Point out how his behavior has damaged your record.

SITUATION II

You are the manager of the design engineering department of a manufacturing company. One member of your engineering staff has come up with a very innovative way to redesign a critical component of the company's product. You're in favor of the innovation, but know that the director of manufacturing engineering, Bill Wendell, likes things the way they are. You are an organizational peer of Bill's; you and he both report to Sam Jenks. Sam won't do anything unless Bill agrees with it. You know that if you just let the new design idea drop, your staff member will resign. You don't want to lose him since he is one of your best men.

What kinds of influence options do the following responses represent? (Column I) Which would you try first? Second? Last? (Column II)

Col. I	Col. II	
		A. Ask Bill to support this change with the understanding that, if it fails to improve cost and reject rates, you'll stop making waves.
		B. Share with Bill your thoughts on how the new design might help in Bill's process engineering efforts, asking him for any suggestions on modifying the new design.
		C. Share with Bill your fear that your staff member may quit if the design isn't introduced, asking him to help you keep a good man on board.
		D. Tell Bill you'll do him a favor sometime if he'll support the new design.
		E. Tell Bill you'll make a more conservative change than was originally suggested if he'll keep quiet about his reservations.

SITUATION III

You are the manager of a component assembly unit. You have repeatedly told your employees that you believe the manager's major job is to be teacher, guide, and counselor to employees. One of your people, Sally Jones, has taken you at your word. She began coming to you for advice about personal problems around a year ago. While you didn't give her any direct advice, you were a good listener. So good a listener, in fact, that now Sally is in the habit of coming to you first thing every morning with coffee for both of you. It almost seems that she can't begin her day until she has had a real heart-to-heart talk with you. The other employees are beginning to think she is your "favorite." They seem to resent both of you for it. You've noticed Sally generally eats lunch alone, and has few friends among the other employees. You want Sally to discontinue or at least cut back on morning sessions.

What kinds of influence options do the following responses represent? (Column I) Which would you try first? Second? Last? (Column II)

Col. I	Col. II		
		A.	Explain to Sally how her regular visits are hurting both you and herself, and ask her to stop coming to talk with you each morning.
		B.	Give Sally more work so that she won't be able to keep up her work and visit with you in the mornings.
		C.	Explain the problem to Sally, and ask her for her ideas on how to best solve it.
		D.	Suggest to Sally that if she'll cut down on the morning visits, you'll take her to lunch once in a while.
		E.	Tell Sally, "Enough is enough. You're paid to work, not to talk."

How do your answers compare with those others have given? The majority of people who have considered these three incidents have identified the responses as follows:

SITUATION I

A. INVOLVEMENT—using Expert Power (your knowledge of the unit) to encourage the boss to sit down and problem-solve with you.

B. ENLISTMENT—requesting a specific change on the basis of information.

C. DIRECTION—using Indirect Coercive Power to demand a specific outcome.

D. NEGOTIATION—using Reward Power (the power to return to high productivity levels) to set up a trade.

E. ENLISTMENT—using Associative and Indirect Expert Power to achieve a specific behavior change on the part of the boss.

Response "A" is generally regarded as the best response from among those that were provided. It is important to establish an agreement with the new boss, to reach some level of mutual understanding. The influence strategy most likely to contribute to feelings of mutual understanding is Involvement.

SITUATION II

A. NEGOTIATION—using Reward Power to set up a contest.

B. INVOLVEMENT—using Expert Power to get Bill to engage in joint problem-solving.

C. ENLISTMENT—asking for a specific outcome on the basis of need and shared goals (Referent Power).

D. NEGOTIATION—setting up a trade (reward for reward). Outcome is somewhat certain (i.e., kind of favor you will eventually do).

E. NEGOTIATION—compromise (giving a little on your original objective in order to get some support).

Response "B" is generally regarded as the best response, since it represents a high level of Involvement. There is a likelihood that the approach will work, since it focuses on goal interdependencies, and admits that long-term commitment is sought. Responses "E" and "A" are generally regarded as the worst. Both represent negotiating tactics. ("A" is a contest, while "E" is a compromise.) The contest may damage the relationship as it sets up a win–lose situation. The compromise will not accomplish the manager's objectives.

SITUATION III

A. ENLISTMENT—relying on Referent Power ("you wouldn't want to hurt me") to achieve a specific change in Sally's behavior.

B. DIRECTION—relying on your Legitimate Power to give out work to block Sally from visiting you.

C. INVOLVEMENT—relying on Referent Power to get Sally to discuss the issue with you. Outcome is uncertain.

D. NEGOTIATION—"Let's make a deal."

E. DIRECTION—relying on Legitimate, Reward, and Coercive Power to order Sally to discontinue her visits.

Response "C" is generally favored, with "A" regarded as a close second. In both cases, the supervisor maintains his Referent Power over Sally, which is presumed to be desirable since she will continue to work in the unit.

RECONSIDERING THE STRATEGIES YOU TEND TO USE

Now that you're familiar with the options available to you as you attempt to influence others, I suggest you take a few minutes to reconsider the results of the Influence Styles Profile (Appendix D), if you chose to complete it.

You can interpret your scores by referring to your scoring sheet. To use the scores, look first at your "a," "b," "c," and "d" totals. These figures represent the extent to which you use a particular influence strategy. If your score is 0–19, you have a low level of reliance on that strategy. If your score is 20–54, you have a moderate level of reliance on that strategy. A score of 55–84 indicates a heavy reliance on that strategy. Then, look at your "e" scores. Divide your Part I "e" score by 2. Compare the result to your Part I "a" totals, "b" totals, etc., to get an indication of the degree to which you prefer *not influencing the situation* to any of the influence modes.

Whether your scores are "good" or "bad" depends on your situation. In some organizations, where tasks and situations change rapidly, flexibility (represented by having approximately the same score for each strategy), is critical. Only you can determine the effectiveness of the strategies you currently use.

To begin doing so, look back at the table on page 107. To use the chart, put an "X" next to all those conditions that describe your present situation. Do most of the marked conditions fall under the strategy you tend to use most often (as indicated) by your profile results)? If not, perhaps your effectiveness would be improved by using another strategy. The chart will be most helpful to you if you go through this interpretive exercise three times; once with your subordinates in mind, once with your organizational peers in mind, and once with your boss in mind.

In applying this chart, we sometimes find that the strategy we should be using is not one that we are comfortable using. Considering the primary outcomes of each influence strategy can be helpful in identifying why one strategy makes us comfortable, while we avoid another.

Outcomes of Influence Strategies

| STRATEGY | OUTCOMES | |
	POTENTIAL COMFORTS	POTENTIAL DISCOMFORTS
DIRECTION	☐ Gets things done in a hurry. ☐ Gets things done your way.	☐ The other may learn to dislike and mistrust you. ☐ The other will comply only when you're around to observe his or her compliance.
NEGOTIA-TION	☐ You know precisely what you can expect of the other person. ☐ You know precisely what you have to give (or give up) to get the behavior you want. ☐ Requires that little time be spent in building trust or closeness.	☐ Flexibility diminishes as responding to change is slowed by having to re-negotiate the contract. ☐ You have to keep struggling to maintain the rewards or sanctions that are motivating the other person to deal with you. ☐ "Rules" must be developed to deal with every contingency.

STRATEGY	OUTCOMES POTENTIAL COMFORTS	POTENTIAL DISCOMFORTS
ENLIST-MENT	☐ You get what you want without incurring the other person's resentment. ☐ You don't have to give up anything in exchange for the other person's support.	☐ You have no control over the other person's changing his or her mind. ☐ You make yourself vulnerable as you let the other person know you "need" his or her help.
INVOLVE-MENT	☐ The other person feels accountable and responsible for what happens. ☐ The other person is committed to what you're trying to do. ☐ Innovation and creativity are likely, as everyone builds on everyone else's ideas.	☐ A lot of time must be spent in solving problems and resolving conflicts. ☐ Things could fall apart if the other person decided (s)he didn't like you or couldn't trust you. ☐ When numbers of people who must be involved become large, decision-making grinds to a halt.

To use the chart, define a single person or group of persons with whom you wish to be more effective. Then, check the five "comforts" that are most important to you. Then, check the five "discomforts" that you can tolerate least well. The strategy that has the most "comfort" checkmarks and the fewest "discomfort" checkmarks is the one you probably attempt to use whenever possible.

Too often, the influence strategy we want to use and the one we actually use are different because we don't have the power we need, the time we'd like, because our goals don't mesh, or because of the kind of commitment or contribution we require. In those cases, it may be possible to change situational constraints (time, power, and goals) and, in so doing, to open up other influence options.

For example, making Involvement an effective strategy requires that you: (1) change the time constraints you're working under, so that you have more freedom to spend time resolving conflicts and solving problems; (2) work with the other person to define shared goals; (3) build informal leverage over the other person by increasing the ties of friendship or expertise; (4) open yourself to considering the ideas of the other person.

Moving toward Negotiation requires that you build a sufficient reward or punishment base to equal (but not to surpass) the clout of the one you need to influence. For example, management is rapidly becoming aware of the benefits of dealing with strong unions—unions that have clout comparable to management's leverage. The "weak" union, in its attempts to appear stronger than it is and to avoid being "railroaded," often makes more unrealistic, nonnegotiable demands than a strong union.

If Direction is the strategy you want to use, then it is critical to swing the balance of power in your direction. Corner the market on what the other feels is rewarding, and you will be in a position to be directive. Or, build up a more impressive arsenal by putting yourself in a position to demand compliance "or else."

If Enlistment is the strategy you prefer, then it is important to gain the respect, friendship, or political support of those whom you hope to influence: "Help me because you like me; because you respect what I know or what I can do; or, because you believe in what I stand for." When appeals are hedged with Formal Power, they are not effective. People rarely respond to the appeal, "Help me because you like me, and on top of that, because if you don't . . . ."

It is sometimes possible to alter conditions (e.g., by defining shared goals or altering the balance of power) in order to make it possible to actually do what you prefer to do. Other times, situational constraints are unalterable, and it would be unwise to follow the strategic choice that makes you most uncomfortable.

Power is at once your greatest asset and, probably, the source of one of your greatest dilemmas. Using power constructively requires the capacity to apply the appropriate influence option. None of the options will be effective, however, unless those abuses that lend credibility to the belief that "power corrupts" are avoided. Among these abuses is **hedging**—gathering ammunition just in case your Referent Power proves to be inadequate and you need to move from Enlistment to Direction.

A second abuse, often committed unintentionally, is **confusing the other party.** For example, implying that Negotiation is acceptable and then coming on with Direction tactics may win you a short-lived victory, but will build longer-term resentment. Confusing the other party is a form of manipulation; it backfires as often as it works.

Manipulation is the subject of the next chapter. What is it? Is it necessary? Does it work? How can we avoid being manipulated?

5

Another Option: Manipulation

Some people attempt to influence outcomes through the manipulation of others. Manipulators would generally deny that they use this approach, however; manipulation has a bad name in our society. People are supposed to be "straight," not devious; ambitious, but not artful. Later in this chapter, we'll take a close look at manipulation— is it good or bad? Does it work? Should people ever manipulate? If so, when? What happens when manipulators get caught? Is there a way to avoid being manipulated? Before exploring these issues, spend ten minutes or so completing the self-profile that follows. The results will give you some indication of your own manipulative tendencies.

The profile consists of six situations with alternative responses. To complete the profile, read each of the situations. Then, distribute 20 points to show the extent to which you favor one response over another. If you greatly prefer Response A to the others, but would consider, in this order, C, D, and E, then you might spread your 20 points this way:

A	10
B	0
C	4
D	3
E	3
F	0

Remember, you are to assign a total of 20 points for every situation! Use whole numbers only.

Manipulation Self-Profile

SITUATION I

You are a young, single woman with a boss who has a reputation for "making it" with all his female employees. You have nothing against him as a boss, but he holds no personal attraction for you. He has made several attempts to get you to have dinner with him, but you've always managed a polite excuse. Yesterday, he let one of your friends know that he didn't like being rejected and thinks you feel that you're "too good" for him. You know he can (and will) block your efforts to secure a promotion if you don't do something to make him feel better about you. What would you do? Spread 20 points to indicate your preferences.

_____ A. Ask him for advice on how to deal with your boyfriend, hoping he'll assume a fatherly or avuncular role with you after that.

_____ B. Openly tell your boss that his invitations upset you and that you would like him to stop putting both of you in an awkward position.

_____ C. Let your boss know that you'll consider resigning if he doesn't stop.

_____ D. Let your boss think you are interested in him but that you are afraid that if you let a relationship develop, you would never really know whether your career progress was a function of merit or pull.

_____ E. Do everything you can to make yourself socially and personally unattractive to the manager.

_____ F. Make him believe that you have four adopted children and a sick mother, and therefore would love to get involved with a man who could help you support the brood.

SITUATION II

You are a landscaper who has had a very difficult time getting new customers. You know your work is of the highest quality, and that your prices are competitive. You've tried mailers, but the response has been low, so you've decided that the personal contact that comes with calling on people in their homes is the way to approach the problem. What are you going to do? Spread 20 points to indicate your preferences.

_____ A. Ask homeowners to give you a chance to show what you can do with the understanding that if they aren't fully satisfied, you'll refund 25 percent of the payments made to you.

_____ B. Conduct a survey of local landscape needs and desires in order to get an opportunity to talk to homeowners long enough to begin to build a relationship and to demonstrate your expertise in the field.

_____ C. Explain to prospective customers how great their yards could look. Then, state that it's too bad you won't have time to get to it this season.

_____ D. For each home you plan to call on, draw a picture of what the yard could look like, given a team of gardeners and a significant investment. Show your picture to the homeowner as an illustration of what you can do for him with a modest investment on his part.

_____ E. Tell homeowners that you are struggling to get better established in the landscape business, and appeal to their desire to help you on your way.

_____ F. Present yourself as an office worker who is sick of the "routine" and wants to try outdoor work. Try to get the homeowner to give you a chance to learn a new trade.

SITUATION III

You are the owner/manager of a travel agency. Several months ago, you took on a new travel agent. Unfortunately, there has been a great deal of disruption in your office since then because your new agent just can't seem to get along with your other employees. You want the new agent to leave your employ, but you want to do it in such a way that there are no bad feelings—the agent is capable, and you would like to retain his respect for you so that he will refer business to you. What would you do? Spread 20 points to indicate your preferences.

_____ A. Tell him that finances are forcing you to cut back on overhead, and that since he is the most recent person to be hired, you have no choice but to let him go. In the process, do your best to convince him that this is something you're sorry you have to do.

_____ B. Shift his responsibilities so that he is forced to perform functions that he doesn't like to do, and will voluntarily resign.

_____ C. Convince him that he is far too talented to waste his time in your small agency, and that you care enough about him and his future to urge him to find a more challenging position with a greater potential for advancement.

_____ D. Tell him directly that the employment situation is not working out for you, and suggest that he work as an outside agent, referring business to you and taking a finder's fee in exchange for referrals.

_____ E. Explain the situation as you see it, and ask for his resignation.

_____ F. Start being grumpy, moody, and difficult to be with, making him dislike you, while still giving him reason to respect your expertise.

SITUATION IV

You are the company's manager of human resource development. You report directly to the personnel manager who knows little about your field, is tight with the budget, and is aware that your competence could make her look bad by comparison. You perceive the need and readiness for an executive development program. You know that, by running the program, you will have a chance to demonstrate your competence to those who really make things happen in the organization. Your boss keeps putting off or avoiding a discussion about the matter with you. You want her to agree to let you design and conduct the program. What would you do? Spread 20 points to indicate your preferences.

_____ A. Write a memo telling your boss that the need exists but that unfortunately you don't have time to respond to it.

_____ B. Make your boss believe you are afraid of being asked to design and run an executive development program, that you are not sure you could handle it.

_____ C. Design the program on your own time; on a one-to-one basis tell people of its availability, and get commitments from potential participants. Then, tell your boss that you are going to conduct the program.

_____ D. Convince your boss that she should do something to make herself appear to be highly responsive to the needs of the organization. Suggest you've got some ideas that would put her in the limelight.

_____ E. Suggest that the boss do an informal needs analysis with the top executives to find out what kinds of training and development needs they have. Assure her that you will be happy to provide anything she wants as a result of the analysis effort.

_____ F. Write your boss a memo outlining why you feel there is both a need for and a readiness for an executive development program. Ask her to let you do it, in order to both satisfy your own job needs and the needs of the organization as a whole.

SITUATION V

You are the chief executive officer of a large organization. When you assumed your position, the company was experiencing difficulties due to excessive overhead, mismanagement, and "deadwood." During your first year in office, you fired 30 percent of the staff, and maintained tight surveillance over what happened throughout the organization. Now, three years later, everyone is afraid of you—afraid that if they report any bad news at all, it will mean their job. As a result, you find out very little. You've heard rumors of trouble in the Colorado plant, and you feel you've got to learn what is happening there. How would you go about it? Spread 20 points to indicate your preferences.

_____ A. Go to the plant, dress in work clothes, assume a false name, and mingle with the workers.

_____ B. Call the head of the Colorado plant to your office, and insist that he tell you what is going on out there.

_____ C. Go to Colorado and spend some time getting to know the head of the plant on an informal basis. Let him know that underneath it all, you are really a nice guy. Then, explain why you need to know the full story and ask him to share it with you.

_____ D. Tell the manager of the Colorado plant that you are attempting to do career and succession planning and that you need to understand more about his operation in order to identify a suitable successor for him.

_____ E. Tell the Colorado manager that you respect his expertise and want to learn more from him on how to create highly productive work environments.

_____ F. Send a consultant out to the plant. Tell the consultant to pretend that he knows nothing about the situation, and really isn't in a position to make any recommendations. Suggest that the consultant go in the guise of a student doing research on plant operations.

SITUATION VI

You are an interviewer, interviewing a job applicant who has favorably impressed several of your coworkers. Your own intuition tells you that this woman would create problems for your organization. Furthermore, you don't like her. Unless you can find out more about her weaknesses, you know she'll be offered full-time employment. The woman is alert and very perceptive and, thus far, has succeeded in giving the "right" answers to all your questions. You've got to make her open up. But how? Spread 20 points to indicate your preferences.

_____ A. Deny your expertise in an area, and then ask her to explain the area to you, hoping she'll feel safe about talking to a novice, allowing you to pinpoint her weaknesses without her knowing that you are able to identify them as such.

_____ B. Imply that you are subordinate to the people she has already talked with, and that your vote doesn't count much.

_____ C. Explain to her that taking a job with an organization in which she doesn't really fit would be as damaging and costly to her as to the organization. Then, ask her to talk with you more openly about concerns you both have.

_____ D. Pretend that you really like the woman, and that you think the two of you could really work well together. Then, just let her talk.

_____ E. Tell her that your gut reaction to her is negative, and that unless she will talk openly about her weaknesses as well as her strengths, you will block her hiring.

_____ F. Convince her that it would be to her advantage to work on a short-term project with the company before making the commitment to become a permanent employee. Then, set up the project so that she's bound to fail.

Manipulation Self-Profile Score Sheet

ITEM	RESPONSE TYPE I	ITEM	RESPONSE TYPE II	ITEM	RESPONSE TYPE III
I-B	_____	I-C	_____	I-A	_____
II-E	_____	II-A	_____	II-B	_____
III-E	_____	III-D	_____	III-C	_____
IV-F	_____	IV-C	_____	IV-D	_____
V-C	_____	V-B	_____	V-E	_____
VI-C	_____	VI-E	_____	VI-D	_____
TOTAL _____		TOTAL _____		TOTAL _____	
INVOLVEMENT/ ENLISTMENT		DIRECTION/ NEGOTIATION		SEDUCTION	

ITEM	RESPONSE TYPE IV	ITEM	RESPONSE TYPE V	ITEM	RESPONSE TYPE VI
I-D	_____	I-E	_____	I-F	_____
II-D	_____	II-F	_____	II-C	_____
III-B	_____	III-F	_____	III-A	_____
IV-E	_____	IV-B	_____	IV-A	_____
V-D	_____	V-A	_____	V-F	_____
VI-F	_____	VI-A	_____	VI-B	_____
TOTAL _____		TOTAL _____		TOTAL _____	
ENTRAPMENT		DISCLAIMER		CAMOUFLAGE	

After completing your rank order selections, fill out the scoring format on the previous page. Simply copy the number you put beside each response in the appropriate place on the chart.

The lowest possible score you could have generated for any single Response Type is 0; the highest is 120. **High scores indicate a strong preference for the response type. Low scores indicate a weak preference for the response type.** To get a picture of your manipulative tendencies, construct a bar graph following this example:

Let's assume you had the following total scores: Type I: 40, Type II: 30, Type III: 30, Type; IV: 15, Type V: 25, Type VI: 2. You would graph your scores this way:

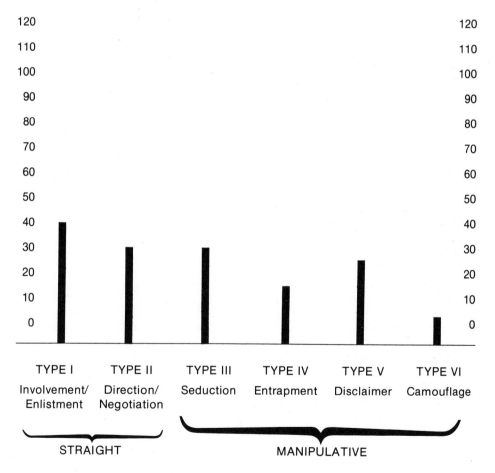

Sample Manipulation Profile

A blank format for your use follows.

Manipulation Profile

120						120
110						110
100						100
90						90
80						80
70						70
60						60
50						50
40						40
30						30
20						20
10						10
0						0

TYPE I	TYPE II	TYPE III	TYPE IV	TYPE V	TYPE VI
Involvement/ Enlistment	Direction/ Negotiation	Seduction	Entrapment	Disclaimer	Camouflage

STRAIGHT   MANIPULATIVE

The tallest bar represents the strategy you most prefer to use; the shortest bar represents the option you are least likely to select. Is your tallest bar a straight influence strategy (Type I or II)? Or is your tallest bar a manipulative approach (Type III, IV, V or VI)? Which of the manipulative strategies do you most prefer: Types III, IV, V or VI?

Next, construct a bar graph to compare the extent to which you rely on a straight influence strategy rather than a manipulative option. To prepare this chart, find the following totals:

(Type I total + Type II total) × 2 = _____

Total of Type III + Type IV + Type V + Type VI =_____

Put these new totals on the following bar chart.

Straight vs. Manipulative Influence Strategy

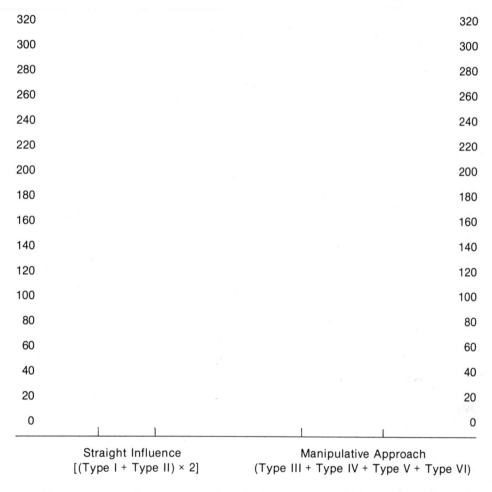

320		320
300		300
280		280
260		260
240		240
220		220
200		200
180		180
160		160
140		140
120		120
100		100
80		80
60		60
40		40
20		20
0		0

Straight Influence
[(Type I + Type II) × 2]

Manipulative Approach
(Type III + Type IV + Type V + Type VI)

Next, compare the extent to which you use your Informal Power in a straight rather than manipulative fashion. To do so, graph these figures:

Type I total × 2 = _____

Type III + Type V = _____

Straight vs. Manipulative Informal Power

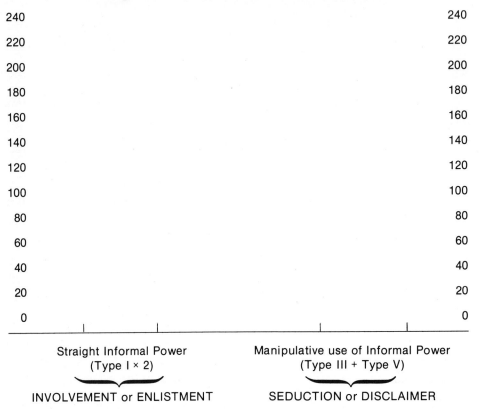

240	240
220	220
200	200
180	180
160	160
140	140
120	120
100	100
80	80
60	60
40	40
20	20
0	0

Straight Informal Power
(Type I × 2)

INVOLVEMENT or ENLISTMENT

Manipulative use of Informal Power
(Type III + Type V)

SEDUCTION or DISCLAIMER

Next, compare the extent to which you use your Formal Power in a straight rather than manipulative fashion. To do so, graph these figures:

Type II total × 2 = _____

Type IV + Type VI = _____

Straight vs. Manipulative Formal Power

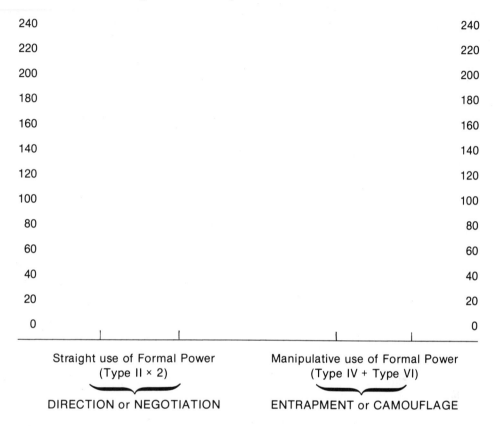

240		240
220		220
200		200
180		180
160		160
140		140
120		120
100		100
80		80
60		60
40		40
20		20
0		0

Straight use of Formal Power
(Type II × 2)

DIRECTION or NEGOTIATION

Manipulative use of Formal Power
(Type IV + Type VI)

ENTRAPMENT or CAMOUFLAGE

To what extent do you use the "double whammy" (which we will discuss later in this chapter) in your dealings with others? Chart these totals:

Type III + Type IV = _____

Type V + Type VI = _____

Type I + Type II = _____
(Note: do not multiply by 2)

The Double Whammy

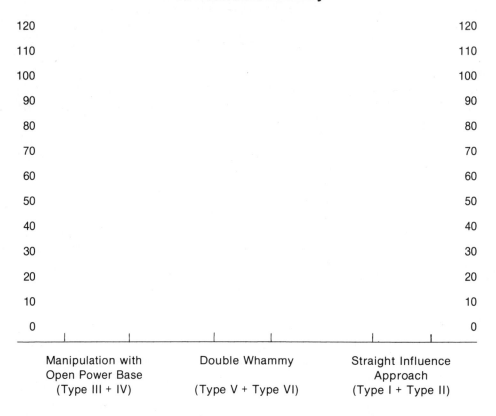

120			120
110			110
100			100
90			90
80			80
70			70
60			60
50			50
40			40
30			30
20			20
10			10
0			0

| Manipulation with Open Power Base (Type III + IV) | Double Whammy (Type V + Type VI) | Straight Influence Approach (Type I + Type II) |

During the following discussion of each manipulative approach refer back to the charts to gauge the extent of your reliance on the approach in question. You will probably want to pay particular attention to the sections dealing with your preferred approaches.

WHAT IS MANIPULATION?

The dictionary defines manipulation as an attempt to "control by artful, unfair, or insidious means to one's own advantage." But what do the terms "artful," "insidious," and "unfair" mean? They are subjective terms, depending on your point of view for interpretation. What seems unfair to me may seem entirely fair to you. What seems insidious to you may appear to be simply necessary to me. In general, we appear to be increasingly willing to accept anything that accomplishes our objectives. The means are becoming less and less of an issue.

The important difference between manipulation and other forms of influence is not moral, but behavioral in nature. **The difference lies in the extent to which the influencer is open about his or her agenda, or about the objectives s(he) hopes to accomplish.** As we have seen, there are some major differences in approach and impact between the Involvement, Enlistment, Negotiation, and Direction strategies. There is also a critical similarity—**directors, negotiators, involvers, and enlisters all let the target of influence know (or, at least, do not attempt to preclude him or her from knowing) about the ultimate objective.** As management and union negotiate, the union is aware that management wants to keep labor costs low; management is aware that the union wants the best employment package it can get. When you involve another in a problem-solving activity around an issue that you feel requires the resources and commitment of both of you, then you certainly do not attempt to conceal your objective (to solve the problem) from your associate.

    Manipulators do attempt to conceal their objectives from their targets of influence. In all cases, they pretend to pursue one objective while actually pursuing another. This holds true whether the manipulator is relying on an Informal Power base (Referent, Expert, or Associative), or on a Formal Power base (Legitimate, Reward, or Coercive). Either is possible:

RELYING ON
INFORMAL POWER

INVOLVING OR ENLISTING	MANIPULATION: SEDUCTION OR DISCLAIMER
INFLUENCER'S OBJECTIVE IS OPEN	**INFLUENCER'S OBJECTIVE IS HIDDEN**
NEGOTIATING OR DIRECTING	MANIPULATION: ENTRAPMENT OR CAMOUFLAGE

RELYING ON
FORMAL POWER

Influence and Power Bases

Two varieties of manipulations involve the use of Informal Power. These manipulations involve pursuit of a hidden agenda either through a direct use of Referent, Expert, or Associative Power, or through denial of friendship, expertise, or contacts. We call the first tactic manipulation through Seduction. The second is manipulation through Disclaimer.

MANIPULATION THROUGH INFORMAL POWER

SEDUCTION	DISCLAIMER
POWER BASE IS OPEN OR ADMITTED	POWER BASE IS HIDDEN OR CONCEALED (The Double Whammy)

Manipulation Through Informal Power

Similarly, there are two tactics available to the manipulator who relies on Formal Power. When hidden objectives are accomplished through the open use of Reward, Coercive, or Legitimate power, we have **entrapment**. When these hidden objectives are accomplished through refusal to use the power at the manipulator's disposal, we witness manipulation through **camouflage**.

POWER BASE IS OPEN OR ADMITTED	POWER BASE IS HIDDEN OR CONCEALED
ENTRAPMENT	CAMOUFLAGE

MANIPULATION THROUGH FORMAL POWER

Manipulation through Formal Power

Presented graphically, the manipulator's four options look like this . . .

MANIPULATION THROUGH INFORMAL POWER

SEDUCTION	DISCLAIMER
POWER BASE IS OPEN OR ADMITTED	POWER BASE IS HIDDEN OR CONCEALED (The Double Whammy)
ENTRAPMENT	CAMOUFLAGE

MANIPULATION THROUGH FORMAL POWER

Manipulation: The Four Options

In the pages that follow, we'll take a closer look at all four types of manipulation.

Seduction: The Hidden Agenda Combined With Open Use of Informal Power

> My Seduction score is:
>
> Possible Range: 0–120 (see page 124)

Picture the little child who sits on Daddy's knee, gives him an unexpected hug and kiss and a touch of flattery, and then asks to be taken to the store to buy some candy. Was the father harmed in any way? Not likely. Was the father manipulated? Definitely. The child's actual objective (to get candy) was hidden behind the apparent objective of giving Daddy some tender loving care. Why did the father comply with the child's wishes, and take him or her to the store? What was the child's power base? It was Referent in nature. Daddy loves the child, and wants the same in return. Because of his affection (and his needs for affection), the child was able to manipulate him into going out together for candy.

One professional I know was periodically challenged early in his working life to "stretch" by a supervisor/mentor who understood his love for challenge and prefaced a few critical assignments with, "I don't think you've got what it takes to handle this, but right now I've no other options." While this might have weakened the self-confidence of some, it spurred this professional to such a level of effort that he mastered skills that even he thought were beyond his province. The professional very much wanted to be admired and respected by his mentor and did indeed stretch to exceed the latter's expectations.

Matchmaking is another form of seduction that can end happily for everyone involved. Jane invites bachelor Carl to a dinner party, telling him she is having other guests who would be interested in hearing his opinions on a few questions. Her hidden agenda is to have Carl meet (and then date) her sister Sue. She invites Sue for the weekend, saying it's about time they had a good visit and that the only "distraction" will be a small dinner party on Saturday night.

The little child's manipulation was innocent enough. The mentor's manipulation produced a positive outcome. The matchmaker got Carl and Sue together. No one really got hurt.

Other individuals not quite so benevolent, manipulate through a clever blend of Referent and Expert Power, such as the unqualified persons who play psychiatrist. Most of us have been exposed to a "shrink player" at least once in our lives. This is the person who, out of apparent concern, tells us what we *really* think or feel, or should:

"You're not really angry at me; you're feeling guilty for letting this happen, which is producing a lot of anxiety. You're just letting this anxiety out in the form of anger."

"You are avoiding the task because you have an extreme case of fear of failure."

"You would be a lot more effective if you could understand that your behavior reflects a lot of pent-up anger that you are afraid to express."

As psychology becomes popularized through such programs as Marriage Encounter, EST, Transactional Analysis, consciousness raising groups, etc., the potential for "shrink" manipulations is bound to increase. It is not unusual today to hear such psychobabble as "you're not tuned in"; "I've got it"; and "Can you relate?" in general usage. The terms themselves are harmless, and the programs that promote them are often helpful to individual participants, whose levels of self-insight increase. When they become ammunition for the manipulator, however, they become potentially dangerous. The damage occurs when the manipulator has enough Referent Power to convince the target of influence that (s)he really cares, when the target of influence believes the manipulator's knowledge exceeds his or her self-knowledge (Expert Power), and when the statements are used to accomplish a hidden objective.

Consider two persons at the same hierarchical level in an organization. One person is perceived to be so competent as to threaten the other's chances for promotion. The latter's true agenda is to create a situation in which the other must fail. His expressed agenda is to meet a series of deadlines. He manipulates his peer into compliance through reference to the other's motivations, hangups, etc.:

Competent Peer: "We have to find ways to stagger these deadlines. I'm overcommitted, and I know that the quality of my work will suffer if I turn out products under this kind of time pressure. In the end, our organization will suffer for it."

Threatened Peer: "Now, Stanley. Put it into perspective. You always panic when you have to think about more than one thing at a time. You don't give yourself enough credit; you should have more confidence in yourself. We both know you are an alarmist. You get a kick out of telling others that you're going to fail, and then succeeding. You should understand that people won't think any less of you if you stop making a bigger deal out of everything than is necessary."

People who threaten illness or suicide in order to accomplish their objectives are relying on Referent Power to seduce others into action. In discussing this chapter, a friend of mine brought up the example of his grandmother, who apparently threatened to kill herself at least five times a week. Would she ever carry it out? Not at all likely, according to my friend. Did her threat work? It definitely did, as family members scurried around to make life more pleasant and less stressful for Grandma. No matter how much scurrying was done, however, Grandma persisted in her threats. It seemed that no effort was great enough, and no comfort sufficient enough, to satisfy her. This was because Grandma's true objective was not to have more life comforts. Instead, she may have wished to exercise tighter control over the household or to get attention in a household where she felt unwelcome.

Grandma exercised the double Referent Power of being a family member and being sufficiently weak, sick, and needy to support her manipulations. She exercised a kind of tyranny—not that of the strong and mighty, but the tyranny of the weak. The tyranny of the weak tends to be exercised by non-assertive people who, in Transactional Analysis terms, play the manipulative role of victim. Weak or dependent people have almost a built-in Referent base, since most of us have absorbed a cultural value that says "the sick, needy, and dependent deserve to be cared for by those of us who are strong," or "Be thy brother's keeper." We then feel extremely guilty when we turn our back on the weak or infirm. Young children can be highly effective manipulators, sending their mothers into a tailspin trying to figure out what they really want. Clumsy people who are continually apologizing for being "stupid" or "careless" succeed not only in demanding forgiveness (their upfront objective), but also in getting an undue amount of attention (their hidden objective).[1]

Seduction, or the combined use of a hidden objective and an Informal Power base, can leave the other person uncertain about what really happened: "I was sure he knew what he was doing; how come it turned out this way?"; "I did exactly as he asked me to do, and now he's furious with me"; "If I had only known. ..." The element of surprise and bewilderment is even greater when the manipulator both negates his or her Informal Power base and pursues a hidden objective. The target of the manipulation, in this case, experiences the full impact of a double whammy.

Double Whammy, or Disclaimer: Pursuing a Hidden Agenda While Denying the Informal Power Base

> My Disclaimer score is: (see page 124)
>
> Possible Range: 0–120

---

[1]For further discussion of manipulations performed by Non-Assertive people, see George Bach and Herbert Goldberg, *Creative Aggression* (Garden City, NY: Doubleday and Co., Inc., 1974), pp. 17-132; also see Muriel James and Dorothy Jongeward, *Born to Win: Transactional Analysis with Gestalt Experiments* (Reading, MA: Addison-Wesly Publishing Co., 1971).

Manipulations that involve denial of Informal Power (Disclaimers) are costing the government and the taxpayers a tremendous amount of money each year, as people on unemployment decide to maintain their leisure. One young woman I know left her job in March and decided she didn't really want to find work until the end of the summer. She carefully concealed this objective from the state unemployment department. However, they persisted in finding job interviews for her, regarding her as someone who would be easy to place in a clerical/receptionist position, given her appealing looks, her immaculate grooming habits, and her good clerical skills. But when she went to interviews, Ms. X donned unironed, tight pants, and replaced her generally conservative makeup with flashy red lipstick, glittering eye shadow, and harsh rouge. Throughout the interview, she chewed a stick of gum with such vigor that every smack could be heard in the next office. When time came for the typing test, she intentionally placed her hands one key over, so that ninety percent of her work was in error. When asked how she would answer the office phone, she responded, "Hi there!" In short, she did everything in her power to convince the interviewer that they had nothing in common, socially or intellectually. She fully negated both her Referent and Expert Power and successfully achieved her hidden objective.

One interviewer I know uses Disclaimer very effectively. He is actually a brilliant management analyst who frowns heavily on what he regards as "social excesses"—all night parties, heavy drinking, extensive dating, etc. Part of his function is to recruit and hire students in their last semester, and his overt objective is to spot people with analytical ability; his hidden objective is to make sure the company rosters are filled with people like himself who are extremely conservative in their life habits. He has been fooled often enough by young people who know what he wants to hear to believe firmly in the wisdom of a manipulative approach. At some point in the interview, he opens his jacket, slouches down a little in his chair, puts on his best devil-may-care smile and begins to reminisce about his "good old days at college." His stories are filled with references to beer parties and crazy party stunts. The manipulation "works" when the interviewee responds in kind, and, attempting to build Referent Power, tries to convince the interviewer that (s)he, too, is a good "party person." If (s)he is convincing enough, then (s)he knocks himself or herself out of the running for the position.

Parents often use Disclaimer to manipulate their children into performing, or into "doing the best they can":

Johnny: "Dad, I can't solve these algebra problems. Would you help me with them?"

Dad: "I'd be happy to help you, but I really don't remember anything about algebra."

Johnny: "I'm sure you'd remember if you just worked on a few."

Dad: (makes a half-hearted attempt) "No, my mind is a blank. Why don't you show me how you would solve the first one; maybe that will help me remember."

Johnny: "Okay, here's how I would approach it. I don't know if it's right, but that's where I would begin."

Dad: "Hmm . . . right . . . I think it's beginning to come back. What would you do next?"

Johnny: "Well, I would . . ."

Dad: "Great; doesn't really look like you need my help, does it?"

Dad's apparent objective was to remember how to work algebra problems. His hidden objective was to show Johnny that he could do them himself. He accomplished this by disclaiming his Expert Power.

Disclaiming Expert Power is not always so well intended. It is sometimes done to get others to do work the manipulator can but doesn't want to do. Consider the case of the manager who is behind in his paperwork and doesn't want to spend all his evenings catching up. He writes for a hobby, but this talent is little known among his peers since his function rarely requires reports of any magnitude.

Manager #1: "I really admire people like you who can express themselves in writing. Me, I'm more of a verbal person."

Manager #2: "Oh, it's nothing. I find writing very easy. It's speaking to groups that I don't do very well."

Manager #1: "It takes me forever to put my thoughts in writing. I've got a report due tomorrow that is at most five pages long, and I'll probably have to stay up most of the night to get it done."

Manager #2: "I'd be happy to stay a little late tonight to help you with it."

Manager #1: "That's really nice of you. Unfortunately, it's my daughter's birthday today, and I've got to get home on time for her birthday dinner. I probably won't even get to the report until ten o'clock or so."

Manager #2: "What's the report about?"

Manager #1: "Oh, it's just a summary of what our division has been doing for the last three months."

Manager #2: "I guess I could do that as well as you. I'll tell you what. You make some notes, and I'll write the thing for you. Maybe you can return the favor some day when I've got a group presentation to make."

Manager #1: "I hate to have you do that. I mean, I don't want to spoil your evening. I got myself into this; I guess I should be able to get myself out of it."

Manager #2: "Really, I'd be happy to do it for you. I insist."

Manager #1: "Well, okay. Since you insist..."

In this case, Manager #1 denied his expertise in order to get out of doing work he didn't want to do. It worked beautifully.

Disclaiming expertise is a favorite manipulative tactic of the participant in a training program who seeks to gain visibility by embarrassing the trainer. This participant asks a question in an area in which (s)he is expert and assumes the trainer is not. When the trainer tries to answer the question, the participant can then point out ways in which the answer was insufficient. The overt objective is to get some information. The hidden agenda is to embarrass the trainer and to simultaneously set up a situation in which the participant can demonstrate expertise to the group.

Sometimes Seduction and Disclaimer are used simultaneously to effect a manipulative outcome. Consider the poker hustler who relies on Referent, and sometimes Associative Power to seduce the victim into playing the game. At the same time, expertise is disclaimed. The hustler's stated objective is to have the privilege of playing with an "expert"—to learn, even if it costs a few dollars. The actual objective is to win a large amount of money. The line goes something like this: "Mr. Poker (Associative) told me if there was anyone who could teach me how to play the game, it was you" (Referent). "How many cards do you deal?" (negation of Expert).

Both Seduction and Disclaimer involve Informal Power—either its use or its denial.

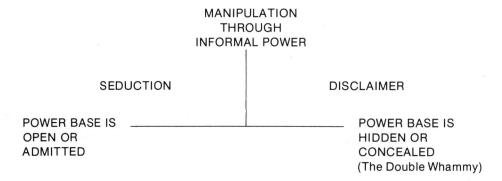

When the manipulator relies on the use (or denial) of Formal Power, we witness Entrapment or Camouflage.

Entrapment: A Hidden Agenda Supported By Open Use of Formal Power

My Entrapment score is: (see page 124)

Possible Range: 0–120

Manipulators who use Entrapment as a tactic are quite open about their ability to reward or coerce the target of influence, or about their "legitimate right" to do so. All that is hidden is the agenda. One executive found the animosity between his Manufacturing and Research and Development personnel disruptive to the work of the organization as a whole. Believing that absence of daily communication was partially to blame, he exercised his Legitimate Power to relocate both groups so they worked in close proximity to one another. His stated objective was to use physical space more efficiently. His actual agenda was to force members of both functions to get to know one another better. The "entrapment" worked to the benefit of all concerned.

Another popular form of Entrapment is teasing—holding out the promise of reward, and then when the other gets close to achieving it, moving it just out of reach, or denying it altogether. Managers sometimes use the promise of a large raise or bonus to inspire a subordinate to work harder. Somehow, the end of the rainbow never appears; the bonus is never significant; the salary increase will always happen next month.

In another form of Entrapment, the manipulator suggests the availability of a reward, only to severely criticize the other person when (s)he decides to claim it:[2]

> **Secretary:** "I know you're under a lot of pressure to meet that deadline. I'd be happy to work late every night this week, and to take work home this weekend if it will help."

> **Boss:** "I don't know what I'd do without you, Sue. I wouldn't have a chance in the world of getting this done without that kind of support. I know you've got a family, though, and they have a right to your time. I think I'll call in a temporary service to get us through this crisis."

> **Secretary:** "Oh, you know what happens with temporaries. They really don't care what happens. They'll cut any corners they can, and you'll end up paying for it. I don't think you should rely on them when the job is this important, and we won't have time to redo it if they mess it up."

> **Boss:** "I see your point. Okay, Sue. We'll do it your way. I'll miss my dinner, so run down the street and get me some sandwiches."

> **Secretary:** (sarcastically) "I suppose tomorrow night you'll expect me to prepare dinner at home and bring it in for you! I certainly hope you remember my commitment when it's time to review salaries—after all, I work like two people! I ought to be paid like two people!"

The secretary made clear her power to get her boss out of a scrape. She put forth the objective of wanting to help. In reality, she had a hidden agenda—to position herself as "victim" to a "persecuting" boss and, in the process, to enhance her Arsenal (to get "one up").[3]

The dynamic of Entrapment through reliance on the power to reward can explain why people are sometimes given a raise and a promotion, only to be fired for "inadequate performance" a short time later. What at first appears to be indecisive or poor management on closer inspection may be a highly clever form of manipulation. For example, an employee's contribution to a specific project is seen as critical. The employer wants the employee to give the project all he's got. At the same time, the employer doesn't like the employee and feels that, on balance, his contribution to the

---

[2]For an interesting discussion of other "games" with a similar theme, see James and Jongeward, *Born to Win*, pp. 197-212: also see Eric Berne, *Games People Play* (New York: Grove Press, 1964), pp. 126-129.

[3]For a description of the roles of victim, persecutor, and rescuer, see James and Jongeward, *Born to Win*, pp. 79-84; also see Stephen Karpman, "Fairy Tales and Script Drama Analysis." Transactional Analysis 7 (April 1968): pp. 39-43.

organization is insufficient. The employee, sensing his real situation, begins to lose motivation. He begins to devote less quality time and energy to the critical project. The employer, hoping to temporarily arouse the employee's commitment and enthusiasm, gives him a raise. The project gets done. The employee is fired. He was manipulated by the raise into doing his best on the project.

People who want a reward badly enough will often be blinded by the glitter of a particular reward and fail to see the underlying manipulative attempt. Similarly, people who want to avoid punishment badly enough may not be aware that they are being manipulated. Coercive Power can also support manipulative attempts.

Probably the most lucid example of Entrapment through Coercion is provided by the brainwashing of prisoners of war. During the Korean War, American prisoners were physically and intellectually starved almost to the point of death due to lack of contact and stimulation. At the point of total alienation, they were placed in reeducation classes. As their bodies and minds began to rebuild, so did their philosophies. Regaining a state of physical and mental well-being became associated with Chinese Communist doctrine; the two became inseparable in the minds of the POW's. Being part of something was "good"; therefore, the doctrine was also "good."

A similar form of manipulation through deprivation is reportedly used in a popular consciousness-raising program. One participant described the event as follows: "People seeking awareness and self-insight are forced to remain in an auditorium for hours on end. Smoking is prohibited. So are restroom breaks." Presumably, as the participants' level of physical deprivation and anguish grows, they become increasingly vulnerable to receiving and believing the message that "You are nothing; you are worthless." Psychological pain begins to accompany and overshadow physical distress. The "trainer," according to the participant, then begins to be perceived as a kind of "savior." (S)he starts suggesting new values, new beliefs and, at the most effective moment, uses his or her power to permit the participants to use the bathroom and take a smoke. The sequence of events is so well timed that the participants see the trainer not as a punitive egotist, but as someone who is totally "put together" and worthy of emulation and respect. The result is an army of ex-participants who subsequently spend incredible amounts of time and energy convincing others to pay several hundred dollars so that they, too, can benefit from the experience. The sponsors need no paid marketers; the same people who paid to endure the pain and humiliation are willing to serve as apostles, free of charge.

A milder form of Entrapment through the use of Coercive Power is used by the crisis-making boss who makes every infraction grounds for dismissal. The apparent objective is to get employees to adhere to the rules and regulations; the hidden agenda is to stifle all initiative and all independence of action, as employees become terrified of inadvertently breaking a rule of which they were unaware. As initiative and independence of action is diminished, the boss secures the position as the most capable of the group, and may even use the apparent "incompetence" of the workers as an excuse to add more staff—to enlarge the office "empire."

Legitimate Power can also support manipulation through Entrapment. A manager has the "legitimate" right to critique and edit an employee's report. Under the guise of attempting to help the employee prepare a better report, the manager nit-picks, pointing out a whole series of inconsequential "mistakes." Important problems are given no more attention than minor problems. The employee despairs, feeling that the report never will be right. He gives up the project in despair, leaving it to the manager to finish the report; since most of the work has been done, the manager needs expend only a small amount of effort to finish the job. If the employee persists in trying to satisfy all the manager's criticisms, chances are he will spend an undue amount of time on the lesser problems, and the result will still be unsatisfactory. The employee slowly becomes convinced that he is less capable than the manager—and the manager's hidden objective has been achieved.

Manipulation through the use of Legitimate Power has increasingly been applied to women who have taken what have historically been regarded as "male jobs," such as the courageous woman who took a job as a maintenance worker in a factory. The supervisor was against her hiring from the beginning, but was backed into a corner by an Equal Employment Opportunity Commission quota system. After she began to work, a male backlash began to confirm the supervisor's prejudices. The only way out of his dilemma appeared to be to encourage her to resign (his hidden agenda). He used his Legitimate Power to post job routines, and assigned her to the men's rest-room detail. Every time the woman tried to perform her job, she was confronted by a barrage of sexual innuendoes and other forms of verbal abuse. Further, the men on the shift made it a point to use the facilities while she was cleaning. She was slowly, but surely, manipulated out of the system.

Similarly, a female mine worker was widely resented for "taking a job away from a man who needed to support his family." Her supervisor privately agreed with this point of view. He, too, tried to manipulate her into resigning by exercising his Legitimate Power to assign her to the night shift, knowing full well that her family responsibilities would make it virtually impossible for her to be away from home five nights a week.

As the examples have shown, all three forms of Formal Power can be used to support manipulations. The examples we have discussed thus far involved the open use of rewards, coercion, and legitimacy. More subtle manipulations occur when, as part of the manipulative attempt, the Formal Power of the manipulator is intentionally camouflaged.

Another Double Whammy—Camouflage: Pursuing Hidden Agendas While Denying the Formal Power Base

My Camouflage score is (see page 124)

Possible Range: 0–120

Persons using Camouflage as an influence tactic put out any of three messages as they pursue their hidden agendas...

- "I would really like to help you (give you rewards) but I can't ..."

- "While I can't force (coerce) you to do it, I suggest ..."

- "It's too bad, but I really don't have the authority (the Legitimate Power) to do anything about it ..."

In each case, the speakers are denying a power base they actually possess. In essence, they are lying. Both the power base and the agenda are hidden or veiled in the Camouflage manipulation.

Parents who are trying to encourage their adolescent children to stand on their own, and to understand the value of money often resort to a manipulative camouflage of their power to reward...

> "I'd give you an increase in your allowance if I could. We just don't have the money. I understand your desire to save for a car. It's too bad—I mean, I really feel badly about this—but I think you're going to have to look for a part-time job after school. Financially, this has been a tough year on us."

The parents in this example state that they want to help their son acquire the things he wants. The hidden agenda is to get him to stand on his own. Their device is withholding additional allowance money to camouflage their real financial situation.

Persons collecting money for charities are often faced with a similar manipulation, as the potential donor makes up excuses for not giving:

> "I really believe that is a worthy cause. In fact, I try to give something each year. This year, I'm afraid I can't. My mother has been quite sick and the medical bills have taken their toll on our discretionary income. Of course, if things change and our financial situation improves, you'll be the first to hear. Make sure to come back next year. Again, it upsets me more than you to have to say no to your request...."

The stated objective in this case is to work to get in a position to contribute. The hidden objective is to get rid of the solicitor while simultaneously protecting the image of being a concerned, giving person.

Camouflage can involve denying that funds exist. It can also involve denial of the ability to do something others need or want. In one famous experiment,[4] involving two warring boys' camps located on the same island, the camp directors turned off the water and denied that they knew how to fix the problem. Their hidden agenda was to force the two sets of campers to work together more cooperatively. The scheme succeeded—as long as the common problem existed, the boys worked together. The manipulation was only a success in the short term, however. Once the boys figured out how to fix the water problem, their energies reverted back to forming warring factions.

---

[4]M. Sherif et al, *Intergroup Conflict and Cooperation: The Robber's Cave Experiment* (Norman, OK: University Book Exchange, 1961.)

Hiding or camouflaging the ability to help occurs often in the workplace. Supervisors are often identified as persons in the middle who are expected to uphold management's policies and procedures and yet simultaneously relate well to the workers. This often creates a situation rife with contradictory expectations and demands. One way to satisfy management while simultaneously maintaining a "good guy" image with the workers is to camouflage the ability to provide the rewards:

> "I know how badly you want those days off. You know that I'd get them for you if I could. But management has a strict policy against excessive "personal time" off. If it were up to me, though, you'd have those days off."

While this statement may have been "straight" (i.e., devoid of manipulation), it becomes manipulative if the supervisor, in reality, has the power to grant or withhold time off at his or her discretion. The ability to do so is veiled, as are the true objectives—to keep production rates up and absenteeism down, to appease management, and still remain a "good guy" in the eyes of subordinates.

Another option open to Camouflage users is to deny their ability to harm, punish, or hurt. A vivid example of this kind of manipulation is provided by the "little guy" who picks a fight with the "big guy," but doesn't reveal that he is carrying a weapon: "I'm not afraid of you, no matter how big you are. Let's step outside and settle this once and for all." A more relevant example is provided by the manager who has a hidden arsenal in the form of the total support of the top brass. Assume the manager finds himself or herself unable to get the resources or contribution (s)he needs from another manager on the same hierarchical level. Presumably as a way to resolve the conflict, (s)he suggests they let the higher-level manager rule in favor of one or the other: "Look, we're just wasting a lot of time over this. Let's go talk to the guy who really knows. He is unbiased, and can probably resolve the issue since he sees the bigger picture. I'll go along with whatever he suggests. How about you?"

The international arms race has been accomplished by manipulations of this variety. One nation takes pains to camouflage or deny that it has and/or is developing increasingly lethal weaponry. The stated objective is "detente"; the actual, hidden objective may be to lull the potential adversary into complacency regarding arms development. Camouflage of the Coercive Power base, in this case, is often combined with denial of the Legitimate base: "We don't feel we have the right to continue spending the taxpayers' money for an elaboration of our defense system when there is such a pressing need to invest in social programs."

Legitimate Power is often denied when it is necessary to remove any feelings of social distance or hierarchy in order to accomplish the hidden objective. A chief executive officer goes into a plant in workers' garb, and casually sits down with the workers in the plant cafeteria. He adopts their jargon and listens to their conversation. His surface agenda is to pass the lunch hour in a pleasant manner. His hidden objective is to find out "what is really going on."

Consultants hired by top management to assess the employee/labor relations climate sometimes rely on the same tactic. They adopt an artificial role (e.g., student, coworker) to get people to provide them with the information they need to support their recommendations to top management. They disguise their identity because the power of that role would be counterproductive, given their true objectives.

Camouflage involves a lie—a denial of the power to help, reward, or punish. It is not the same as a lie, however. Camouflage is a lie coupled with a hidden agenda. When a child falsely denies breaking a lamp, his or agenda is clear—to stay out of trouble. When an employee falsely denies padding an expense account, (s)he is not manipulating; (s)he is simply lying.

Four distinct types of manipulation—Seduction, Entrapment, Disclaimer, and Camouflage—have been discussed.

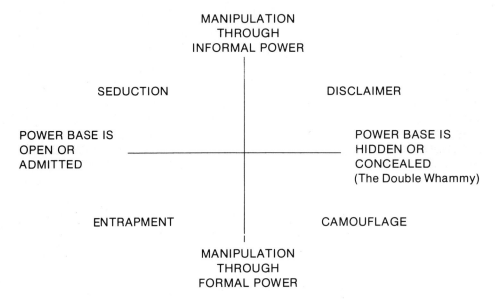

In the examples that have been cited, some of the manipulations worked; others didn't. Some were highly damaging to the persons involved; others would have been applauded by the staunchest moralist.

In the pages that follow, manipulation will be considered both from the point of view of ethics and effectiveness.

IS MANIPULATION EVER APPROPRIATE?

As we know, some people think that power is a dirty word. Many think of manipulation as a negative or unethical approach, and disparage those who rely on manipulative tactics:

"You've got to watch yourself with her; she's a real manipulator."

"That contractor is a real shark; before you know it, he's manipulated you into contracting for more than you need or want."

"He's really a devious person; you think he's doing you a favor and then, all of a sudden, you find you've been set up."

Manipulation is not, in and of itself, a dirty word. **There are times when manipulation is appropriate: when hiding your true agenda (and possibly concealing your power base) is a realistic way to approach the situation.**

Manipulation can be appropriate when people are flatly denied the chance to prove what they can do. Women and minorities once had no choice but to resort to manipulative tactics to get a "real" opportunity in the work place. In applying for my first job after college, I denied that I could type (a true disclaimer since I had paid many of my college expenses by typing theses). Why did I make this disclaimer? Because I wanted the position of an insurance underwriter and believed that a display of typing ability would have landed me first in a secretarial seat. To disclaim my ability would mean one of two things: that I wouldn't get a job at all, or that I would succeed in being named an underwriter trainee. On the surface, this appears to be simply a lie by omission, and not a manipulation. After all, my objective—to be named an underwriter—was open. The manipulation lay in my not really aspiring to be an underwriter. My true objective was to make as much money as I could in a short period of time in order to help put my husband through business school and to then get a position in the field that truly interested me—applied psychology. The company believed both my disclaimer about typing ability and my surface objective (to be an underwriter). I got the position, and held it for several years. Was the manipulation inappropriate? I think not, since I am certain I could not have secured the position had I been "straight." Was the manipulation "wrong" or "unethical"? Not in my perception. Since I maintained the position long enough to return the organization's initial training investment in me, no one was harmed either by the disclaimer or the hidden agenda. Would the company disagree with me? Did they feel wrongly manipulated? I have no reason to believe so, since they have given me work since my departure.

Manipulation may also be appropriate when we or others are in danger—psychologically, physically, or professionally. Few would argue that the manipulation perpetrated by undercover police as they attempt to gather evidence to convict pushers of hard drugs is either inappropriate or unethical. To be open about their objective (to gather evidence) would undeniably end in failure. To dismiss the objective as something that cannot be accomplished because it cannot be pursued in a "straight" fashion is equally indefensible, since the psychological and physical safety of others is at stake.

Danger to one's professional well-being can also create a situation in which manipulation is the most appropriate option. One manager I know had the misfortune of having the president's son-in-law working for him. The son-in-law's performance was marginal at best; he was inept and disrupted the work of the unit as a whole. The manager tried to deal with the son-in-law as he would have with any other employee, but he discovered that the president had no intention of adhering to standard operating procedures and policies when it came to his son-in-law. The manager was criticized for submitting negative performance evaluation forms to Personnel, and was told in no uncertain terms that a critical posture toward the "crown prince" would not be tolerated.

The manager was in a "damned if I do; damned if I don't" situation. He firmly believed that if he overlooked the son-in-law's poor performance, the morale in his work unit would decrease and, with it, productivity levels would fall. If he dealt directly with the issue, he was certain he would be fired. He determined that the only approach available to him was to manipulate the son-in-law into resigning, or at least into requesting a transfer. He did so by using his Legitimate Power to entrap the son-in-law. He withheld assignments he knew the son-in-law enjoyed and gave him assignments that were both difficult and peripheral to the work of the unit as a whole. In that way, he slowly eroded the son-in-law's feeling of self-confidence while diminishing the need for the son-in-law to interact directly with others in the unit. Within a few months, the son-in-law chose to resign.

While manipulation may be sometimes necessary, it is never the best route to take when a "straight" form of influence (Involvement, Negotiation, Direction, or Enlistment) would do the job. Persons who discover that they have been the subjects of manipulation inevitably end up feeling negative toward the manipulator. These negative feelings create hostility, caution, and a defensive posture that make it difficult to influence that person (manipulatively or otherwise) in the future. Once their cover is blown, undercover police lose their ability to infiltrate criminal groups. Once a child discovers that a parent has manipulated him or her into taking an action, the child will begin to question the parent's subsequent motivation. Manipulation and trust are never compatible. For this reason, manipulators are closing off other influence options even as they manipulate.

Manipulations are particularly dangerous when the outcome involves a loss for the other person. While no one likes being manipulated "for their own good," manipulations that end in loss are never forgiven and are rarely forgotten. Manipulation should be regarded only as a last resort. Ethics aside, the manipulator takes a tremendous risk, as (s)he increases the likelihood of a hostile backlash, and diminishes possibilities for building and using Expert and Referent Power in the future. Manipulation can thus be as dangerous for the manipulator as it is uncomfortable for the manipulated.

What if someone is trying to manipulate you? Is that necessarily something to be avoided? The bad feelings that can be created as a result of being manipulated are energy-draining; to be manipulated is often to be distracted from pursuing our own objectives. People who succeed tend to be highly adept at blocking others in their attempts to manipulate them.

TO AVOID BEING MANIPULATED

Understanding why someone might be attempting to manipulate you represents the first step in blocking the manipulation. People manipulate when: (1) they feel their objective would be unacceptable to you, and/or (2) they don't trust you not to harm them in some way, and/or (3) they perceive themselves to be unempowered, unable to deal with you and the resistance you might pose. There are times when you would not consider complying if you knew their true agenda. Other times, the would-be manipulator has misjudged you or your intentions. **In either case, in order to stop the manipulation attempt, you must openly "call it like it is": state that you're feeling manipulated, and why.**

Confronting the manipulation involves a direct, straightforward mention of the behaviors that make you uneasy:

> "Every time you do something "extra" for me, you ask a favor in return. I'd be a lot more comfortable if you'd just come right out and ask me what you want without setting me up first."

> "I can't be totally open with you if you continue to badmouth me to other managers. I don't understand what you really want from me."

Having pointed out that you have picked up a double or confusing message, ask the other person to state what (s)he is really trying to accomplish. Once you've heard (or reheard) the agenda, then specify the behaviors or conditions that must occur for you to have any confidence that the restatement represents the actual agenda:

> "Okay. You want us to be totally honest with each other. I'd like that too, but I will be cautious because of the problems we've had in the past."

> "I'm all in favor of your being more independent, but I guess I've heard about your good intentions too often to really believe you mean what you say. I'd like to see you start to take some responsibility for your own life."

Occasionally, confronting the manipulator will stimulate a total restatement of agenda:

> **Confrontation:** "Your behavior doesn't make sense to me. First, you complain to others about being overworked, and then you volunteer to take work home every night. What's going on?"

> **Response:** "Okay, I guess I'd better level with you. I want a raise and I thought the best way to make sure I got it was to become so indispensable to you that you would have no choice but to grant me what I want."

The restatement may represent the real agenda, or it may represent another manipulative attempt. How do you know? One clue lies in the consistency of the statement with past behavior—was the individual really trying to become indispensable? Do you have reason to believe that the individual thought you would turn down a raise if (s)he had been open about it?

Let's assume that the would-be manipulator responds to your confrontation with a restatement that you believe does, in fact, represent a true agenda, and that you have no reason to block the individual in his or her efforts to achieve the objective. **Your objective at this point should be to give the individual a reason to be more straightforward with you in the future.** Doing so requires that you build trust (a Referent Power base) or that you clarify those objectives you would support and those you would not support.

Now let's assume that the would-be manipulator indicates that his or her true objective is something you would not want to support, even though he or she finally leveled with you. Reinforcing the honest statement of objective while clearly stating your objections and the basis for your refusal is important. To do otherwise is to respond to a manipulative attempt with another manipulation—a situation in which everyone ends up losing.

> **Open Refusal:** "I am pleased that you finally decided to level with me. I really appreciate that, and hope you will continue to be as honest in the future. I'm afraid, however, that I cannot grant your request for a raise. Your performance simply does not warrant an increase at this time. I am quite willing to work with you to clarify ways in which you can become eligible for an increase in the future."

> **Manipulative Refusal:** "I'm glad you decided you could be honest with me. I want you to believe that I'd give you a raise if I could, but it's just not in the budget at this time."

The open refusal in the example is likely to generate two positive outcomes: the manipulative attempts are likely to stop, and the employee is likely to try to improve his or her performance. The probable outcomes of the manipulative refusal are less positive. The employee does not know the real reason the request was denied, and (s)he may be aware that the manager does, in fact, have the power to grant a raise. If so, the employee is likely to lose respect for and trust in the manager. Performance improvement is unlikely; new manipulative attempts are a possibility.

The person who succeeds avoids unnecessary manipulation of others and is able to confront others who would try to involve him or her in their manipulations. Discriminating between necessary and unnecessary manipulations, and blocking manipulative others, requires that you be **assertive,** rather than **aggressive,** and **responsive** rather than **non-assertive** in your dealings with others. In the next chapter, the differences between these behaviors will be considered along with the underlying life attitudes they represent. Some guidelines for giving and receiving feedback, and for communicating effectively with others will be presented. Mastery of these skills will both diminish your need to manipulate and will enhance your ability to confront manipulators in a constructive manner.

6

Interpersonal Effectiveness: A Prerequisite

In the last several chapters, we've looked at a number of options that are available as you attempt to influence others in order to accomplish your goals. We've seen that Direction gets rapid action, but rarely commitment. Conversely, Involvement generates commitment but can take a great deal of time. Similarly, Negotiation and Enlistment have both advantages and disadvantages. All of the Influence Strategies are appropriate in some situations and inappropriate in others; success depends on our ability to select an appropriate Influence Strategy. **It is also important to develop and use sound interpersonal skills.**

Interpersonal Effectiveness is a characteristic of every individual who succeeds. However, "leaders" are as different in personality and style as are the organizations they represent. To be effective interpersonally is to identify and use your most productive resources while simultaneously encouraging others to contribute—it is not to fit into a predetermined personality mold.

It is difficult to define precisely the discrete behaviors that will guarantee that you will be regarded as interpersonally effective by all persons with whom you work. Persons who are hard of hearing may feel that you should speak louder. Conversely, persons who hate noise may feel you would be more effective if you spoke more softly. Some people most enjoy persons who express their anger openly. Others are extremely uncomfortable with conflict, and fear open expression of anger.

Definitions of what constitutes Interpersonal Effectiveness are, therefore, somewhat individual in nature. These definitions also tend to be somewhat situational. When you are facing a deadline, you might most enjoy working with a person who is totally task-focused and efficient. On the other hand, you might find such a person uninteresting and dull at a cocktail party.

What is Interpersonal Effectiveness? It can be defined as the ability to stimulate others to behave in ways that are desirable to you while simultaneously maintaining a relationship characterized by mutual good feelings. Are you interpersonally effective if others consistently seek you out only to make selfish use of your resources? No. Are you interpersonally effective if others consistently attempt to avoid engaging with you? No. You are interpersonally effective if others seek you out, and if you are able to make things happen your way while simultaneously making it possible for others to feel generally positive about events and outcomes.

Individual preferences and situational demands notwithstanding, some behaviors can be consistently associated with Interpersonal Effectiveness. All have one thing in common: They project an "I'm okay–You're Okay" attitude.[1]

To what extent do you project an "I'm Okay" feeling as you communicate with others? To get an indication, respond to each of the following statements by circling the one number to the right of each item that most accurately describes your behavior in the kind of situation described:

Do I Project That "I'm Okay?"

	Never	Rarely	Sometimes	Usually	Always
1. When I have to make a decision that my peers won't like, I make the decision I believe is right regardless of the conflicts that may result.	0	1	2	3	4
2. When I am asked to join my peers at an after-hours social function, I know I can add a lot to their enjoyment.	0	1	2	3	4
3. When a peer's action creates a problem for me, I express my opinion even though it may make me unpopular.	0	1	2	3	4
4. When I need the cooperation of my peers, I freely ask for whatever assistance I need.	0	1	2	3	4

---

[1]Eric Berne, "Standard Nomenclature, Transactional Nomenclature." *Transactional Analysis Bulletin* 8 (October 1969): p. 112.

	Never	Rarely	Sometimes	Usually	Always
5. When a peer compliments me, I accept the compliment and am comfortable doing so.	0	1	2	3	4
6. I am confident that my work will impress my boss.	0	1	2	3	4
7. When my boss asks me a question that I can't answer, I tell him or her that I don't know without embarrassment.	0	1	2	3	4
8. I feel my boss can benefit from working with me.	0	1	2	3	4
9. When my boss asks for my advice, (s)he benefits from my thinking.	0	1	2	3	4
10. When I can't meet a deadline, I am comfortable asking that the deadline be extended.	0	1	2	3	4
11. When I need to ask a subordinate to do a job that I know he or she won't like doing, I am comfortable asking that the task be done.	0	1	2	3	4
12. When I believe that a subordinate is not working up to capacity, I am comfortable discussing my beliefs with that person.	0	1	2	3	4
13. I find it easy to compliment subordinates for a job well done.	0	11	2	3	4
14. I am confident that I know how to manage people.	0	1	2	3	4
15. I give subordinates credit where credit is due.	0	1	2	3	4

To find your total "I'm Okay" score, complete the following chart:

ITEM	SCORE	ITEM	SCORE	ITEM	SCORE
1		6		11	
2		7		12	
3		8		13	
4		9		14	
5		10		15	
TOTALS					
"I'm okay with peers"		"I'm okay with my boss"		"I'm okay with subordinates"	

To interpret your "I'm Okay" scores, consider that:

- The possible score range for any one section ("peers," "boss," "subordinates") is 0–20.

- It is worthwhile to attempt to achieve a score of 20 in each section.

- A low "I'm Okay" score regarding the boss may indicate a lack of self-confidence as you deal with authority figures or persons in hierarchically superior positions.

- A low "I'm Okay" score regarding subordinates may indicate a mistrust of your own managerial skills.

- A low "I'm Okay" score regarding peers may indicate discomfort with relying on the Informal Power bases that equal hierarchical positions encourage.

If your "I'm Okay" scores need improving, then attempt to display more of the following "I'm Okay" behaviors:

- Show you value your resources (ideas, opinions, feelings).

- Stand up for your rights.

- Recognize and accept your mistakes *without rationalizing or projecting blame.*

- See the humor in difficult situations.

- Ask for assistance as needed *without inappropriate apology.*

- Openly express negative feelings (such as anger, fear, and hurt) in constructive ways.

- Let people know when they don't live up to your expectations.

- Try to understand negative feedback, *neither projecting nor rationalizing.*

- Receive positive feedback graciously, *without denial or feigned modesty.*

- State clearly what you expect of others.

- Hold your head erect.

- Maintain consistent eye contact while talking to the other person.

- Take care to look the best you can.

- Be relaxed while energetic.

- Use gestures, body stance, hand motions, etc., to reinforce verbal messages.

To what extent do you project "You're Okay" feelings? Complete the following mini self-analysis to get one indication. Once again, circle one number to the right of each item.

Do I Project That "You're Okay?"

	Never	Rarely	Sometimes	Usually	Always
1. When my peers resist acting on a decision I've made, I assume they have a valid reason for their reaction.	0	1	2	3	4
2. When I am asked to join my peers at an after-hours social function, I assume that they will add to my enjoyment.	0	1	2	3	4
3. When I don't agree with what my peers are doing, I am confident they will accept my criticism non-defensively.	0	1	2	3	4
4. When I need the cooperation of my peers, I know they will be willing to give it to me.	0	1	2	3	4
5. When peers compliment me, I know they really mean it.	0	1	2	3	4

	Never	Rarely	Sometimes	Usually	Always
6. When my boss does not like some aspect of my performance, I assume (s)he has a legitimate reason for his or her complaint.	0	1	2	3	4
7. When my boss asks me a question that I can't answer, I trust (s)he will accept an "I don't know" without punishing me.	0	1	2	3	4
8. I know I can benefit from working with my boss.	0	1	2	3	4
9. I assume my boss will give me a fair chance to show what I can do.	0	1	2	3	4
10. When I can't meet a deadline, I am confident my boss will understand why.	0	1	2	3	4
11. When I need to ask a subordinate to do a job that I know he or she doesn't like doing, I trust (s)he will understand the necessity of doing the task.	0	1	2	3	4
12. When I feel a subordinate is not working up to capacity, I am confident he or she would want to hear and would respect my views.	0	1	2	3	4
13. When a subordinate resists doing something I want him or her to do, I assume (s)he has a good reason.	0	1	2	3	4
14. I am confident subordinates will do their best.	0	1	2	3	4
15. I trust that subordinates will give me credit where credit is due.	0	1	2	3	4

To find your "You're Okay" scores, complete this chart:

ITEM	SCORE	ITEM	SCORE	ITEM	SCORE
1		6		11	
2		7		12	
3		8		13	
4		9		14	
5		10		15	
TOTALS					
"My peers are okay"		"My boss is okay"		"My subordinates are okay"	

To interpret your "You're Okay" scores, consider that:

- The possible score range for any one section (i.e. "peers," "boss," "subordinate") is 0–20.

- It is worthwhile to attempt to achieve a score of 20 in each section.

- A low "You're Okay" score regarding the boss may indicate a basic lack of trust of those in positions of authority over you—or—it may indicate that you do, indeed, have a problematic boss.

- A low "You're Okay" score regarding subordinates may indicate contempt for or impatience with persons hierarchically inferior to you—or—it may indicate a true lack of capacity on the part of your subordinates.

- A low "You're Okay" score regarding your peers indicates either unfounded contempt for their ability—or—justified lack of respect.

Is it possible to project "You're Okay" attitudes when the other person in your opinion, *is* actually "not okay"? Can a manager project "you're okay" attitudes toward a subordinate who is late every day and botches most assignments? Can a peer treat another peer as "okay" who manipulates and plays political games to everyone's detriment? Can you treat your boss as "okay" if he devotes all his energies to blocking your efforts to reach your objectives for fear that you might outshine him? If we believe another individual or group is really "not okay," are we doomed to interpersonal ineffectiveness with that person or group? Fortunately, Interpersonal Effectiveness is far more a matter of behavior than of attitude. **While we may have difficulty altering our attitude about someone, we can control our behavior. Self-control, or purposeful modification of behavior to reach objectives, is a characteristic of the successful person.** To project "not okay" behaviors (even toward a person we are convinced is "not okay") is to elaborate those very behaviors that we find problematic in the first place. Regardless of your situation, then, if your "You're Okay" scores need improving, then attempt to display more of the following "You're Okay" behaviors:

- Respect the rights of others.

- Take time to make sure you *understand* the other person's ideas, opinions, and feelings.

- Listen objectively to understand the other person's position before accepting or rejecting his or her point of view.

- Be reliable and dependable; live up to any promises you make to the other person.

- Take the other person's needs and feelings into account.

- When you have conflicting needs, look for ways to satisfy both.

- Give the other person constructive feedback regarding your relationship.

- Openly discuss feelings and behaviors that may be detracting from your mutual effectiveness.

Projecting "I'm Okay–You're Okay" behaviors is extremely important to Interpersonal Effectiveness. The following examples illustrate the importance.

"I'm Okay–You're Okay" Salesman to Customer: "I understand your desire to have the product by next Tuesday. In order to deliver the quality of product we know you expect, we cannot commit to delivery until the twenty-fourth."

This salesman portrayed positive regard for the customer in implying that the latter's need is legitimate, and his or her request worthy of attention. Contrast this with the "I'm Okay–You're Not Okay" salesman:

"I'm Okay–You're Not Okay" Salesman to Customer: "Your demand is unrealistic. You just can't expect to have delivery until the twenty-fourth."

This salesman openly accused the customer of being unrealistic ("not okay") and, in cutting off the conversation, clearly implied that the customer's request was not even worthy of discussion (another "You're Not Okay" message).

Slight modifications in behavior can make the difference between success and being unable to influence events. To succeed, we have to distinguish between those behaviors that are effective and those that are ineffective. In the pages that follow, a model of behavior will be presented to assist you in your efforts to select the most effective way to deal with others.

MAPPING YOUR OWN BEHAVIORAL PROFILE

There are four distinct behavioral modes we can use as we engage with others. Which do you tend to use? To get one indication, think of a specific individual with whom you wish to be more effective. Then, read each of the items that follow and, in the box to the right of each item, place a number from 0 to 5 to indicate the extent to which the behavior describes you. Use this scale:

0	1	2	3	4	5
I never display this behavior	**I rarely** display this behavior	**I occa-sionally** display this behavior	**I often** display this behavior	**I usually** display this behavior	**I always** display this behavior

1. I make my opinions and objectives known. ☐

2. I draw out the needs, feelings, and opinions of the other person. ☐

3. When arguments arise, I drop the argument in order to keep peace. ☐

4. I discourage disagreement with my point of view. ☐

5. I express my feelings openly. ☐

6. I build on or elaborate the ideas of the other person. ☐

7. I go along with what the other person wants to do even when I don't want to do so. ☐

8. I poke fun at the other person's suggestions or ways of doing things. ☐

9. I persevere, standing up for my point of view. ☐

10. When the other person is expressing an opinion, I suspend judgment, listening objectively and attempting to really understand. ☐

11. When the other person does something that makes me angry, I keep quiet about it. ☐

12. I make the other's efforts or capacities seem small, minor, or weak by comparison to mine. ☐

Now, to begin to map your behavioral preferences, perform these additions:

Behavioral Preference Score Sheet

ITEM	YOUR SCORE	+	ITEM	YOUR SCORE	+	ITEM	YOUR SCORE	=	BEHAVIOR	YOUR TOTAL
1	☐	+	5	☐	+	9	☐	=	ASSERTIVE	☐
2	☐	+	6	☐	+	10	☐	=	RESPONSIVE	☐
3	☐	+	7	☐	+	11	☐	=	NON-ASSERTIVE	☐
4	☐	+	8	☐	+	12	☐	=	AGGRESSIVE	☐

In the pages that follow, each of these four behavioral modes—Assertive, Responsive, Non-Assertive, and Aggressive—will be discussed. Given the relatively narrow range of the test you just completed, I suggest that if you are interested in developing a more situationally-specific profile of yourself, spend twenty to thirty minutes completing the more elaborate Behavioral Styles Profile in Appendix E. **If you do plan to complete the profile, please do so before continuing with this chapter.** Familiarity with the model to be discussed tends to skew the profile results.

YOUR BEHAVIORAL OPTIONS: TO BE ASSERTIVE, RESPONSIVE, AGGRESSIVE, OR NON-ASSERTIVE[2]

Consider a manager dealing with a subordinate who has failed to carry his fair share of the work load. The subordinate commits himself to projects, and then doesn't complete them. The manager is held responsible by the customer for the subordi-

---

[2]For further discussion of Assertive, Responsive, Non-Assertive, and Aggressive behavior, see Robert Alberti and Michael Emmons, *Your Perfect Right: A Guide to Assertive Behavior* (San Luis Obispo, CA: Impact, 1974); Arthur Lange and Patricia Jakubowski, *Responsible Assertive Behavior* (Champaign, IL: Research Press, 1978); and Sharon Anthony Bower and Gordon Bower, *Asserting Yourself: A Practical Guide for Positive Change* (Reading, MA: Addison-Wesley Publishing Co., 1976); Malcom E. Shaw, *Assertive-Responsive Management: A Personal Handbook* (Reading, MA: Addison-Wesley Publishing Co., 1979).

nate's failure to perform, and the customer has become highly critical of the manager. Here are the manager's options:

Assertion: "I am disappointed by your failure to perform, and don't appreciate the position you have put me in with the customer. I want you to _____ in order to correct the situation."

Responsiveness: "I'd like to talk with you about your performance. I want to understand why you've been unable to complete your projects in the last few months."

Aggression: "You obviously don't care at all about me or the unit. You're one of those people who will take a free ride whenever you get a chance to do so."

Non-Assertion: "I don't understand why you haven't been completing projects. I probably wasn't clear about the assignment. Maybe I should have been more available to answer your questions."

The outcome surely would have varied depending on the behavioral option selected by the manager.

Behavioral Options and Likely Outcomes

OPTION	MANAGER'S BEHAVIOR	LIKELY OUTCOME
ASSERTION	Clearly expresses wants, needs, feelings Stands up for own rights without violating the other person's rights Does not insult, put down, or attribute motivation to the other person Maintains "I'm Okay-You're Okay" posture	Subordinate knows how his/her behavior is affecting manager. Subordinate understands consequences of his/her behavior.
RESPONSIVENESS	Listens Tries to understand other person's point of view Tries to get information Does not apologize for self Maintains "I'm Okay-You're Okay" posture	Subordinate explains his/her point of view, needs, objectives. Problem-solving is possible. Mutual good feelings are established or maintained.

Behavioral Options and Likely Outcomes (cont'd.)

OPTION	MANAGER'S BEHAVIOR	LIKELY OUTCOME
AGGRESSIVENESS	Attacks, insults, puts down the other person Patronizes Shows contempt Attributes motivation Shows other person (s)he thinks the other is "not okay"	Subordinate feels hurt, defensive, or fearful. Subordinate attacks or withdraws. Mutual problem-solving becomes impossible.
NON-ASSERTION	Does not stand up for own rights Puts self down Apologizes inappropriately Takes blame when not really believing it Projects an "I'm Not Okay" posture	Subordinate feels guilty or loses respect for manager. Subordinate feels manipulated. Open communications and problem-solving become extremely unlikely.

As the chart indicates, persons who select the Aggressive or Non-Assertive behavioral options are unlikely to effect their desired outcomes. Aggression leads to fear, anger, or withdrawal. Non-Assertion leads to guilt and loss of self-esteem. Neither leads to mutually effective problem-solving.

The behaviors depicted in our manager-subordinate episode were blatant; Aggression and Non-Assertion often take more subtle forms. It is these behavioral subtleties that enhance or detract from a person's level of Interpersonal Effectiveness. To understand these subtleties, let's take a closer look at the behavioral options.

The Assertive Approach

The primary characteristic of Assertive behavior is the predominance of "I-messages":

- I am angry.
- I like you.
- I have a deadline to meet.

- I don't understand your behavior.
- I don't want to feel guilty.
- I want your help.
- I can do it alone.
- I'm going to make it happen.
- I need that information.

The person who is behaving assertively is focusing on self, not other. At the same time, **the other person is not put down, attacked, nor explicitly excluded from stating his or her wants, needs, feelings, and goals.** In focusing on the self, the Assertive individual behaves in a self-oriented—though not egocentric—manner. Assertive behavior is aimed at **winning, but not at the other's expense.** In other words, the assertive individual wins, but not because the other loses. The "top dog"/ "bottom dog" relationship plays no part in the assertion. The balance of social power is intentionally maintained, as the asserting individual takes responsibility for his or her own life, feelings, and situations and urges the other party to the interaction to do the same.

To work with an Assertive individual is to know where you stand. Interpersonal ambiguity is diminished as needs, wants, and expectations are clarified. Conflict is replaced by problem-solving as the impact of each person's behavior on the other is identified in an objective fashion. Mutual feelings of self-esteem are enhanced as discussion centers around dysfunctional behavior rather than challenges as to the inherent worth or value of the other. Assertions, in effect, clear the air in relationships: second-guessing, manipulative power plays, hidden agendas, and subtle "put-downs" are absent.

Earlier, the impact of behavioral subtleties was considered. In the following Assertive Response Quiz, all of the items are heavily loaded with "I-messages." Can you pick out the one Assertive response? Can you identify what the remaining three responses have in common?

Assertiveness Response Quiz

SITUATION: You've just delivered some bad news to someone—conclusions (s)he didn't expect and didn't want to hear.

YOUR DESIRED OUTCOME: To get the other person to understand, accept, and act upon your conclusions.

RESPONSES:

(A)   "I feel very strongly that you would have drawn the same conclusions had you done a thorough job of analysis last year."

Assertive Response Quiz (cont'd.)

(B) "All I know is that I have done my job; what you do with the results is up to you."

(C) "I am sorry that our conclusions are upsetting to you. However, I am convinced that to ignore the results would be a big mistake. It is my hope that you'll act upon the results."

(D) "I know this comes as unwelcome news to you. But, I don't want you to be too concerned. I know I can explain the situation to your boss in such a way that he'll continue to respect your ability."

THE ASSERTIVE STATEMENT IS _____

The other responses have this in common: _____

_____

_____

_____

_____

Response "C" is the only Assertive response. It is the only response that clearly projects an "I'm Okay–You're Okay" position. **By definition, assertions are characterized by a projected attitude of mutual "okayness."**

Responses "A," "B," and "D" all contain subtle elements of aggression, in spite of the preponderance of "I-messages." "A" contains an element of contempt. "You couldn't do a decent analytical job." "B" contains a trace of belligerence: "If you won't do it my way, then tough luck. I couldn't care less." "D" projects a patronizing attitude: "You're so weak and vulnerable that you'd probably lose your job without my help." Contempt, belligerence, and patronage are aggressive behaviors—they depict a "You're Not Okay" message. Assertive behaviors depict an "I'm Okay–You're Okay" message.

As the proliferation of assertiveness training programs illustrates, Assertive behaviors, while productive, can be difficult to display. The blocks to behaving assertively are both psychological and social in origin.

Being assertive requires that an individual possess self-confidence and self-esteem, or a belief in his or her inherent value and in the rightness of what (s)he seeks. A person who has a low level of confidence in either himself or herself or in the appropriateness of his or her request or statement is likely to hedge—to be other than straight about his or her agenda. The person who suffers from a low level of self-esteem is likely to seek the continual reenforcement of others regarding his or her inherent worth, and to fear rejection. To assert yourself is to risk rejection. To openly declare your needs, wants, and feelings is to risk having the other person ignore, put down, or ridicule your statements. Only if an individual has a high level of self-esteem can (s)he tolerate the possibility of rejection.

Cultural barriers compound the psychological blocks. Students are often taught that it is "wrong" to start a paragraph with the word "I." Many parents teach their children that to openly express a preference in a social situation is rude. As a result, many frustrated hosts and hostesses are forced to second-guess the true desires of their guests: "Would you like Coke, ginger ale, or Seven-Up?" "I don't care."

Still other experiences teach us to forego assertive statements with persons holding certain status positions. Many of us have been taught to obey unquestioningly our political leaders, to follow without question the mandates of religious leaders, and to take on faith and with silent acceptance the judgments of physicians.

Fortunately, few of us possess these blocks to such a degree that we consistently fail to be Assertive. An important step in becoming more Assertive is understanding *when* you have the most difficulty displaying these behaviors—in what *situations,* around what *topics,* and with persons of what *status* do you experience difficulty in being Assertive? Check all of the following that represent behaviors you find difficult to display:

SITUATION	SAMPLE ASSERTION
☐ In a retail establishment, when the clerk begins to wait on someone who has not been there as long as you:	"I was next."
☐ In a restaurant, when your food is served cold or badly prepared:	"I am not satisfied with this, and want you to take it back to the kitchen."
☐ When you are kept waiting:	"I want you to know that I don't like being kept waiting like that."
☐ When a neighbor persists in doing something that annoys you:	"Your behavior is upsetting me. I would like you to stop."
☐ When a friend borrowed something and has failed to return it:	"I would like my _____ back, please."

TOPIC	SAMPLE ASSERTION
☐ Your **objectives:**	"I am trying to accomplish this and this and this . . . ."
☐ Your **opinions:**	"I disagree with you. In my opinion . . . ."

TOPIC	SAMPLE ASSERTION
☐ Your **positive feelings**:	"I care a great deal about you."
☐ Your **negative feelings**:	"When you do that, I get very angry."

STATUS OF OTHER PERSON	SAMPLE ASSERTION
☐ To someone hierarchically superior:	"I disagree with the way you're going about this." –or– "I want to tell you how I view the matter."
☐ To your physician:	"I don't like being kept waiting. My time is also very valuable." –or– "I have a right to understand why you are prescribing this treatment."
☐ To a policeman:	"I want to tell you my side of the story."
☐ To a celebrity:	"I admire your work, and would like to talk with you about it."
☐ To a manipulative family member:	"I find your constant demands unfair and annoying."

If you have difficulty being Assertive in any of these situations, or with these persons (or others), then take a few minutes to consider the reason for your reluctance or hesitation. Frequently, a simple questioning of our assumptions enables us to behave differently.

How do people behave who are not Assertive in the situations we discussed? Let's take the example of a patient whose physician is late for an appointment. The Non-Assertive patient can be:

Responsive: "It must be difficult to stay on schedule when you have medical emergencies coming up all the time."

Non-Assertive: "Good afternoon. I won't take much of your time."

Aggressive: "Look, Doc, either you see me when I get here, or I'll find myself another physician."

The element of mutual "okayness" is strongest in the Assertive and Responsive approaches. It is noticeably absent in the Non-Assertive and Aggressive approaches.

The Responsive Approach

Responsive behavior is extremely effective when contributions from the other person are sought. The desired contribution may be feelings, attitudes, information, opinions, or perceptions. The implication is that I, in being Responsive, am open to change as a result of your inputs. Responsiveness is characterized by a preponderance of explorations, questions, and seeking behaviors:

- "What do you think of . . . ?"

- "I would like to better understand what you mean."

- "Let me restate what I think you're feeling."

- "Let me make sure I heard you right. You said . . . ."

The person who is behaving responsively is focusing on the other person, without simultaneously deprecating the self. The projected attitude is "I'm Okay–You're Okay." The element of "You're Okay" is stated explicitly. The following "messages" are typically associated with Responsive behaviors:

Responsive Messages and Behaviors

MESSAGE	BEHAVIORS
Explicit: "I value what you think." Implicit: "I also value what I think."	• Asking questions • Asking the other person to give an opinion or to suggest a course of action • Listening
Explicit: "Your feelings matter." Implicit: "So do mine."	• Noticing when the other person is upset, angry, happy, etc., and commenting on it • Clarifying how the other feels • Trying to avoid behaviors that cause unnecessary pain or stress for the other

Aggressive Messages and Behaviors (cont'd.)

MESSAGE	BEHAVIORS
Explicit: "You are strong and capable." Implicit: "So am I."	• Asking the other for help, without claiming to be weak, dependent, or unable • Clearly and without apology sharing your limits and your "weaknesses" with the other person

The Responsive approach seeks out the resources of the other person; it asks him or her to influence the situation. It is in no way a weak or passive approach. On the contrary, only a very self-confident individual can allow himself or herself to be guided by others; to state, without apology, that others might be more skilled or informed in an area. Self-confidence and self-esteem are as characteristic of Responsive persons as they are of persons who tend to prefer the Assertive approach. Persons who are comfortable being Assertive rarely find it difficult to move into a Responsive mode. (For an excellent in-depth discussion of the relationship between Assertive and Responsive behaviors, I suggest you read Malcolm E. Shaw's *Assertive–Responsive Management: A Personal Handbook,* published in 1979 by Addison-Wesley.) Responsive behaviors leave open the possibility for input, influence, or contribution from the other party. While the "You're Okay" message is predominant, the "I'm Okay" component is very much intact.

Frequently, both the "I'm Okay" and "You're Okay" messages are made equally explicit. The result is the Assertive/Responsive approach. This approach epitomizes the problem-solving process, as it encourages a give-and-take and mutual exchange of resources:

Assertive: "I would like to go over the report with you at lunch."

Responsive: "Can you be available?"

Assertive: "I want to find out more about your product."

Responsive: "Can you suggest someone I might talk to?"

Assertive: "I am feeling angry right now."

Responsive: "I want to find out why you treated the situation the way you did."

The Assertive individual contributes resources and shapes events. The Responsive individual effectively utilizes the resources of others.

The person who balances Assertive and Responsive behaviors is most likely to succeed, as (s)he not only shapes events but stimulates others to contribute. Persons who are Interpersonally Effective are both Assertive and Responsive. Persons who tend to experience difficulty with others tend to be either Non-Assertive or Aggressive, or both.

The Aggressive Approach

When many people first see the terms "Assertion" and "Aggression," they assume that to be Aggressive is simply to be "Over-Assertive." This is an oversimplification. It is true that persons who are continually Assertive and rarely Responsive are annoying to be around. Few of us enjoy the company of someone who is perpetually concerned with his or her own needs, wants, and objectives. Even such a person, however, is easier to tolerate than the Aggressive individual. While highly Assertive persons may give you little opportunity to contribute, they do not explicitly devalue or deny your ability to do so. All Aggressive behaviors contain the messages "You're Not Okay" and "I am better than you."

There are many ways with which to convey the feeling, "You're Not Okay." Violence or physical aggression is the most blatant: "You are so 'not-okay' that you deserve to be hurt or killed." Less blatant, but often of equal impact, are Aggressions against self-esteem:

Aggressive Messages and Behaviors

MESSAGE	BEHAVIORS
"You're weak, helpless, and dependent."	• Patronizing • Humoring the other person • Doing things for the other person that (s)he *can* and wishes to do for himself or herself • Refusing to tell the truth for fear the other person can't take it
"You're stupid, incompetent, and irresponsible."	• Restricting the other person's freedom of movement; unnecessarily specifying the means as well as the ends • Refusing to involve the other person in solving a problem which concerns him or her • Reminding the other person that his or her results are less perfect than yours would have been • Continually finding fault in what the other person does or how it is done

Aggressive Messages and Behaviors (cont'd.)

MESSAGE	BEHAVIORS
"You're irrational, out of control, and not responsible for your own actions."	• Treating the other person as un-changing and as perpetually weak regardless of the situation • Avoiding discussion of the real issues between you • Avoiding all unnecessary contact with the other person • Protecting yourself from the ac-tions of the other person
"You're not worthy of my time and attention."	• Cutting off conversation • Maintaining an unusual physical distance when talking with the other person • Beginning to walk away while the other is still talking • Consistently failing to return calls • Refusing to listen to the other per-son's point of view • Withdrawing; expressing a lack of concern. "Do it your way—I don't care." • Continually being late for appoint-ments • Prefacing conversations with men-tion of how busy you are

Each of these messages, and the associated behaviors, portray the "You're Not Okay" feeling. They also depict the "I'm better than you" attitude. For example:

Refusing to return calls: "My time is more important than yours."

Over-programming the other person's activities: "I know how to do it better than you, so I'm going to tell you what to do in a step-by-step fashion. Don't question, just do as I say."

Being overly-protective: "I am wiser and more capable than you."

Limiting the other person: "Now *this* is something I *know* you can do."

Each of these behaviors involves an active put-down of the other. Aggressive persons say through their behavior, "If I don't protect my rights, you'll surely abuse them" (You're Not Okay). They may *also* be saying, "I can't take the risk of being open with you, because you would discover my weak points and take advantage of them" (I'm Not Okay). People who feel truly "okay" about themselves do not *need* to resort to win–lose behaviors and to attacks. Aggressive behavior usually indicates an "I'm Okay–You're Not Okay" position; sometimes it indicates an "I'm Not Okay and Neither are You" position.

The Non-Assertive Approach

The Non-Assertive response projects the feelings, "I'm not okay," and "Since I can't win, why bother?"

The Non-Assertive response represents a failure to stand up for one's rights, an inability or refusal to contribute or to use one's own resources. The objective of the Non-Assertive person is to play it safe, to avoid conflict, and to refuse to take responsibility.

Persons who suffer from generalized non-assertiveness (as opposed to situation-specific non-assertiveness) see themselves as unempowered, insignificant, and unworthy. They rarely establish or meet goals. They lack the conviction that they can succeed. They rely heavily on fate or luck rather than initiative. Here's how the Non-Assertive individual would deal with the following situations:

> **Situation:** A physician keeps a patient waiting for two hours.
>
> **Patient's Non-Assertive response:** To say nothing; to act as though the doctor had a right to disrupt the patient's plans for the day.
>
> **Situation:** A subordinate fails to complete a report as promised.
>
> **Manager's Non-Assertive response:** To say nothing, or to apologize for putting undue pressure on the employee.
>
> **Situation:** A superior delegates a piece of work giving inadequate instructions, and then refuses to answer the employee's questions. The superior then criticizes the employee for doing an inadequate job.
>
> **Employee's Non-Assertive response:** "I guess I'm just not good enough for the job. I know I bother you, and I'm sorry."

The truly Non-Assertive individual really believes (s)he has few rights and resources. Fortunately, few of us have such a pervasive sense of personal insignificance. More often than not, the Non-Assertive response represents in part a feeling of powerlessness and, in addition, an attempt to reach one's goal through manipulation of the other person.

How does the Non-Assertive individual manipulate others? Primarily through guilt. Our cultural and religious backgrounds reinforce the notion that we who are strong should help those who are weak or oppressed. Witness welfare programs, the unemployment compensation system, Affirmative Action legislation, and punitive alimony judgments. All four provide examples of an institutionalized norm—those who are able must help those who are not.

The power of the Non-Assertive response lies in its ability to make other persons assume responsibility for the life, situation, and feelings of the passive or dependent party. The ability to inspire guilt in another person is a distorted form of power. Recall the "tyranny of the weak" discussed in Chapter 5.

Why is the Non-Assertive individual, who seeks to appease others, often comfortable inspiring bad feelings in others? Primarily because the Non-Assertive individual does feel his or her rights have been violated, and is, therefore, angry, but sees openly expressing anger as being too dangerous. It is thus almost impossible to really know where you stand when dealing with the Non-Assertive individual. The result for the other person is often feelings of frustration, entrapment, guilt, and confusion.

While Aggression involves an open attempt to dominate, Non-Assertion is more covert. The outcome is similar, however; only the behavior differs. Non-Assertion can be regarded as passive Aggression, particularly when the "I'm Not Okay" position is blended with the "You're Not Okay" position:

Non-Assertive Messages and Behaviors

MESSAGE	BEHAVIORS
"I'm weak, helpless, dependent and you won't or didn't help me."	• Refusing to ask for assistance when assistance is needed • Refusing to "stretch"—to take on challenging projects
"Anything we attempt to do together will turn out badly."	• Procrastination • Saying you'll do something that you have no intention of doing to get the other person off your back • Holding back resources
"I am not responsible for what I do or for what happens to me."	• Placing blame on others • Refusing to be held accountable • Refusing to initiate • Refusing to take a clear position

MESSAGE	BEHAVIORS
"I can't trust you with my real feelings, which are probably not very valid anyway."	• Showing anger in subtle, indirect ways (e.g., starting rumors, political backstabbing) • Going along with an opinion you don't hold; refusing to disagree openly
"If you're so good, then prove it—figure out what I *really* want (since I'm not sure I know myself)."	• Setting the other up to fail by making him or her second-guess your wishes. • Putting the other in a "damned if I do; damned if I don't" position

The Non-Assertive individual in these examples projects a feeling of mutual "not okayness": "I am weak or dependent (Not Okay). You are the kind of person who would abuse me (You're Not Okay). All I can do to lessen the likelihood of my being abused is to comply, to refuse to take a position, or to be artificially 'nice'."

Non-Assertion, like Aggression, is a win–lose proposition. Often, the "winner" is the compliant, non-asserting party, as (s)he forces the other to bear sole responsibility for the "problem."

The Non-Assertive subordinate is the manager's nightmare. The "yes-man" syndrome immediately inhibits effective problem-solving, and leaves bad feelings at the conclusion of any interaction. Similarly, the Non-Assertive customer is the salesman's nightmare. Parents have a difficult time communicating with the Non-Assertive child, since the child takes orders without revealing his or her feelings. The relationships in all these cases becomes increasingly tenuous as:

• Excessive energy is expended in second-guessing what the other person wants.

• The relationship becomes fraught with unexpressed anger and resentment.

• The "strong" one begins to hedge on delivering bad news to avoid hurting the "weak" one.

Non-Assertion and Aggression:
Opposite Sides of the Same Bad Penny

Those who are comfortable with the "passive–aggressive" or Non-Assertive mode generally find it far easier to shift into the Aggressive than into the Assertive or Responsive mode. This often happens when so much anger has been accumulated that it can no longer be concealed.

Having gotten openly hostile, discomfort with conflict reemerges, and the Non-Assertive mode is resumed. The behavior shifts resemble a pendulum swing.

I refuse to put forth my true wants, feelings, or needs. (Non-Assertive) ⟶ You step on my rights once too often, and I get hostile. (Aggressive)

I become uncomfortable because my true feelings are on the table and that is unsafe, so I try to appease you, putting down my own anger in the process. (Non-Assertive) ⟶ You accept my apology (which I didn't really mean), and that makes me very angry, because you aren't admitting you were unfair. So, I get hostile again. (Aggressive)

The greater the Aggressive shift, the more momentum is provided (through fear of open conflict) to move to an equally extreme Non-Assertive position.

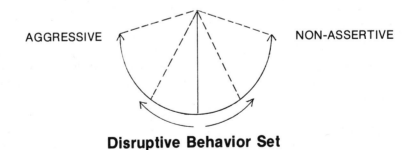

AGGRESSIVE   NON-ASSERTIVE

Disruptive Behavior Set

The Assertive-Responsive pattern also can be visualized as a pendulum swing. The Responsive individual eventually learns enough about, or from, the other person to establish an Assertive position. Conversely, having made an assertion, the effective individual generally tests out the impact of that assertion on the other by moving to a Responsive mode.

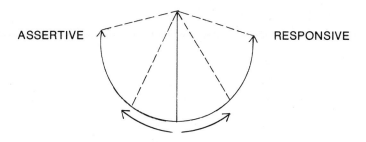

ASSERTIVE   RESPONSIVE

Constructive Behavior Set

We all have a choice as to the pendulum our behavior represents. A person who has been operating primarily in the Aggressive mode will find it easier to move to the Assertive mode than to the Responsive mode, given the "take charge" aspects of both. Similarly, the person who has been behaving primarily in the Non-Assertive mode will find the move to Responsiveness more comfortable than a move to Assertion, given the reactive aspects of both.

Given the destructive pendulum swing dynamic, is it possible to work with Aggressive or Non-Assertive individuals in a mutually productive manner? It definitely is possible. The ability to do so is an important characteristic of the individual who is able to succeed. By following the **rules of giving and receiving feedback,** it is possible to make the large majority of interpersonal relationships more productive.

GIVING AND RECEIVING FEEDBACK

The ability to give and receive feedback is one of the most important characteristics of the Interpersonally Effective individual. In a real sense, men and women are cybernetic systems: they have the capacity to interact with their environments, to sense what is happening as a result of that interaction, and to self-correct. Interpersonal Effectiveness is a direct result of a series of self-corrections which are "on target" in terms of what the individual hopes to accomplish. **If we refuse to receive feedback from others, we are increasing our "blind spots," and diminishing our ability to self-correct. If we refuse to give feedback to others, we are depriving them of information that can be critical to the self-correction process.**

What is feedback? It should be an objective, non-judgmental description of another individual's behavior and how that behavior affects you. It need not, and should not, be regarded as a threat. When people give feedback, they are creating a **change opportunity,** not a mandate.

There are three forms of feedback: sensory, verbal, and nonverbal. When we momentarily touch a hot stove, we get immediate feedback from our nervous system telling us that unless we move our hand, we'll get burned. When we embarrass someone, we may get nonverbal feedback if we cause him or her to blush. Similarly, when people start to sigh, yawn, or cast their eyes to the clock during a presentation, we are receiving rather pointed nonverbal feedback. As a result of this feedback, we are often able to shift our emphasis or to change the pace of the presentation to reinterest the audience.

Verbal feedback is the most difficult to give and to receive constructively. However, it is critical to our personal effectiveness and to the quality of our relationships with others. There are some useful ground rules for making the verbal feedback process effective.

First, **feedback to another person should be descriptive. It should not be judgmental, nor should it attribute motivation.** Let's assume you're in a crowded elevator, and someone is standing on your foot. The constructive way to give feedback would be to say, "You are standing on my foot, and it hurts." Chances are, the other person would apologize and get off your foot. But what if you said, "You're really oblivious. You're standing on my foot, you dumb oaf." Chances are pretty good that the other would remove his foot in order to get in a better position to punch you in the nose! Or, let's assume you're talking to a subordinate who has let you down in some way, making it difficult for you to meet a deadline:

> **Constructive Feedback:** "I am angry that you didn't finish the job, and even more upset that you didn't let me know earlier that you were having difficulty. At this point, it's going to be very difficult to get the deadline changed."

> **Destructive Feedback:** "You're one of the most irresponsible people I've ever met. You don't seem to have any idea of what it means to make a commitment."

In this example, the constructive feedback was *descriptive*—it described the other person's behavior and the impact of that behavior. The *person* was not judged or evaluated. In the destructive feedback sequence, the speaker judged the worth of the person. People cannot disagree with a description of how you feel, but they have a lot of room to disagree with evaluative statements about the worth of their being.

One way to avoid being judgmental as you give feedback is to avoid *attributing motivation*. None of us are qualified to explain to another *why* he or she has chosen or not chosen to do something. When we do attribute motivation, we are necessarily beyond the province of fact (i.e., how we feel) and everything we say is then open for dispute...

> **Feedback that Attributes Motivation:** "You wouldn't get in here at the crack of dawn if you didn't think that would help you get the promotion."

> **Predictably Defensive Response:** "You have no way of knowing why I come in early, and I have no intention of telling you. Just stay out of my way, will you?"

Feedback should be descriptive; it should also be **expressed out of concern** for the other person. To give feedback is to give the other an opportunity to self-correct; to do so is a sign of concern. To withhold feedback is to deny the change stimulus. Even though giving feedback shows concern, we all have a tendency to withhold negative feedback, even with persons we love or respect. This is largely because our Judaic-Christian heritage instructs us to "turn the other cheek" and to "say nothing if you can't say something nice," ignoring disruptive or unproductive behavior on the part of others. Turning the other cheek is to deny others an opportunity to be more effective.

Because feedback is difficult to give, and because it is a sign of concern, **it should not be received defensively**. If you become defensive when someone gives you feedback, (s)he will simply stop—the risk is too high and the personal rewards too low:

> **Feedback:** "You speak too rapidly during meetings. People just stop trying to follow what you're saying."

> **Defensive Reaction:** "You would too if you were in my situation. They give me 20 points to make and 2 minutes to make them in. And, on top of that, I always speak rapidly. I happen to think that is a positive attribute."

> **Feedback Giver:** (To him- or herself): "I'm sorry I said anything; why bother!"

Feedback should also be **two-way**. Persons who give feedback to others should also expect to receive feedback. Feedback is also a two-way street in that it not only reflects the behavior of the "actor," but also the value system of the "observer." Behavior that is acceptable for one person may be unacceptable to another. Personal value differences as well as individual behavior must be considered.

Finally, feedback should be **current** and **relevant**. Feedback about occurrences that happened four or five months ago or even a week ago are often viewed with suspicion by the receiver. The receiver simply suspects that you got up on the wrong side of the bed on this particular morning, assuming that if his or her behavior had *really* upset you, you would have mentioned it when it occurred. Feedback should also be relevant to the relationship you have or seek to establish with the other person. It is inappropriate to give feedback to a person with whom you work only occasionally about their choice in clothing, automobiles, etc. These factors have no impact whatsoever on the relationship you need to develop with this person.

To illustrate the application of the rules of feedback we've discussed, let's look at a manager attempting to deal with the problem of a solid performer who is always late to work:

> **Manager:** "You are continually late. I think you just like to show off—to prove you can get your work done in half the time it takes others."
> (Feedback attributes motivation)

> **Subordinate:** "You don't know what I'm trying to do and not do, and you have no idea why I'm late as often as I am."   (Reaction is defensive)

> **Manager:** "Look, work hours are set for a good reason. Your not respecting the system is just another sign that you are oblivious to the rights and needs of others."
> (Feedback is evaluative)

> **Subordinate:** "I don't feel that way at all. I do think that you're making a lot of accusations without knowing the facts. My work record is unimpeachable, and I'm going to request a transfer."
> (Manager has inspired a defensive and threatening posture)

Now, let's look at how the dialogue might have progressed had the "Rules of Feedback" been followed:

Manager: "When you are late so often, it makes me feel that you really don't respect me or what we're trying to do here."
(Feedback is descriptive—it does not evaluate the person)

Subordinate: "I am sorry you feel that way. I do get my work done, and really didn't think I was causing a problem by coming in a little late."

Manager: "I can understand that—your performance can't be criticized. However, there have been a lot of times when I've needed your input early in the day and you were not around. By the time you arrive, I'm up to my neck in the day's crises, and not in a position to problem-solve around the work issue that concerned me."
(Feedback focuses on the task at hand—it is relevant)

Subordinate: "I understand that. I really will try to get in on time in the future. I've been going to school nights and working pretty late on my thesis. You seem a lot more relaxed during the middle of the day when the start-up hassles are out of the way. Could we plan a couple of working lunches during the week to discuss some of the issues you want to cover with me?"

Manager: "I think I'd agree with that, but I would appreciate your making more of an effort to get in on time. I need you around when the shift starts."
(Manager has permitted feedback to be two-way)

REFLECTING ON YOUR OWN BEHAVIOR

Did you take the time to complete the Behavioral Styles Profile in Appendix E? If so, remove the scoring sheet in order to interpret your scores. Complete the following:

I. **As you engage with subordinates, do you rely primarily on Assertive-Responsive or Non-Assertive-Aggressive Behavior?** To answer this, total your a + b scores for Part I, and compare the result with your total for the c + d scores.

Assertive-Responsive

My "a" score ☐ + My "b" score ☐ is ☐

Non-Assertive-Aggressive

My "c" score ☐ + My "d" score ☐ is ☐

II. **As you engage with your peers, do you rely primarily on Assertive-Responsive or Non-Assertive-Aggressive behavior?** Referring to Part II, compare your a + b total with your c + d total.

Assertive-Responsive

My "a" score ☐ + My "b" score ☐ is ☐

Non-Assertive-Aggressive

My "c" score ☐ + My "d" score ☐ is ☐

III. **As you engage with your boss, do you rely primarily on Assertive-Responsive or Non-Assertive-Aggressive behavior?** Total your Part III a + b scores and compare the total with your c + d total.

Assertive-Responsive

My "a" score ☐ + My "b" score ☐ is ☐

Non-Assertive-Aggressive

My "c" score ☐ + My "d" score ☐ is ☐

IV. **Do you tend to be the kind of person who tries to shape events, or are you the kind of person who prefers being shaped, letting others take the initiative?** To get one indication, compare these totals:

With Subordinates:
    My "a" score ☐ + My "d" score ☐ is ☐ Take-Charge Behavior
                    — as compared to —
    My "b" score ☐ + My "c" score ☐ is ☐ Following Behavior

With Peers:
    My "a" score ☐ + My "d" score ☐ is ☐ Take-Charge Behavior
                    — as compared to —
    My "b" score ☐ + My "c" score ☐ is ☐ Following Behavior

With the Boss:
    My "a" score ☐ + My "d" score ☐ is ☐ Take-Charge Behavior
                    — as compared to —
    My "b" score ☐ + My "c" score ☐ is ☐ Following Behavior

These scores should be fairly balanced. Those who are most effective at taking charge are aware of the needs, feelings, and opinions of others. Similarly, those who enjoy letting others take the initiative devote much effort to letting others know their feelings and opinions so that the others have the benefit of their knowledge and perceptions. **If there is a wide difference between your scores, then reconsider the approach you take.**

V. **When you are taking charge do you tend to be Assertive or Aggressive?**

	Assertive	Aggressive
With Subordinates:	My "a" score ☐ compared to my "d" score ☐
With Peers:	My "a" score ☐ compared to my "d" score ☐
With the Boss:	My "a" score ☐ compared to my "d" score ☐

If your "a" scores in each case are not a lot greater than your "d" scores, then your interpersonal relationships could probably be improved.

VI: **When you are letting others take the initiative, do you tend to be Non-Assertive or Responsive?**

	Responsive	Non-Assertive
With Subordinates:	My "b" score ☐ compared to my "c" score ☐
With Peers:	My "b" score ☐ compared to my "c" score ☐
With the Boss:	My "b" score ☐ compared to my "c" score ☐

If your "b" scores in each case are not a lot greater than your "c" scores, then your interpersonal relationships could probably be improved.

When high levels of interpersonal ability are combined with an appropriate use of power and influence style, the result is an individual who can truly succeed. In the final part of our discussion, we'll look at the relationship between Influence Style and the Assertiveness Behavioral Model.

USING POWER TO ENHANCE EFFECTIVENESS

In an earlier chapter, four basic modes of influencing others—Involvement, Enlistment, Negotiation, and Direction—were considered. Because Involvement and Enlistment tend to be regarded as "nicer" forms of influence, it is easy to assume they are the only workable strategies to use if maintaining the interpersonal relationship is your objective. **All four strategies are workable and depend for their effectiveness on maintaining an Assertive or Responsive approach.** Directing need not be done Aggressively, as the following examples illustrate:

Assertive Direction: "I want that analysis by Friday. As you know, your performance record has not been good. You need to do a good job on this one."

Aggressive Direction: "In spite of your lousy work habits, you had better find a way to get that analysis done by Friday. I can get you fired, and would almost enjoy doing so."

Similarly, Involvement can be done in an Assertive-Responsive or Non-Assertive manner:

> **Assertive-Responsive Involvement:** "I want to share with you some of our ideas on ways the company's products could be marketed more effectively. I'd like your reactions."

> **Non-Assertive Involvement:** "I know I've been pestering you a lot, but I just can't seem to get this. I need your ideas."

The outcomes of Negotiations vary dramatically, based on the underlying behavioral approach:

> **Assertive Negotiative:** "If I'm to continue to put in these long hours, then I feel it is only fair that my salary be increased to match my output."
> **Outcome:** You will get a clear, non-defensive answer.

> **Responsive Negotiative:** "I'd like you to describe to me what you perceive as a fair day's work for a person at my salary level."
> **Outcome:** You will understand the attitude of the person you're negotiating with.

> **Aggressive Negotiative:** "You're a great one for taking advantage of people. I'm not about to let myself be had."
> **Outcome:** You will probably be fired!

> **Non-Assertive Negotiative:** "I probably shouldn't ask for a raise, but I've got to because of some outside pressures that I can't handle."
> **Outcome:** Your salary may be decreased!

Enlistments, which are based on the Informal Power base (Referent, Expert, or Associative), can also be approached from any of the behavioral modes. Only the Assertive or Assertive-Responsive modes are likely to be effective:

> **Assertive:** "I need to see the work sheets you prepared last week."

> **Assertive/Responsive:** "I think the work sheets you prepared last week would save me a lot of time on this project. Could we go over them today?"

> **Aggressive:** "You're so smart and tidy—compulsive, if you know what I mean. I'm sure your work sheets are in terrific shape. How about sharing them with me?"

> **Non-Assertive:** "I must be really slow. I'm at a loss as to how to approach this job. I know it's a bother, but could I see those work sheets you prepared last week?"

Think of someone you know who builds effective interpersonal relationships and, as a result, is successful. Chances are, this individual is someone who:

- **Projects an "I'm Okay–You're Okay" feeling,** indicating that (s)he values both him- or herself and others;

- **Rarely displays Aggressive or Non-Assertive behavior;**

- **Is capable of being Responsive as well as Assertive;**

- **Is able to give and receive feedback in a constructive manner;**

- **Uses the most appropriate Influence Strategy** after assessing the task, the people, and the relative balance of power;

- **Avoids unnecessary manipulations and knows how to avoid being manipulated.**

Further, the maximally effective person is a communications expert. (S)he knows how to stimulate others to share information. We'll look closely at these skills in the next chapter.

7

On Getting Information: The Decision-Maker's Bloodline

Without a plow, the farmer can't work. Without concrete, the builder can't build. Without drugs, the physician can't heal. Without information, the manager can't manage.

Regardless of company or industry affiliation, the manager's job is to make decisions. (S)he doesn't directly produce products, but decides what products are to be produced. (S)he doesn't directly use services, but decides what services are to be offered and at what price. While not technological experts, many managers make the decisions that determine what technologies are to be used. If decisions like these are based on insufficient data, then they are likely to have severely negative consequences. The ability to access data and to acquire information is critical to the success both of the individual and of the organization of which (s)he is a part.

Similarly, whether or not you perform a management function, you need to make decisions. Without sufficient information, your decisions are likely to be less than optimal.

Some of the information you may require can be acquired through printed material and observation. Most of it, however, is gleaned through face-to-face communications. Face-to-face communications are regarded as so vital to Litton Industries, for example, that management has taken pains historically to discourage memos and letters. They urge employees to communicate directly as often as possible, and have helped promote this by making corporate planes available solely to permit travel between plants.

We are not all equally adept at using face-to-face communications to get the information we require. People are frequently reluctant to share what they know; information is power, and some people feel that sharing it diminishes their own Expert Power base. Others fear that sharing a certain piece of information compromises their own position. Still others behave in a way that precludes the possibility of an open give-and-take.

To get information from these people requires that you develop skills in communicating clearly and in building trust and diminishing the perception of risk on the part of the person from whom you need information. In this chapter, each of these skills will be discussed.

THE COMMUNICATIONS HIERARCHY

The responsibility for making a communication "work" rests with you, the sender of a message. A communication is only as effective as the action it produces. If you want someone to give you a financial forecast, and only succeed in getting him or her to hand you a copy of the latest published market figures, communication did not work. **It is up to you to make sure the other person understands what you want and is willing to respond in kind.**

Efforts to build understanding and produce desired responses occur continually throughout our lives. In effect, our communications can be visualized as a continuing spiral through the various steps of the Communications Hierarchy. The hierarchy looks like this:

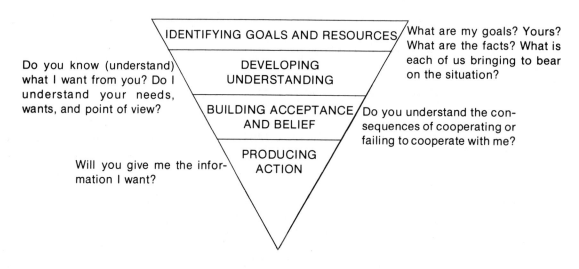

The Communications Hierarchy

The process outlined in the hierarchy is inviolate. Each level must be satisfied in sequential order if effective communication is to occur. Consider the manager who, in the process of attempting to get cost data from suppliers, simply identifies herself and her company and proceeds to ask a series of questions. Chances are this simple process of Identifying Goals will not be sufficient to assure understanding on the part of the supplier. Or, if he does understand, he may not see any good reason to answer the questions. The result is a communication "misfire" because two critical steps of the hierarchy were omitted:

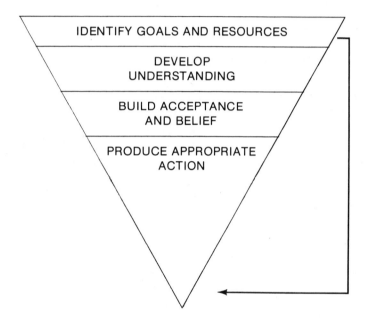

Skipping Steps in the Communications Hierarchy

The Communications Hierarchy is **logical**—one step must precede the other. It is not **linear**, however, but **spiral** in nature. In other words, it is frequently necessary to revert to earlier steps in the hierarchy before progressing. For example, as you attempt to Develop Understanding during a communication, you may uncover feelings, attitudes, or knowledge that have a bearing on the situation that were not disclosed during the identification step. You may find it desirable to return to that step instead of proceeding directly to an attempt to Build Acceptance and Belief:

Identifying Goals and Resources (Prospect): "We are looking for a supplier who will be able to guarantee delivery of a minimum volume each month. In exchange, we are willing to guarantee an agreed upon minimum monthly payment, even if our actual requirement is less than the volume represented by the payment."

Identifying Goals and Resources (Supplier): "I think you'll find our prices are highly competitive. Because we have a lot of customers, we can offer advantageous prices."

Developing Understanding (Prospect): "Getting the lowest possible price is not as important to us as the guarantee of delivery."

Developing Understanding and then beginning to try to build Acceptance and Belief (Supplier): "I understand that, after all, your business is dependent on meeting delivery dates, regardless of the fluctuations in the supply of the raw materials. We offer such a guarantee to many of our customers."

Return to Identification of Goals and Resources (Prospect): "If you offer widespread guarantees, how can you be sure you'll be able to live up to all of them?"

Return to Identification of Goals and Resources (Supplier): "Because we do such a large volume of work we are able to get guarantees from our own suppliers."

Sometimes, we progress even farther through the steps of the hierarchy and find a need to return to the first step of Identifying Goals and Resources. Frequently, while attempting to Build Acceptance and Belief as to the desirability of pursuing a certain course of action, we find that the other person holds certain attitudes or beliefs that would cause him or her to hedge on answering a certain question. Exploring these attitudes (which are also "resources," albeit negative in impact) represents a return to the first step of the Communications Hierarchy.

As we have noted, the communications process is logical, but not linear. While steps may be repeated, no step should ever be omitted:

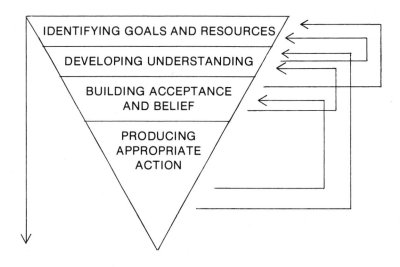

Proceeding Through the Communications Hierarchy

Communications tend to be maximally effective when goals and resources are identified in an Assertive-Responsive manner, followed by an attempt to develop and check for Understanding. These "checks" are, by and large, Responsive in nature:

- "I want to see you succeed here. Do you believe that?"

- "I can't commit to that delivery date because we use independent trucking firms who set their own schedules. Does that pose a problem for you?"

Establishing Acceptance and Belief requires Assertive behavior:

- "If you don't do something to increase your sales volume, I'll have no choice but to recommend that someone else be promoted to sales manager."

- "If you keep me waiting another time, I will find another supplier."

The introduction of Aggression into the Communications Hierarchy by the *sender* of a message will abort the communication. The *receiver* who feels put down or abused is unlikely to attempt to understand the communication. His or her energies are more likely to be devoted to self-defense or counterattack.

When the Sender is Aggressive

MESSAGE SENDER IS AGGRESSIVE	MESSAGE SENDER IS ASSERTIVE/RESPONSIVE
Identifying Goals and Resources: "I know you probably can't handle it, but I want you to attempt to do this analysis."	**Identifying Goals and Resources:** "I want you to work up the analysis on this project. I don't have a lot of time to work with you and must ask you to do as much as you can on your own."
Developing Understanding: "You know I don't like to be bugged every other minute with trivial questions. You do understand that, don't you?"	**Developing Understanding:** "Do you understand the scope of the project I'm asking you to do? Are you uncomfortable about any of the parts?"
Establishing Acceptance and Belief: "This is your last chance to show whether you are at all capable."	**Establishing Acceptance and Belief:** "The analysis must be done by Friday. Otherwise, we'll jeopardize the account. This is an opportunity to show what you can do."
Likely Action: Subordinate will fail.	**Likely Action: Subordinate will do his or her best.**

Non-Assertive behavior on the part of the message sender is also likely to be unproductive, since the message that is put out rarely coincides with the sender's true objective:

> **Sender's Non-Assertive Message:** "I'm really sorry to have to ask you to do this research for me—I'd do it myself if I could."
>
> **Sender's Hidden Message:** "I know I could do it, but I don't want to. I really don't care if I inconvenience you, but I don't want to tell you that since you might get angry."
>
> **Receiver:** "I know you can do it. You don't give yourself enough credit. In fact, I think the sooner you learn you can do it, the better off you'll be. So, for that reason, I'm not going to do it for you."

But what if the message receiver is Aggressive or Non-Assertive? The Communications Hierarchy can be used to encourage more cooperative behaviors on the part of the receiver *if* the content of the communication addresses the problematic behavior. In this case, the process involves:

- **Identifying Goals and Resources:** What you want to accomplish, how you're feeling, and the impact of the other's behavior on you.

- **Developing Understanding:** Around those aspects of the situation that have led to the tension-provoking behavior.

- **Establishing Acceptance and Belief:** As to the negative consequences to both of you of continuing in that vein.

- **Producing Appropriate Action:** Around what you can both do more of and less of to build a more productive relationship.

Let's assume you have to deal with an Aggressive coworker who would rather see you leave the organization and who takes *every* opportunity to criticize you to others. Here's how you might address the issue:

- **Identifying Goals and Resources** (feelings, in this case): "I feel you don't welcome my involvement. That makes it difficult for me to work as effectively with you as I'd like. I'd like to understand why you behave toward me as you do."

- **Developing Understanding:** "I'd like to understand why you seem to feel that I'm trying to look better than you. Is it because of that opening in Sales?"

- **Establishing Acceptance and Belief:** "Unless we can resolve our difficulties, we'll continue to diminish each other's efforts, and we'll both end up losers. We could both be more effective if we worked together."

- **Producing Action:** "Would you be willing to set aside a time to discuss specific ways to improve our relationship?"

The antagonistic coworker's interim responses would undoubtedly alter your responses. It is likely that the response to the statement designed to Establish Acceptance and Belief could result in an exchange of additional information. If so, the conversation might return to Level I, and progress once again through each successive level to some mutually acceptable conclusion.

Using the Communications Hierarchy to discuss feelings and dysfunctional behaviors may cause discomfort at first. There are times, however, when the issue at hand (e.g., getting the information you need) cannot be addressed until bad feelings or behavioral barriers are resolved.

The willingness to confront behavioral barriers to productive face-to-face communications is critical. Equally critical is understanding the feelings, attitudes and perceptions of the person from whom you hope to get information. As people enter a face-to-face communication, they inevitably bring with them a perception of the degree of risk involved in talking openly with you, and a feeling about the degree to which you can be trusted. **Risk** and **trust** are critical, as both affect simultaneously the willingness of the other person to exchange information. Risk refers to the degree to which the other party feels endangered or jeopardized by talking with you. Trust refers to the confidence (s)he has in your character, ability, strength, or expertise. The result is any one of four possible entry positions:

- High trust level, combined with a perception of low risk.

- Low trust level, combined with a perception of low risk.

- High trust level, combined with a perception of high risk.

- Low trust level, combined with a perception of high risk.

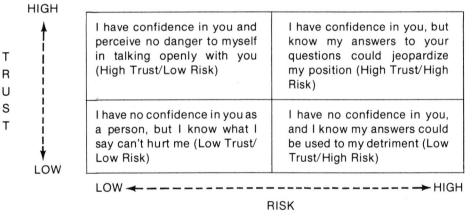

Trust/Risk Elements

The person who begins a dialogue with a High Trust/Low Risk position is generally willing to talk openly and at length with you. Stated differently, this type of person begins with a willingness to move directly into a **Collaborative** mode. For example, if you call on a former professor to find out some industry specifics, chances are the professor feels low risk (or danger) and high trust (or confidence) and will be willing to Collaborate.

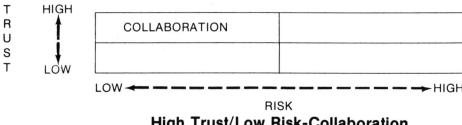

High Trust/Low Risk-Collaboration

A different picture is presented by the person who begins the conversation with a Low Trust Level combined with a perception of Low Risk. This individual has no reason to talk at length, and yet has no reason to fear the proposed interaction. Pollsters and market research people often deal with people in this position. Their attitude tends to be, "I'll do as you ask as long as your information requests don't inconvenience or threaten me." These interviewers can expect **Cooperation**.

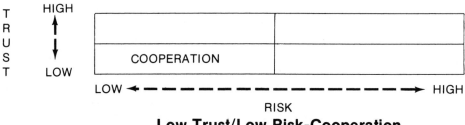

Low Trust/Low Risk-Cooperation

When a High Trust Level is combined with a perception of High Risk, the other person's position is, "I'll talk with you, but I'll need a lot of reassurances." Consider a dialogue between an individual who has a highly innovative idea (in this case, an invention) and an employer who wants to understand the invention and its underlying technology. The inventor may enter the conversation with High Trust ("the company's always been fair in the past") and High Risk ("but if I tell them about this, I stand to lose a lot of money"). It is likely that the interview will be characterized by **Reservations** on the part of the inventor.

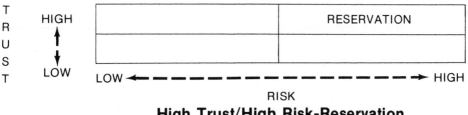

High Trust/High Risk-Reservation

While the exchange can be difficult when the interviewee has Reservations, it is possible to accomplish the objectives due to the level of trust in the relationship. This is not true, given a Low Trust Level combined with a perception of High Risk. The inventor, in this case, would exhibit **Resistance**. In effect, he would be saying, "I don't want to tell you anything. I'll hedge and conceal when I can. I'll disclose as little as I can because I know from past experiences that I'll get a poor deal."

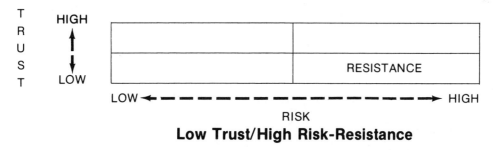

Low Trust/High Risk-Resistance

The four possible entry positions can be visualized as follows:

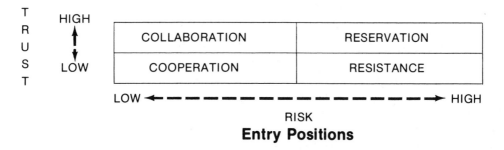

Entry Positions

The only entry position that precludes any kind of meaningful information exchange is Resistance, or the High Risk/Low Trust combination. If you need to get information from a resistant individual, then it is necessary to either diminish or counterbalance the perception of risk (moving to a Cooperative mode) or to increase the level of trust (moving to a Reservation mode), or both increase trust and reduce perceived risk (moving to a Collaborative mode).

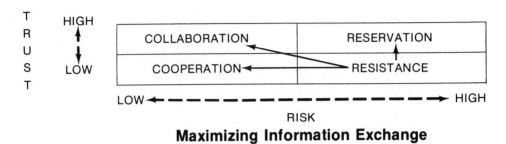

Maximizing Information Exchange

Resistance, then, represents the only mode that is inherently counterproductive to an exchange of information. The other three modes may or may not be acceptable. If you need to engage the other person in a lengthy discussion, and want to get answers to questions in sensitive areas, then it may be necessary to move the other person out of the Cooperative mode and into the Collaborative mode. You must select a mode according to your objectives. The following chart summarizes when each mode is most effective:

Entry Mode Effectiveness

DISCUSSION MODE INDICATED	WHEN
COLLABORATION	• your purpose is to establish an on-going relationship in order to implement a long-term and totally open exchange.
COOPERATION	• your purpose is to get answers to a few questions which are not regarded as sensitive by the other.
RESERVATION	• actual risk for the other person is such that neither a true Collaborative mode nor a Cooperative mode are possible, and yet you need the other person to talk with you about sensitive issues.

As the Entry Mode Effectiveness table indicates, you may find it necessary to shift the entry position from the Cooperative to the Collaborative mode. For example, let's assume you are a manager charged with cutting costs. You want to talk with the purchasing officer about the volume of business placed with different suppliers. Let's further assume the purchasing officer sees no threat or risk in supplying this information, nor does he have a reason to trust you. Now assume that, in addition to questions about volume, you want the officer to tell you the real reasons he occasionally selects the more expensive suppliers, and that you want to establish a relationship that will permit subsequent information exchanges. To accomplish these objectives, you need to move the purchasing officer from the Cooperative to the Collaborative mode. This can only be done by taking steps to increase Trust.

Increasing Trust—Low Risk

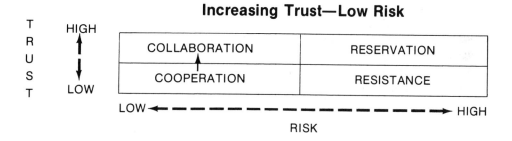

It is occasionally necessary to attempt to move the other person away from Reservation toward Collaboration. Assume you are a personnel counselor. One of your client managers has already learned to trust your discretion. His perception of risk, however, is high as he contemplates the possibility that you could damage his promotion opportunities if you shared what you know about him. In order to develop an ongoing, open relationship with the manager, you need to move the manager out of the Reservation mode and into the Collaborative mode. While this is difficult to do if you are truly in a position to use the information to damage the other person, it is sometimes possible to minimize the degree of perceived risk.

Decreasing Perceived Risk

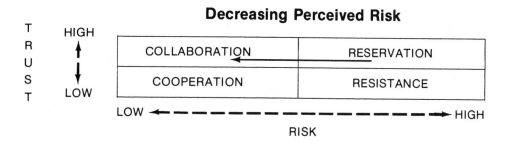

The last type of shift you may find it necessary to make is moving the other person from the Resistance to the Reservation mode. The consultant who has to get information about costs, prices, etc., from a client manager can anticipate encountering the Resistance mode, particularly if the manager is aware that (s)he has made some bad decisions. It is unlikely that it will be possible to diminish or counterbalance the manager's perception of risk, particularly if honest answers could be damaging. It *is* possible to increase the degree to which the manager trusts the consultant's ability, judgment, or character. By working to increase trust levels, the consultant moves the information exchange into the Reservation mode.

Increasing Trust—High Risk

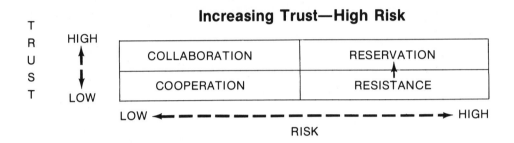

Sometimes you may need to move the other from a Resistant mode to a Collaborative mode. As a young go-getter, newly hired as assistant to the president, let's assume that you have been charged with working with a division manager to devise a strategic plan to turn around a division that has experienced a declining profit margin. The division manager is highly resistant, however. He has a low trust level, perceiving only your youth and inexperience. He also perceives a high level of risk, given the possibility that you can do what he has not been able to do—namely, to reverse a profit decline trend. In order to gain access to the information required to comply with the president's directive, you need to establish an informational give-and-take with the division manager. In summary, you need to shift the division manager from the Resistance to the Collaboration mode. To do so, it is necesssary to simultaneously increase the level of trust and diminish the perception of risk.

Increasing Trust while Decreasing Risk

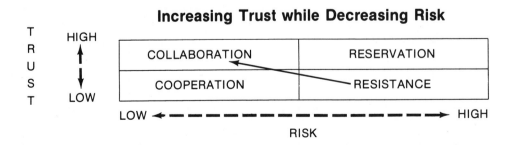

TECHNIQUES: BUILDING TRUST

There are several rules of thumb regarding the formulation of questions and phrasing of statements that increase the level of trust between two parties to an exchange, and, as a result, enhance the flow of information. In the paragraphs that follow, specific trust-building techniques will be presented as they apply to each step of the Communications Hierarchy.

Building Trust: Identifying Goals and Resources

A technique frequently used in building trust is **giving Positive Information** in the beginning of the discussion. This minimizes the other person's fear of the unknown. Examples of Positive Information openings are:

"I have been looking forward to having an opportunity to talk with you."

"As you know, Joe Smith suggested that I talk with you. He said if anyone could help us, it was you."

The positive statement of information is most effective when it: (1) is stated in an Assertive-Responsive manner; and (2) clarifies or enhances your Informal Power base.

As you probably recall, in making an Assertive statement, you state your goals, needs, wants, or perceptions without explicitly inviting the other person to do the same. Since you want to begin the information exchange process as soon as possible, the simple Assertion may be inappropriate. Similarly, the simple Responsive opening can be problematic. Chances are the other person will resist having to declare his or her position first. (S)he probably needs to learn a little about you before revealing anything about himself or herself. Responsive statements can be highly disruptive, particularly when they appear too early in the process. Imagine the outcome if:

- You are talking with a job applicant who very much wants the job (high risk) and you open with, "I can tell you are nervous. Let's talk about why."

- You, as a consultant, are talking to an employee of a client organization and you open with, "I'm very interested in finding out about the problems you are facing."

Chances are, the other person would feel somewhat defensive and attempt to reveal as little as possible in his or her answers. The Assertive-Responsive opening both reveals something about you and invites the other to do the same:

"I am working on an analysis that I hope will help you make plans for next year. I have been told that you are the most knowledgeable person in that area. I believe you can help me learn more about product and plant-specific costs."

In the above example, the speaker provided positive information, stated his objective, and asked for a response. He was Assertive-Responsive in his approach.

The second technique useful in building trust while identifying goals and resources is to point out your Informal Power base while avoiding reference to, or use of, a Formal Power base.

Do this:

INFORMAL POWER

Expert: "Tell me what I want to know because you respect my ability, what I know, and what I can do with the information."

Referent: "Tell me what I want to know because you like me or feel we have a lot in common."

Associative: "Tell me what I want to know because I am acquainted with persons whom you respect or admire."

Not this:

FORMAL POWER

Legitimate: "Tell me what I want to know because of who I am."

Coercive: "Tell me what I want to know because I can and will hurt you in some way if you do not."

Reward: "Tell me what I want to know because I will give you something you value if you do so."

Here are examples of attempts to build Informal Power during the Identification of Goals and Resources:

Manager (interviewing a job applicant): "There is a job opening here that I would like to discuss with you (Positive Information). I have interviewed a number of candidates (beginning to establish Expert Power), and know that many of the experiences you've had here are well matched with the services we provide (establishing Referent Power)."

New Manager of Sales (having a dialogue with a salesman): "I understand your sales record is one of the best in the company (Positive Information). Sales reps I've talked to in other regions have indicated that their sales volumes could increase dramatically if costs could be lowered and prices reduced somewhat (beginning to establish Referent Power). I know this was true at the company I left— when we cut costs by X percent, our sales volume tripled. (Again, establishing Expert Power). It is my hope that, as a result of discussions like this, we will be able to significantly increase our sales volume (establishing Referent Power). I'd like to know what you think; to hear your opinions on the impact of price, product quality, etc., on our sales volume. (Assertive-Responsive)."

It is likely that these openings will establish a sufficient trust level to begin to get information. Two types of questions can be used to get information relevant to Goals and Resources—Positive Overhead Questions and Positive Probes.

Positive Overhead Questions are general, and provide the respondent with an opportunity to talk about those positive events or accomplishments that (s)he chooses to discuss: "Can you tell me why you feel this company outperforms its competitors?" "What did you most enjoy at school?" "What aspects of your job are most satisfying?" In selecting which topics to address, the respondent reveals a great deal. The nature of the respondent's answer provides a measure of the extent to which trust has been established. Brief, nonrevealing answers indicate that you should try to reaffirm or to further enhance your Expert or Referent Power base.

Positive Probing Questions ask for very specific pieces of information that the respondent would classify as "positive": "Which product feature is most appealing to you?" "When will you be in a position to make a decision about our job offer?" **The most effective probing questions are those that avoid the possibility of a "yes" or "no" answer, and encourage the respondent to talk.** A poorly stated Probing Question is, "What did you like most about your last job?"

All the techniques just discussed are helpful when you need to give the other person a reason to trust you—when you need to shift the entry position from Cooperation or Resistance to Reservation or Collaboration. They are particularly suitable during your initial effort to Identify Goals and Resources.

Building Trust: Developing Understanding

After Identifying Goals and Resources, the next step in the Communications Hierarchy is to Develop Understanding. Two forms of response are particularly suitable to Developing Understanding while simultaneously Building Trust: the Reflective Response and the Empathetic Response.

Reflective Responses restate or mirror back feelings, attitudes, and opinions: "A price increase would be advantageous, then"; "I gather, then, that we need to increase our R&D budget." There is often a temptation to preface Responsive statements with "You said..." or "You think..." or "You feel..." These prefaces can be highly inflammatory, and should be avoided. One consultant I know said to a prospective client, "You said your managers don't know how to keep track of costs." The client responded, "I know what I said and what I didn't say, and certainly don't need you to tell me...." Telling someone what (s)he "said" or "thought" or "felt" is contemptuous, or at least perceived to be so by the other person.

The use of well-phrased Reflective Responses accomplishes two objectives: it leads to a better understanding of the respondent by encouraging him or her to comment further about the issue, and demonstrates your interest in his or her thoughts, thus Building Trust.

Empathetic Responses are indications on your part that you understand fully how the other person feels. These statements should be designed to make the other feel that you have his or her best interests at heart: "I know how difficult it can be to give a picture of your total life in thirty minutes"; "I understand that you may be concerned that the things you're telling me may reach others"; "I know that it is difficult to answer these questions without the benefit of preparation"; "I can sense your enthusiasm over this project." While Empathetic Responses in and of themselves do not yield information, they tend to reinforce the willingness of the respondent to be more open.

Positive Probes and Overheads are as helpful in Developing Understanding as they are in Identifying Goals and Resources. They are used to further clarify areas that were previously mentioned.

The trust building techniques useful in Developing Understanding, then, include Positive Probes and Overheads and Reflective and Empathetic Statements.

Building Trust: Establishing Acceptance and Belief

After Developing Understanding, the next level in the hierarchy is **Establishing Acceptance and Belief.** If your objective is to Build Trust, then the other person must be given a reason to accept your expertise—to believe in you as a friend, or in the inherent "goodness" of your objective in asking for information. This can be done by reminding the other person that you care, by pointing out ways in which you can and would like to help, or by pointing out how providing the information you seek will contribute to both of your goals.

> "I know that by working together, we'll be able to solve this problem before the press gets hold of it."

> "I am confident that, by working together, we will be able to achieve some significant competitive gains."

> "I think you will find our data base very helpful to you."

When you are faced with the need to Build Trust with a person who perceives a high level of risk in talking with you (Resistance), then there is an additional technique that should be considered as you attempt to Establish Acceptance and Belief— **Levelling.** Levelling involves risk-taking on your part. (You take a risk when you disclose something "in confidence" about yourself or your situation.) Often, Levelling takes the form of sharing something personal with the other individual—letting him or her get to know another aspect of you or your life: "(S)he likes or trusts me if (s)he's willing to tell me a thing like that." **When you take a risk yourself, the other person is much more likely to believe in the sincerity of your preceding Empathetic Statements.** The Levelling technique should be used cautiously, and should not be manipulative, insincere, or fake. **The price of being caught in such a manipulation is total deterioration of any trust that has begun to emerge.**

Building Trust: Producing Action

Even as you move to **Produce Action,** you can continue to build trust. It is important to remember that trust at an "action" level is still untested. All the other person knows is what you've said; your behavior has yet to confirm your statements. In asking for a commitment, it is important that you also make a commitment. By definition, trust building is required to move the other person *out* of the Resistance or Cooperative modes and into Collaborative or Reservation modes. Collaboration requires a mutual commitment, and Reservations can only be managed through ongoing reassurances. These reassurances begin to ring hollow if they never get beyond the stage of "nice words."

Trust Building: In Summary

The techniques that are used in applying the Communications Hierarchy to Building Trust are summarized in the table below:

Building Trust

COMMUNICATION LEVEL	TECHNIQUE
IDENTIFYING GOALS AND RESOURCES	• Make Positive Assertive-Responsive Statements • Clarify Informal Power Base • Use Positive Overheads or Probes
DEVELOPING UNDER-STANDING	• Give Reflective Responses • Give Empathetic Responses • Use Positive Overheads or Probes
ESTABLISHING ACCEPTANCE AND BELIEF	• Reaffirm shared goals to convince the other person of the need for mutual support • Use your Expert and Referent Power • Level: take some risk yourself
PRODUCING APPROPRIATE ACTION	• Make a commitment • Ask for a commitment

Trust Building is necessary when you want the other person to move from a Cooperation or Resistance mode to a Collaboration or Reservation mode. When you need to move the other person from the Resistance or Reservation mode to the point of Cooperation or Collaboration, then it becomes necessary to diminish or counter-balance the respondent's perception of the extent of **risk** (s)he takes by providing you with the information you want.

TECHNIQUES FOR DIMINISHING OR COUNTERBALANCING PERCEPTIONS OF RISK

People who feel that they would be taking a risk by sharing information with you will pose obstacles throughout the discussion. These obstacles often take the form of insisting that you have neither the "right" nor the "need" to know. Other times, the obstacles are more subtle and are manifested as evasiveness, or talking around issues. **Whatever their nature, these obstacles always represent the respondent's perception that there is little or no benefit to be derived from answering your questions.** Removing the obstacles requires pointing out the upside gain and, by contrast, diminishing fear of the downside risk. Once again, a communication of upside gain or "benefits" is only likely to be effective when the steps of the Communications Hierarchy are followed.

Diminishing Risk Perception: Identifying Goals and Resources

In Identifying Goals and Resources, you should begin with a strong statement of benefits, which can take a number of forms. Desirable results that the other person can obtain for himself or herself are clearly benefits. So are desirable results that "significant others" (e.g., family or associates) can derive from the respondent's cooperation.

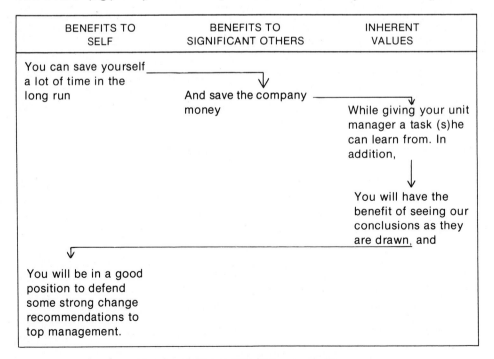

BENEFITS TO SELF	BENEFITS TO SIGNIFICANT OTHERS	INHERENT VALUES
You can save yourself a lot of time in the long run	And save the company money	While giving your unit manager a task (s)he can learn from. In addition,
		You will have the benefit of seeing our conclusions as they are drawn, and
You will be in a good position to defend some strong change recommendations to top management.		

Typical Benefits Presentation

Weaker, but nonetheless motivational, if the other person trusts you, are the values represented by the goal itself. For example, if the respondent believes that consumer action is the key to product improvement, then (s)he is likely to perceive as valuable your desire to "uncover information about product defects." If a person believes it is good to help students in their research efforts, (s)he is more likely to cooperate with a student interviewer because of the inherent value of the effort. An example of the combined use of the various benefits appears on the previous page.

Pointing out benefits as part of Identifying Goals and Resources can significantly increase the other person's willingness to provide information. The benefits that you point out must be selected with care, however. Avoid stating as benefits those outcomes that may not be perceived to be beneficial by the other. To do so puts you in the role of someone who is making a pitch and who does not understand the respondent.

After having provided information on benefits, conclude the Identification of Goals and Resources step by asking Positive Overhead Questions or Positive Probes. These questions should encourage the respondent to confirm his or her interest (or lack of interest) in the benefits you have outlined.

If your respondent has Reservations, but is not Resistant, then the Negative Overhead or Probe might be used to discover relevant concerns. **Negative Overheads** are similar to Positive Overheads in form. They differ only in that the response will most likely involve a discussion of unsuccessful, stressful, or unpleasant facts or perceptions: "Why are you concerned about disclosing information about sales?" or "What is it about your past job that you find unpleasant to discuss?"

Similarly, **Negative Probes** differ from Positive Probes only in the nature of the anticipated response: "Please describe the production policies followed by your employer" or "Please tell me why you left your last job."

Negative Overheads and Probes *can* yield information about the respondent's perception of the risk level at stake and outcomes (s)he hopes to avoid as well as goals (s)he hopes to accomplish. **If the other resists answering these questions, then you would be wise to tread softly, emphasizing benefits, and deemphasizing liabilities.**

Diminishing Risk: Developing Understanding

The next step in Diminishing the Perception of Risk is Developing Understanding. If the respondent has expressed concerns, then use **Reflective Statements** to learn more about the nature and depth of these concerns: "You are concerned that your division managers will refuse to cooperate" or "You are worried about the reaction of the investment community."

If the other person trusts you, you might resort to **Interpretive Statements** as part of your effort to Develop Understanding. When you make an Interpretive Statement, you are adding something to what the respondent has said to check the conclusions that you have drawn as a result of the discussion thus far:

"I gather then, that you prefer to utilize suppliers who offer the lowest cost and can guarantee delivery."

"Can I assume, then, that you would be interested in a job that required extensive travel if the compensation were high enough?"

The respondent's comfort increases as (s)he is made aware of your conclusions and ability to "tune in," and is given an opportunity to correct any false impressions. If your conclusions are correct, (s)he will be more willing to share sensitive pieces of information (to take risks). **If your hypotheses are incorrect, however, you incur a high risk of diminishing trust levels.**

In addition to reflecting back and interpreting what the respondent has said, it is sometimes desirable to provide information to further develop understanding of the actual as opposed to the perceived risks at stake. If you have established a trust rela-tionship (i.e., if the mode is Reservation rather than Resistance), then "playing it straight" by **giving negative information** may be indicated. **Often, the actual risks are far less awesome than the unspoken, unlabelled risks that are preoccupying the respondent:**

"If your people refuse to cooperate, you'll have to mandate the project."

"If our hypotheses are correct, you may have to divest...."

"If the tests are negative, we'll have to stop production for six months."

In giving negative information, it is critical that you avoid evaluative or judgmental comments. Imagine how differently you would react to these statements if you were a manager conversing with another manager:

Evaluative Manager: "The profit margins in your division have been declining as a direct result of unwarranted cost increases."

Non-Evaluative Manager: "It seems that cost increases have been reducing profit margins over the last few years. We need to work to reverse that trend."

The first statement puts the speaker in the role of judge and evaluator, determin-ing what are "warranted" and "unwarranted" cost increases. Most managers would hear the first statement as being highly contemptuous, and react in a defensive, infor-mation-restricting manner. Depending on the style and personality of the receiver, responses would probably take the form of rationalizing or justifying past behavior; projecting blame to others; becoming hostile; or attempting to withdraw from the conversation entirely. **Negative information should be presented only when there is some level of trust. When presented, it should be factual and non-evaluative.**

In Developing Understanding, then, make sure that:

- You are aware of the risks as perceived by the other.

- The other understands the benefits.

- You both agree on the actual as opposed to the perceived risks.

Diminishing Risk: Building Acceptance and Belief

Having developed a level of mutual understanding of benefits and risks, your next objective is to Build Acceptance and Belief around the fact that benefits outweigh risks, and that the benefits will occur if your objectives are accomplished. If the trust level is low (the other person is Resistant), then you need to rely on your Expert Power to illustrate why the benefits outweigh the liabilities. If you are in a position to guarantee a benefit, then do so. This represents a cautious use of Reward Power: "If you help me, I'll see that you get credit for your efforts." If the other person has a reason to trust you, then reassurances that you will not intentionally use the information to his or her detriment are also helpful in Building Acceptance and Belief.

Diminishing Risk: Producing Action

The conclusion of your exchange requires that you Produce Appropriate Action. Appropriate Action, in this case, is getting the respondent to commit to taking the risk—to provide you with the information you are seeking. Here, it is desirable to re-state not only what the other person will do, but what you will do in return.

Diminishing Risk Perception

COMMUNICATION LEVEL	TECHNIQUE
IDENTIFYING GOALS AND RESOURCES	• Give positive information on benefits • Use Positive Probes or Overheads • If trust exists, use Negative Probes or Overheads
DEVELOPING UNDER-STANDING	• Check to see if other person under-stands benefits • Reflect back concerns • If trust exists, use interpretive state-ments (cautiously!) • If trust exists, "play it straight," giving negative information on actual risks
BUILDING ACCEPTANCE AND BELIEF	• Point out how upside gain (benefits) outweighs risk • If trust level is high, offer personal reassurances • Offer "formal" guarantees
PRODUCING APPROPRIATE ACTION	• Restate "contracts"—what both of you have agreed to do

The techniques as discussed can be used in concert with the Communications Hierarchy to Build Trust and/or diminish the perception of risk. If used successfully, these approaches put the respondent in modes most conducive to your information-gathering objectives.

PUTTING WHAT YOU'VE LEARNED TO WORK

Think of one person with whom you'll need to talk in the next week or so in order to get information that could affect the decisions you have to make or the priorities you decide to follow.

Next, determine the entry position this person is likely to assume as your discussion begins. As you do this, consider:

- Reasons (s)he has to trust you.

- Reasons (s)he has to distrust you.

- Benefits (s)he may perceive in talking with you.

- Risks (s)he may perceive in talking with you.

Putting all this together, determine this person's position on the entry position chart:

Entry Positions

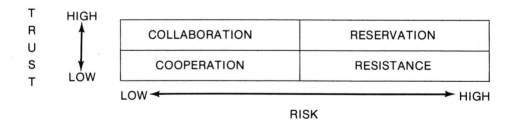

Next, specify the mode you need this person to assume if your information needs are to be satisfied. Consider the following:

DISCUSSION MODE INDICATED	WHEN
COLLABORATION	• Your purpose is to establish an on-going relationship in order to implement a long-term and totally open exchange.
COOPERATION	• Your purpose is to get answers to a few questions that are not regarded as sensitive by the other person.
RESERVATION	• Actual risk for the other person is such that neither a true collaborative nor cooperative mode is possible, and yet you need to talk with the other person about sensitive issues.

Selecting Discussion Mode

Finally, indicate the techniques you plan to use to build trust or diminish perception of risk.

The planning formats that follow should help you put your information-gathering skills to work:

Planning the Information-Gathering Meeting

Person from whom I need information: _____

My information-gathering objectives are: _____

_____

_____

_____

This person trusts me because: _____

_____

_____

This person doesn't trust me because: _____ .

_____

_____

_____

This person will want to share information with me because (perceived benefits):

_____

_____

_____

This person will be reluctant to share information with me because (perceived risks):

_____

_____

_____

I suspect that, as we begin our conversation, this person will be in this mode:

☐   COLLABORATION: (S)he has confidence in me and perceives no danger in talking openly with me. (High Trust/Low Risk)

☐   COOPERATION: While (s)he has no confidence in me, neither does (s)he feel there is any harm in talking with me. (Low Trust/Low Risk)

☐   RESERVATION: (S)he trusts me, but knows his or her answers could jeopardize his or her position. (High Trust/High Risk)

☐   RESISTANCE: (S)he has no confidence in me and has reason to fear talking openly with me. (Low Trust/High Risk)

To meet my objectives, I need this person to assume this mode:

☐   COLLABORATION: To be totally open; to suggest problems and avenues of inquiry; to make a real commitment to the exchange.

☐   COOPERATION: To honestly answer a few predetermined questions.

☐   RESERVATION: To want to talk openly with me despite known and real risks in doing so.

During the conversation, I plan to build trust and diminish perception of risk by:

☐   Making these Positive Assertive-Responsive Statements:

_____

_____

_____

☐   Giving Positive Information on these benefits:

_____

_____

_____

☐   Clarifying my Informal Power base by:

_____

_____

_____

☐   Using these Positive Overheads or Probes:

_____

_____

_____

☐   Using these Negative Overheads or Probes:

_____

_____

_____

☐   Giving these kinds of Reflective Responses:

_____

_____

_____

☐   Giving these kinds of Empathetic Responses:

_____

_____

_____

☐   Making these kinds of Interpretive Statements:

_____

_____

_____

☐   Convincing him or her of the need for mutual support by:

_____

_____

_____

☐   Giving information on these actual risks:

_____

_____

_____

☐   Pointing out how upside gain outweighs risk by:

_____

_____

_____

☐   Taking some risk myself; Levelling by:

_____

_____

_____

☐   Offering these personal reassurances:

_____

_____

_____

☐   Offering these "formal" guarantees:

_____

_____

_____

☐   Making this kind of commitment:

_____

_____

_____

☐   Asking for this kind of commitment:

_____

_____

_____

Appendix F contains additional Information-Gathering Planning Formats.

At this point, almost all of the steps required for succeeding, as *you* define success, have been considered:

- Clarify your values around power

- Gain Goal Clarity and Confidence

- Acquire the power you need to influence others

- Select the most appropriate Influence Strategy

- Avoid unnecessary manipulations on the part of both yourself and others

- Display a balance of Assertive and Responsive behavior

- Give and receive feedback

- Communicate in ways that produce desired action

- Build trust and diminish the perception of risk in order to motivate others to provide you with the information you need

Only one step remains—looking at the organization and organizational unit of which you are (or hope to be) a part. Just as the actions we take affect the success or failure of others, so our fate is partially determined by the groups to which we belong. In the next chapter, we will look at your organizational affiliations and how to make them work in your favor.

8

Your Organizational
Affiliation:
Help or Hindrance?

In the last several chapters, we've looked at a series of behaviors and characteristics that distinguish people who attain their goals from people who don't. People who succeed generally have a high level of Goal Confidence and have become expert at using the most appropriate Influence Strategy. They have developed solid communications skills, and rely primarily on Assertive and Responsive behaviors. In addition, they have joined a group or an organization that is or has the potential to be influential within the organization.

Rarely can an individual be more powerful than the group of which (s)he is a part. If Sales is less powerful than Marketing, then the sales manager is not likely to be more powerful than the marketing manager, regardless of his or her personal style and prowess. A critical step in succeeding, then, is understanding power from a systemic standpoint. This understanding can help you join an organization or a unit within an organization that can help, rather than hinder, your efforts to achieve your goals.

How powerful is the organizational unit you have joined, or are considering joining? On the pages that follow you'll find a self-scoring test to help you answer this question.

The questionnaire asks you to think about an organizational **division, department,** and **function.** If you work for or are planning to join a large organization, you will probably find this distinction easy to apply. Let's assume you work for a bank as a training specialist:

Division: Retail branch
Department: Personnel
Function: Training

Or, let's assume you work in a large department store:

Division: Appliances
Department: Sales
Function: Setting up displays

If you have joined or are considering joining a small organization that does not have divisional distinctions, then skip questions 1–9. Respond to the department questions from the point of view of the work group to which you belong (e.g., a case team, or an account focus).

If you are a member of corporate staff, then skip questions 1–9, and consider "corporate" as your "department" as you answer items 10–18.

To complete the questionnaire, simply put a checkmark in any one of the boxes to the right of each item. For example, if you are in the jewelry division of a firm that specializes in cosmetics and considers jewelry a semiprofitable add-on, you might respond to item 2 this way:

ITEM	True	More True Than False	More False Than True	False
2. As a division, we are in a position or have the resources to enable the organization to respond to those opportunities it regards as most important.	☐	☐	☑	☐

Affiliation Power Profile

	True	More True Than False	More False Than True	False
1. As a division, we are in a position or have the resources to enable the total organization to solve those problems it regards as key barriers to its ability to reach its objectives.	☐	☐	☐	☐
2. As a division, we are in a position or have the resources to enable the organization to respond to those opportunities it regards as most important.	☐	☐	☐	☐
3. The structures (i.e., norms, policies, procedures, relationships, and conditions) that are in place give our division complete freedom to decide what we want to do and how we want to do it.	☐	☐	☐	☐

	True	More True Than False	More False Than True	False
4. Other divisions are unable to a-chieve their objectives without the output or resources of my division.	☐	☐	☐	☐
5. Experience in my division is regard-ed as critical for anyone who aspires to a top management position.	☐	☐	☐	☐
6. The organization as a whole has in-vested or is willing to invest sizeable sums in our division, and we have the ability to generate a high rate of return on that investment.	☐	☐	☐	☐
7. People who have responsible posi-tions in our division would be very difficult to replace.	☐	☐	☐	☐
8. It would be disastrous for the or-ganization if our division made a serious error.	☐	☐	☐	☐
9. Our division holds a central posi-tion in the information network, knowing most everything and de-ciding what information other divi-sions will get.	☐	☐	☐	☐
10. As a department, we are in a posi-tion or have the resources to enable the division to solve those prob-lems it regards as key barriers to its ability to reach its objectives.	☐	☐	☐	☐
11. As a department, we are in a posi-tion or have the resources to enable the division to respond to those opportunities it regards as impor-tant.	☐	☐	☐	☐
12. The structures (i.e., norms, poli-cies, procedures, relationships, and conditions) that are in place give our department complete free-dom to decide what to do and how to do it.	☐	☐	☐	☐

	True	More True Than False	More False Than True	False
13. Other departments are unable to achieve their objectives without the output or resources of my department.	☐	☐	☐	☐
14. Experience in my department is regarded as critical for anyone who aspires to a top management position.	☐	☐	☐	☐
15. The organization or the division has invested or is willing to invest sizeable sums in our department, and we have the ability to generate a high rate of return on that investment.	☐	☐	☐	☐
16. People who have responsible positions in my department would be difficult to replace.	☐	☐	☐	☐
17. It would be disastrous for the organization, or for the division, if our department made a serious error.	☐	☐	☐	☐
18. Our department holds a central position in the organizational or divisional information network, knowing most everything and deciding what information other departments will get.	☐	☐	☐	☐
19. The function I perform can enable the organization to solve those problems it regards as key barriers to its ability to reach its objectives.	☐	☐	☐	☐
20. The function I perform can enable the organization to respond to those opportunities it regards as important.	☐	☐	☐	☐
21. The structures (i.e., norms, policies, procedures, relationships, and conditions) that are in place allow me complete freedom to decide how to perform my function.	☐	☐	☐	☐

	True	More True Than False	More False Than True	False
22. If I failed to perform my function, others would be unable to do their jobs.	☐	☐	☐	☐
23. The organization regards people who perform my function as having skills that are important to managing the company.	☐	☐	☐	☐
24. The organization or the department has invested or is willing to invest sizeable sums in my function, and we have the ability to generate a high rate of return on that investment.	☐	☐	☐	☐
25. People who perform my function would be very difficult to replace.	☐	☐	☐	☐
26. If people performing my function made an error, the consequences for the organization would be severe.	☐	☐	☐	☐
27. My function holds a central position in the information network, knowing most everything and deciding what information others will get.	☐	☐	☐	☐

To score the Affiliation Power Profile, total the number of checkmarks you recorded and multiply as indicated on the format below:

Total checks in "True" boxes ☐ × 6 = ☐

Total checks in "More True Than False" boxes ☐ × 4 = ☐

Total checks in "More False Than True" boxes ☐ × 2 = ☐

Total checks in "False" boxes ☐ × 0 = ☐

TOTAL ☐

The highest score you could have achieved is 6 × 27, or 162. (If you skipped questions 1–9, the highest possible score is 108.) The lowest score is 0.

The following score ranges should help you interpret the meaning of your scores. Before you continue, however, bear in mind that the Affiliation Power Profile was designed to provoke thought only. Until statistical tests are performed, the instrument cannot claim to be scientifically reliable or diagnostically precise. Score ranges assume a normal distribution that has not been verified.

RANGE	SIGNIFICANCE
0–40 (if you answered all questions) –or– 0–27 (if you omitted 1–9)	The work group in question has very little power in the organization; individuals in this work group will probably have a very difficult time exerting any measurable influence on the organization; visibility and, therefore, promotion beyond the work group is unlikely.
41–81 (if you answered all questions) –or– 28–54 (if you omitted 1–9)	The work group in question has only a moderate degree of power in the organization. The truly ambitious individual should probably not seek affiliation with this work group. It is unlikely that individuals will have a say in activities or decisions that affect the larger organization or other units.
82–122 (if you answered all questions) –or– 55–82 (if you omitted 1–9)	The work group in question has a substantial amount of power, though other groups at the same level are more powerful. It is likely that this unit can involve or enlist the support of others; directions will go unheeded more often than not, and to negotiate is to risk losing.
123–162 (if you answered all questions) –or– 83–108 (if you omitted 1–9)	The work group in question is one of the most powerful in the organization. Individuals who belong to this work group will find their organizational affiliation to be an asset in their efforts to achieve their goals within the organization.

The focus of the remainder of this chapter will be what makes one work group more powerful than another, and the options available to those whose organizational affiliation is hindering goal achievement.

DETERMINING RELATIVE POWER: A SYSTEMS MODEL

It is frequently impossible to determine from an organizational chart alone the relative power of one work group over another. Often, the more powerful of two units is the one positioned at a lower hierarchical level. For example, consider the organizational chart of a typical manufacturing plant.

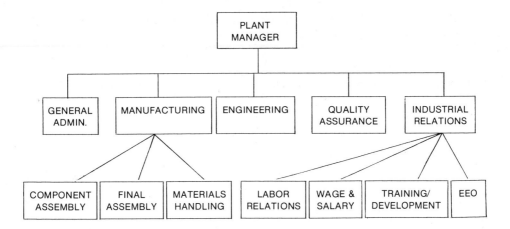

Manufacturing Plant Organizational Chart

The work group that deals with labor relations is on a lower hierarchical level than the work group that deals with quality assurance. The manager of quality assurance reports directly to the plant manager, while the manager of labor relations must report through the manager of industrial relations to the plant manager. However, when the organization is faced with the threat of a major strike, the labor relations expert assumes a great deal of power—more power than counterparts at his or her hierarchical level, and probably more power than the manager of quality assurance. If the scope of the strike is significant enough, the labor negotiator may communicate directly with top management. In such instances, the recommendations of the labor specialist are likely to outweigh those of other executives; his or her demands for additional staff or budget are likely to be attended to more quickly than similar requests made by others.

Similarly, persons responsible for purchasing raw materials in industries in which profit margins are low and the cost of goods can make the difference between profit and loss, often wield a great deal more power than other managers who would appear to be on the same hierarchical level. In industries that depend on the continued smooth functioning of intricate machinery, machine maintenance personnel frequently wield more power than their hierarchical "equals." **The organizational chart does not fully describe the actual distribution of power within an organization.** All the charts can describe with any degree of accuracy are relationships (who talks to whom about what), roles (or functions), and responsibilities.

Assessing the degree of power available to different work groups within an organization requires that we look at the following:

- How vital is the work of the group perceived to be in terms of solving critical organizational problems?

- How indispensable is the work of the group considered to be in terms of responding to major opportunities?

- Who do current structures (i.e., norms, policies, procedures, relationships, and conditions) favor?

- Who is dependent on whom for what?

- Which functions does top management respect and understand?

- What kind of investment has the company made in the work group?

- How scarce are the resources of the work group perceived to be?

- What margin of error does the work group have?

- Who knows what; who controls the flow of information?

The Impact of Perceived Problems and Opportunities

Power tends to reside in those work groups that can solve or avoid those problems the organization regards as critical. Similarly, power flows to those work groups that have the skills and resources to take advantage of opportunities. If a hospital finds it has an opportunity to accept the gift of a new cardiac care wing, then that group of physicians who specialize in cardiology will develop the strongest power base. If a consulting company finds itself in a position to bid for an important account, then those consultants who have a background in the industry in question may assume more power than their peers.

Both problems and opportunities thus play a major role in determining power positioning within an organization. In both cases, however, we may not be dealing with the facts but with perceptions. **Power resides in those people who can solve or avoid problems thought to be critical, and in those people who can respond to opportunities thought to be beneficial.** But why is one problem considered critical, while another is regarded as peripheral? Why is one situation regarded as an opportunity not to be missed, while another is rapidly dismissed as irrelevant to the business at hand? The answer to these questions lies in the **strategy** an organization elects to pursue.

Executives are continually in the process of making **strategic decisions**: to become multinational versus "staying at home"; to make an acquisition or to divest; to rationalize or elaborate the product line; etc. The first level of strategic decisions defines what the organization is seeking **to be, to achieve, to become.** For example, Sears has historically sought to be a multiproduct supplier for homeowners in outlying areas; to achieve market dominance across products; to become the primary mailorder house.

Generally, strategic definitions specify intended competence or specialization regarding the organization's customers and its markets, its products and services, and the technologies to be utilized. The strategic definition is elaborated as the organization establishes objectives around the acquisition and utilization of its critical resources (human, financial, and physical), and around ways to manage interactions with critical environmental groups (e.g., unions, governments, energy conservation groups, and suppliers).[1]

Consider the stated objectives of three banks in the same city:

- We want to be regarded as the "people's" bank—a place where the average homeowner can come; where loan requests are welcome; where friendly bankers ae available to help customers develop financial plans.

- We want to be regarded as the entrepreneur's bank—an organization that understands the needs of the small businessman and the professional in the business for himself or herself.

- Our strategy is to become the primary financial and investment advisor for America's largest, most sophisticated corporations. We plan to develop a solid expertise in inventory management, currency exchange, etc.

The people's bank is likely to regard an increase in local unemployment as a critical problem; the corporate bank is likely to be less concerned about this problem. The entrepreneur's bank is likely to regard the renovation of the downtown business area as a major opportunity, while the corporate bank will become far more excited about a technological breakthrough made by one of its clients.

Strategies have an important effect on definitions and perceptions of problems and opportunities. Work groups seen as key to solving "critical" problems are able to wield more power than groups that are perceived to have no connection to the "crisis at hand."

If an organization regards the introduction of new products by competitors as tantamount to organizational crisis, then the researchers who can potentially outstrip the competition in terms of product development become highly powerful. If a university does not consider student enrollment figures as a problem and is more concerned about getting research grants; then adept lecturers are less valued and less powerful than more research-oriented professors. If a school board has stated as a major objective the academic development of foreign-speaking students, then multi-lingual teachers assume a power edge over teachers who speak only one language.

The extent to which a work group can enable an organization to resolve key problems or respond to critical opportunities, then, provides a measure of relative power. If we plot the importance of a work group re: problems and opportunities as a continuum, then we can begin to discriminate between four Power Levels.

---

[1]For a discussion of management and business strategy, see Peter Drucker, *Management: Tasks, Responsibilities and Practices* (New York: Harper and Row, 1974).

Power Levels as a Function of Strategy

LOWEST DEGREE OF   HIGHEST DEGREE OF
RELATIVE POWER   ←————————————————→   RELATIVE POWER

POWER LEVEL I	POWER LEVEL II	POWER LEVEL III	POWER LEVEL IV
Group's resources have no impact on the organization's ability to solve key problems or respond to key opportunities	Group's resources have minimal impact	Group's resources have significant impact, but others can contribute as much or more	Without this group, the problem could not be solved or the opportunity realized

Sometimes, an organization's strategy is poorly or inappropriately defined, and a discrepancy begins to arise between perceived problems and opportunities, and actual problems and opportunities. If there were, in fact, no difference between perceived and actual, the power distribution in any organization would fluctuate in ways most conducive to organizational health. Those in power at any given time would be those who should be in power, given optimum strategies related to needs and opportunities. This, however, does not always happen. Sometimes, those in power have a leveraged position because of historic strategies, needs, and opportunities. Having achieved a position of influence, they then create structures that are designed to perpetuate and legitimize their use of power, regardless of changing circumstances, and the need to shift strategies.

For example, when an organization must reduce an unacceptable reject rate and meet industry quality and performance standards, Manufacturing, Engineering, and Quality Control may assume dominant positions. Left unchecked, they may try to enhance and then stabilize their positions by establishing unnecessarily rigid product specifications and test procedures. As a result, the organization can face massive delivery problems as Manufacturing becomes unable to keep up with volume demands. The difficulty of meeting unrealistically tight product specifications and stringent test standards becomes insurmountable. **Power distribution that was once functional for the organization can become dysfunctional.**[2]

The federal government offers a number of examples of this dynamic. Agencies are often established to oversee and implement new programs, which then become outdated or no longer important to the country's primary needs. And yet the program continues, because the agency continues. Why does the agency continue to exist? Because its power base has become institutionalized through a mass of Supportive Structures.

---

[2]Gerald Salancik and Jeffrey Pfeffer, "Who Gets Power and How They Hold On To It: A Strategic-Contingency Model of Power." *Organization Dynamics,* Winter 1977, pp. 3-21.

The Impact of Organizational Structures

Structures are composed of those mechanisms which:

- Divide the overall task of the organization into subtasks

- Provide the means and/or incentives for organization units to accomplish the subtasks

- Reintegrate the completed subtasks

The definition of the task, the provision of incentives, and the reintegration of the efforts of diverse groups is accomplished through the establishment of Norms, Policies, Procedures, Relationships, and Conditions.

- **Norms** define appropriate and inappropriate behavior. For example, many industrial and commercial organizations have historically required men to wear white shirts, jackets, and ties. This unofficial uniform has been the organizational Norm.

- **Policies** are decisions made in advance of their execution. They define what will and will not occur. Transfer price policies determine who buys what, from whom, at what price. Personnel policies determine what kind of resources the company will get, at what price.

- **Procedures** are guidelines covering how the work will be performed, or who will do what to whom. In a sense, they are the "means" that are intended to support the policies.

- **Relationships** exist in both a hierarchical (or "formal") and social (or "informal") sense. Hierarchical relationships define who officially has the power and authority in the organization, and make it legitimate for some persons to tell other persons what to do, and how to do it. Social relationships often determine the informal power structure, defining who really gets things done, regardless of the organizational chart.

- **Conditions** are the circumstances that provide opportunities for, or restraints upon, organization members. Some conditions are organizationally imposed (e.g., size of offices, size of the organization, physical location of plants). Others are externally imposed (e.g., unionization or its absence, government regulations, competitors' pricing policies).

Structures inevitably provide some work groups with more power than others. The **policy** of using sales representative organizations can diminish the power of the sales manager as his need to have staff report directly to him is minimized. The **procedure** of having underwriting surveyors inspect all properties to be insured increases the power of the inspectors relative to the underwriters. The hierarchical **relationship** whereby a product manager reports to a geographic head increases the power of the area executives relative to those who have product accountability. The **norm** that encourages employees to be well dressed and stylish at all times gives a power edge to those persons who can afford to buy the best clothes and who are able to wear clothes well. The **condition** whereby marketing personnel are housed in offices adjacent to the offices of the executive committee can increase the power of Marketing relative to that of Sales, which is located four floors below.

Structures, then, affect the relative Power Level of the group. The effects can be shown as a continuum, with Power Level I indicating total restriction and Level IV characterized by total freedom:

Effects of Structure on Power Levels

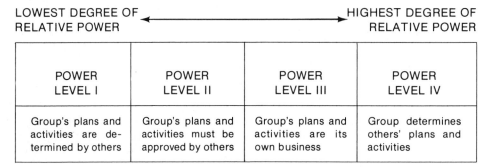

LOWEST DEGREE OF RELATIVE POWER ⟵————————————⟶ HIGHEST DEGREE OF RELATIVE POWER

POWER LEVEL I	POWER LEVEL II	POWER LEVEL III	POWER LEVEL IV
Group's plans and activities are determined by others	Group's plans and activities must be approved by others	Group's plans and activities are its own business	Group determines others' plans and activities

One of the reasons that the structures in place can have such an impact on the relative power of work groups is that they affect one group's dependence on another for acquiring the resources it needs to accomplish its objectives.

The Impact of Resource Dependency

As relative dependency increases, the work group's relative power to achieve its goals decreases. Accordingly, the most powerful work groups in an organization tend to be those that are the least dependent on the resources of other groups.[3] Organizations are, by definition, clusters of interdependent units. Every group in an organization must, to some degree, rely on the output and resources of other groups if it is to achieve its objectives. For example, Marketing has nothing to market if Manufacturing doesn't produce. Similarly, Manufacturing's products gather dust in a warehouse if Sales doesn't perform. While "profit centers" could not (in most cases) function smoothly without the support of "cost centers" (e.g., Data Processing/Management Information Systems, Personnel), the "cost centers" would not exist in the absence of the line operation. The issue, then, is not one of independence vs. dependency, but of the **Relative Degree of Dependency** within an interdependent system.

The concept of Relative Degree of Dependency becomes clearer if we define **dependency as the desire or need to get something done that you don't have**

---

[3]John Kotter, *Power in Management* (New York: Amacom, 1979), pp. 53-66.

the skills, resources, or authority to do yourself. The manufacturing department staff wants to ship enough units to fill customer orders on time. They want the quality of all units produced to be approved, but they cannot approve or "sign off" on each unit themselves—they do not have that authority, and are therefore dependent on Quality Control. The remedial reading teachers in a school system want to purchase special reading aids. They do not have the funds to do so; lacking the required resources, they are dependent on school administration and ultimately the board of education, which is in a position to grant or withhold funding.

On the other hand, if the board of education has remedial reading aids on hand, and wants them used in the school system, they become dependent on the remedial reading staff to use the devices. **The Relative Degree of Dependency of one group as compared with another can be determined only by considering the objectives of the groups involved.**

The Relative Dependency of a work group can be seen as a point along a continuum:

Power Levels as a Function of Relative Dependency

LOWEST DEGREE OF ←——————————————→ HIGHEST DEGREE OF
RELATIVE POWER   RELATIVE POWER

POWER LEVEL I	POWER LEVEL II	POWER LEVEL III	POWER LEVEL IV
Group is heavily dependent on output or resources of others to achieve its objectives; dependency is one way	Group is somewhat more dependent on resources or output of others than vice versa	Other groups are somewhat more dependent on this group's resources and output than vice versa	Other work groups are heavily dependent on resources or output of this work group; dependency is not returned

Some functions tend to have a higher degree of Relative Dependency than others simply by virtue of their responsibilities. Corporate planners, for example, cannot perform their function if they cannot get data from the field; their output remains simply hopes recorded on paper until line managers elect to implement the plan. All too frequently, teachers cannot meet their educational objectives because parents fail to establish a home environment supportive of those objectives.

The Impact of Executive Familiarity with the Function

Top management in most organizations has an opinion (sometimes stated and sometimes not) regarding the experiences that constitute the best training ground for building leadership capabilities. These assumptions often reflect the top executives' own experiences: "Since I am a capable leader, the experiences I had must be important to building leadership capacity." Opportunities for promotion are frequently greater in systems whose top management personnel have come from a variety of functional backgrounds, or whose top managers have been exposed to a wide variety of functions during their career progression. Generally, people tend to place a greater importance on functions they understand than on those they do not; there is a strong tendency to oversimplify, or discount, that which we don't understand or haven't tried. Marketing sometimes thinks of Manufacturing as a "straightforward, logical process... the machinery is in place... all they have to do is put enough people at appropriate points along the line... they don't have to deal with intangibles such as consumer preferences, buying patterns, and all that." Manufacturing, in turn, may think of Marketing in much the same way. "All they have to do is develop some fancy brochures and think of cute names for the products... marketing is just a desk job... the real work happens here."

The tendency of people to underestimate the difficulties of functions unfamiliar to them is reflected in a number of traditional households across the country, as the wife laments, "All he has to do is catch a train, sit in meetings, and take two-hour lunches," and the husband responds, "She has a free ride through life—she really doesn't do anything with her days. I'd switch anytime." Husbands and wives in several households have, in fact, attempted to switch roles, with the wife going out to work and the husband taking care of the house and the children. The experience is often productive, as both learn to appreciate the drawbacks as well as the benefits of the other's responsibilities. Mutual respect and understanding begin to replace resentment and underestimation of the other's capabilities and functions.

Executive Prejudices and Power Levels

LOWEST DEGREE OF RELATIVE POWER ⟷ HIGHEST DEGREE OF RELATIVE POWER

POWER LEVEL I	POWER LEVEL II	POWER LEVEL III	POWER LEVEL IV
Organization leaders do not appreciate or understand how experience in the work group contributes anything to leadership capacity	Organization leaders believe that experience in the work group is marginally useful to building leadership capacity	Organization leaders believe that experience in the work group is useful, though not necessary, to building leadership capacity	Organization leaders believe that experience in the work group is critical to building leadership capacity leadership capacity

The same thing often happens, or fails to happen, in organizations. The chief executive officer who has spent time in Engineering, Marketing, Sales, Manufacturing, etc., is more likely to consider as leadership candidates people from any or all of those functions than is the CEO who has a narrower and more specialized experience base.[4] **Work groups that provide experiences thought to build leadership strengths are likely to have a stronger power base than those that do not provide these experiences.**

The table of Executive Prejudices and Power Levels shows work groups along a continuum ranging from total lack of executive respect for the leadership training inherent in a function to extensive awareness of the function's impact on building leadership skills.

The Impact of Investment in the Work Group

Knowledge and respect for a function by top management tends to swing the balance of power even more when the organization has a significant level of investment in the work group. People like to think that the decisions they have made were good ones. To admit that a decision was bad, and to cut one's losses before they get worse, is a very difficult thing to do. Think of the times you've said, or heard people say, "I can't stop now; I've already put too much time into it," or "I know if I just hold on, the thing will turn around," or "My car has been a lemon all along, but now I've put so much money into it that I've got to keep it."

The same hopes affect the balance of power within organizations: "We just put half a million dollars into new equipment. If the manager thinks he needs more staff to operate the equipment, then we'd be unwise to fail to support him"; "We spent three million dollars investigating the overseas market—if we don't set up an operation there, all that money will be down the drain"; "We've already got two years and twenty million dollars in development of that product prototype. I know it has problems, but if we don't go into production, the whole thing will be a loss. At least we should try to recoup our investment."

The more an organization has invested in a work group, the more that group can get its own way by claiming that its requests represent the only way to make the investment pay off. In one organization I had an opportunity to observe, the training department was able to get a budget increase at a time when most other departments were told to maintain the previous year's budget levels. This was surprising, given the department's historic lack of influence and visibility. The increased leverage came from the company's sizeable investment in videotape equipment that had rarely been used. All the training manager had to do was to point out that the equipment was needed to facilitate corporate communication, but had been underutilized for want of appropriate software and trained operators. Once the manager convinced management of this, the department's budget was increased sufficiently to buy software and hire additional staff members who were trained to use the equipment.

A work group's relative power is measured not only by the size of the organization's investment in it, but by the organization's confidence that the investment will yield a respectable return. To convince management to invest in a function and to

---

[4]Cecil Gibb, "Leadership." *The Handbook of Social Psychology,* ed. Lindzey et al (Reading, MA: Addison-Wesley Publishing Co., 1969), pp. 265-267.

then fail to use that investment to further organizational growth is to *diminish* the power of the work group to affect subsequent investment decisions. These two measures of a work group's power are summarized in the following table.

Investment Leverage and Power Levels

LOWEST DEGREE OF RELATIVE POWER ←——————————————→ HIGHEST DEGREE OF RELATIVE POWER

POWER LEVEL I	POWER LEVEL II	POWER LEVEL III	POWER LEVEL IV
Organization has nothing invested or is unwilling to invest or group cannot guarantee an investment would be recovered	Organization has or is willing to invest a little, and group can promise the investment will be recovered	Organization has or is willing to invest moderate sums, and group can promise a satisfactory return	Organization has or is willing to invest sizeable sums and group can deliver a high rate of return

One measure of the relative power of the work group, then, is the extent to which the organization sees the group as an investment opportunity. The power position of the work group is further magnified as the organization perceives that no entity other than the group in question has the capacity (i.e., skills or knowledge) to make the investment pay off.

The Impact of Resource Scarcity

Resource Scarcity affects the power balance. In the early days of applied computer technology, programmers had a stronger power position in organizations than they do today. The technology is no less critical today to the organization (on the contrary, it has become more critical as the information that must be processed has increased in scope and complexity), but the number of people who can program and debug computer programs has also increased. The resource is less scarce than it was, so the power enjoyed by computer programmers is comparably less.

In the insurance industry, underwriters who deal in risk areas that require judgment (as opposed to application of formulas) often exercise more power than those who can rely on established structures and rating manuals. The power differential may reflect management's belief that finding people who can exercise good judgment is more difficult than finding people who can accurately apply preprinted rates to risk analysis. Whether this is true is beside the point—as long as management *perceives* that one resource is more scarce than another, then a power differential will exist.

Members of work groups that are considered a scarce resource generally have a measure of Coercive Power not enjoyed by others. For example, if I can replace you easily, then the threat that you might resign has a minimal impact. On the other hand, if I believe replacing you would be difficult (because you represent a scarce resource), then I am more likely to go out of my way to make sure things are satisfactory to you. The same dynamic holds true of groups.

The following table shows how resource scarcity affects the relative power of the work group in this way:

Resource Scarcity and Power Levels

LOWEST DEGREE OF ←————————————————→ HIGHEST DEGREE OF
RELATIVE POWER   RELATIVE POWER

POWER LEVEL I	POWER LEVEL II	POWER LEVEL III	POWER LEVEL IV
People in the group could be replaced with little or no cost to the organization	People could be replaced, but a small cost would be involved	People could be replaced, but the cost would be significant	The cost of replacing people in the work group would be enormous

One reason for resource scarcity is the degree of specialization represented by the group's function. The more highly specialized a function, the fewer the number of people who are trained to perform the function. Specialization brings clout, particularly when a need for expertise is accompanied by a high cost of errors.

The Impact of Error Margin

Policemen who operate on the street probably enjoy a greater measure of power than their counterparts with desk jobs. On the street, the margin of acceptable error is narrow. The typical organizational hierarchy illustrates the dynamic that power and a low error margin go hand in hand. The higher the executive is in a hierarchy, the more cost and risk tend to be involved in his or her decisions. The executive who can spend or not spend a million dollars, pounds, or yen is in a position to make a much more serious error than a supervisor who is authorized to spend only a thousand dollars, pounds, or yen.

Logic indicates that people who are in a position to make expensive errors would be more closely watched, and therefore, less empowered, than people who are not in a position to create the same degree of havoc. But just the opposite is generally true; we usually let high risk-takers do things their own way. People are less likely to question the actions of a bomb squad than they are the actions of a traffic cop. Similarly, people offer many tips on training household pets; the same people tend to be silently awed by the efforts of a lion tamer. There appears to be an assumption that "If (s)he'll take that kind of risk, (s)he must know what (s)he's doing."

The following table shows how allowable margins of error affect the relative power of work groups.

Error Margin and Power Levels

LOWEST DEGREE OF
RELATIVE POWER
←————————————————→
HIGHEST DEGREE OF
RELATIVE POWER

POWER LEVEL I	POWER LEVEL II	POWER LEVEL III	POWER LEVEL IV
WIDE MARGIN: Errors would probably not be felt or noticed.	MODERATE MARGIN: Errors would be noticed and would cost something to correct.	SLIM MARGIN: Errors would be noticed and the cost to correct them would be significant.	NO MARGIN: Errors would be disastrous.

One of the reasons that groups with a lower error margin are relatively more powerful is that they can generally access a more comprehensive data or information base than can other work groups in the system.

The Impact of Information

Information is Power. To win in war is to know in advance what moves the enemy is going to make, and to establish strategies accordingly. To win in business is to know what the competition is going to do, what the consumers want to buy, what the government is going to permit, and to establish objectives accordingly. To win in a race for an elective office is to know what the voters want and to build your platform accordingly. Those who are informed are always in a better position to determine effective strategies than those who are not, regardless of the situation.

Why does one work group get more information than another? One answer lies in the **need to know**—a need that is frequently not satisfied. Many work groups may feel they need to know something, and yet remain unable to access the data simply because other groups do not acknowledge this need or right to know. In other instances, one work group may deny access to information to retain a measure of power over the other work group.

Information, then, also plays a part in determining the work group's position along the continuum of relative power:

Information and Power Levels

LOWEST DEGREE OF
RELATIVE POWER
←————————————————→
HIGHEST DEGREE OF
RELATIVE POWER

POWER LEVEL I	POWER LEVEL II	POWER LEVEL III	POWER LEVEL IV
Group can only gain access to information clearly related to its direct activities.	Group can gain access to all information related to its activities and those of related functions.	Group is free to gain access to any information it desires.	Group controls all information and decides who needs to know what and who can gain access to what.

In many organizations, information is used to protect or maintain the existing hierarchy. The firm to which I belong does a great deal of analytical and diagnostic work. Typically, the client will ask for a full report of survey results. Separate department heads then see only their own results. In this way, top management maintains its position as the only group with a global view of the organization. Similarly, in government circles, access to confidential information is a mark of power and, presumably, of trustworthiness.

In Summary

We have considered several factors regarding the balance of power within organizations:

- How vital is the work of the group felt to be in terms of solving problems perceived to be critical or in terms of responding to opportunities perceived to be key?

- What freedoms or restrictions are imposed by organizational structures (i.e., norms, policies, procedures, relationships, and conditions)?

- How dependent is one work group on another for acquiring the resources it needs to achieve its objectives?

- To what extent does management regard experience in the work group as important to building leadership ability?

- In which work groups does the organization have a sizeable investment? Which of these work groups have the ability to make the investment pay off?

Summary of Factors Influencing Power Levels of Work Groups

FACTOR	POWER LEVEL I	POWER LEVEL II	POWER LEVEL III	POWER LEVEL IV
Importance of the work group to solving problems	Group's resources have no impact.	Group's resources have minimal impact.	Group's resources have significant impact, but others can contribute as much if not more.	Without this group, the problem cannot be solved.
Importance of the work group's response to opportunities	Group's resources have no impact.	Group's resources have minimal impact.	Group's resources have significant impact, but others can contribute as much if not more.	Without this group, the organization cannot respond to opportunities thought to be key to implementing organization strategy.
Impact of governing structures	Group's plans and activities are determined by others.	Group's plans and activities must be approved by others.	Group's plans and activities are its own business.	Group determines other groups' plans and activities.
Relative degree of dependency	Group is heavily dependent on resources of others to achieve its objectives; this dependency is primarily one-way.	Group is somewhat more dependent on resources or output of others than vice versa.	Other groups are somewhat more dependent on this group's resources and output than vice versa.	Other work groups are heavily dependent on resources of this group to achieve their objectives; dependency is one-way.
Perceived relevance of work group experience to leadership ability	Organization leadership does not understand or appreciate how experience in the work group contributes to building leadership ability.	Organization leadership believes that experience in the work group is marginally useful in building leadership ability.	Organization leaders believe that experience in the work group is useful, though not necessary, to building leadership ability.	Organization leaders believe that experience in the work group is critical to building leadership ability.

Resource investment in the work group	Organization has nothing invested or is unwilling to invest, and group cannot guarantee an investment would be recovered.	Organization has or is willing to invest a little, and group can promise the investment will be recovered.	Organization has or is willing to invest moderate sums, and group can promise a satisfactory return.	Organization has or is willing to invest sizeable sums and group can deliver a high rate of return.
Professional and technical resource scarcity	People in this group could be replaced with little or no cost to the organization.	People in the group could be replaced, but a small cost would be involved.	People could be replaced, but the cost would be significant.	The cost of replacing people in the work group would be enormous.
Margin for error	Errors would probably not be felt or noticed.	Errors would be noticed and would cost something to correct.	Errors would be noticed and the cost to correct would be significant.	Errors would be disastrous.
Information flow and control	Group can only gain access to information clearly related to its direct activities.	Group can gain access to all information related to its activities and those of related functions.	Group is free to gain access to any information it desires.	Group controls all information and decides who needs to know what and who can gain access to what.

- How do different work groups compare in terms of perceived scarcity or replaceability of their members?

- Which work groups have the tightest margin for error?

- Which work groups can most easily access critical data?

A simultaneous consideration of all these factors makes it possible to place any work group within the organization on one of four Power Levels. These Power Levels are summarized in the chart on pages 228 and 229.

PUTTING AFFILIATION POWER TO WORK FOR YOU

As you began this chapter, you had an opportunity to complete the Affiliation Power Profile. You might find it useful now to analyze the results from the point of view of each of the factors that have been discussed. Doing so will provide one indication of Power Level, as well as the specific areas in which your work group is benefiting or suffering.

To begin this analysis, refer back to the profile itself (pages 210–213) and translate your responses to numerical scores as follows; and then enter the scores next to the items.

- If you checked "True," assign a 6.

- If you checked "More True Than False," assign a 4.

- If you checked "More False Than True," assign a 2.

- If you checked "False," assign a 0.

Here is a format for you to use to record your scores:

ITEM	MY RESPONSE/SCORES	MY SCORE
1	☐ True – 6 ☐ More True Than False – 4 ☐ More False Than True – 2 ☐ False – 0	☐
2	☐ True – 6 ☐ More True Than False – 4 ☐ More False Than True – 2 ☐ False – 0	☐

ITEM	MY RESPONSE/SCORES	MY SCORE
3	☐ True – 6 ☐ More True Than False – 4 ☐ More False Than True – 2 ☐ False – 0	☐
4	☐ True – 6 ☐ More True Than False – 4 ☐ More False Than True – 2 ☐ False – 0	☐
5	☐ True – 6 ☐ More True Than False – 4 ☐ More False Than True – 2 ☐ False – 0	☐
6	☐ True – 6 ☐ More True Than False – 4 ☐ More False Than True – 2 ☐ False – 0	☐
7	☐ True – 6 ☐ More True Than False – 4 ☐ More False Than True – 2 ☐ False – 0	☐
8	☐ True – 6 ☐ More True Than False – 4 ☐ More False Than True – 2 ☐ False – 0	☐
9	☐ True – 6 ☐ More True Than False – 4 ☐ More False Than True – 2 ☐ False – 0	☐
10	☐ True – 6 ☐ More True Than False – 4 ☐ More False Than True – 2 ☐ False – 0	☐
11	☐ True – 6 ☐ More True Than False – 4 ☐ More False Than True – 2 ☐ False – 0	☐
12	☐ True – 6 ☐ More True Than False – 4 ☐ More False Than True – 2 ☐ False – 0	☐

ITEM	MY RESPONSE/SCORES	MY SCORE
13	☐ True – 6 ☐ More True Than False – 4 ☐ More False Than True – 2 ☐ False – 0	☐
14	☐ True – 6 ☐ More True Than False – 4 ☐ More False Than True – 2 ☐ False – 0	☐
15	☐ True – 6 ☐ More True Than False – 4 ☐ More False Than True – 2 ☐ False – 0	☐
16	☐ True – 6 ☐ More True Than False – 4 ☐ More False Than True – 2 ☐ False – 0	☐
17	☐ True – 6 ☐ More True Than False – 4 ☐ More False Than True – 2 ☐ False – 0	☐
18	☐ True – 6 ☐ More True Than False – 4 ☐ More False Than True – 2 ☐ False – 0	☐
19	☐ True – 6 ☐ More True Than False – 4 ☐ More False Than True – 2 ☐ False – 0	☐
20	☐ True – 6 ☐ More True Than False – 4 ☐ More False Than True – 2 ☐ False – 0	☐
21	☐ True – 6 ☐ More True Than False – 4 ☐ More False Than True – 2 ☐ False – 0	☐
22	☐ True – 6 ☐ More True Than False – 4 ☐ More False Than True – 2 ☐ False – 0	☐

ITEM	MY RESPONSE/SCORES	MY SCORE
23	☐ True – 6 ☐ More True Than False – 4 ☐ More False Than True – 2 ☐ False – 0	☐
24	☐ True – 6 ☐ More True Than False – 4 ☐ More False Than True – 2 ☐ False – 0	☐
25	☐ True – 6 ☐ More True Than False – 4 ☐ More False Than True – 2 ☐ False – 0	☐
26	☐ True – 6 ☐ More True Than False – 4 ☐ More False Than True – 2 ☐ False – 0	☐
27	☐ True – 6 ☐ More True Than False – 4 ☐ More False Than True – 2 ☐ False – 0	☐

Next, transpose your scores onto this format:

FACTOR	ITEM/SCORES	TOTAL ALL ITEMS
IMPORTANCE TO PROBLEMS	1 _____ 10 _____ 19 _____	☐
IMPORTANCE TO OPPORTUNITIES	2 _____ 11 _____ 20 _____	☐
IMPACT OF STRUCTURES	3 _____ 12 _____ 21 _____	☐

FACTOR	ITEM/SCORES	TOTAL ALL ITEMS
RELATIVE DEGREE OF DEPENDENCY	4 _____ 13 _____ 22 _____	☐
RELEVANCE OF EX-PERIENCE WITH GROUP TO LEADER-SHIP ABILITY	5 _____ 14 _____ 23 _____	☐
INVESTMENT	6 _____ 15 _____ 24 _____	☐
RESOURCE SCARCITY	7 _____ 16 _____ 25 _____	☐
ERROR MARGIN	8 _____ 17 _____ 26 _____	☐
INFORMATION FLOW AND CONTROL	9 _____ 18 _____ 27 _____	☐

   After recording your totals, graph them by putting a point above the factor and across from the number representing your total for that factor. For example, assume you had these scores:

FACTOR	ITEM/SCORES		TOTAL
IMPORTANCE TO PROBLEMS	1	4	10
	10	4	
	19	2	
IMPORTANCE TO OPPORTUNITIES	2	4	6
	11	2	
	20	0	

Your graph would look like the Power Graph below:

Affiliation Power Graph—First Step

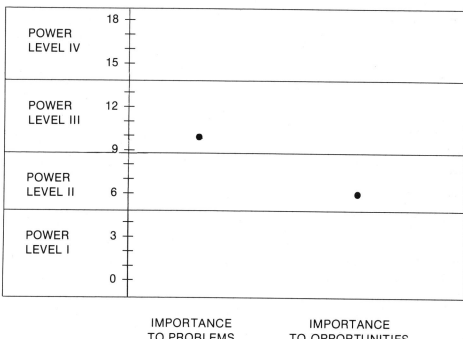

After recording all your totals, connect them. Your completed graph might look something like the Completed Affiliation Power Graph on the next page.

Completed Affiliation Power Graph

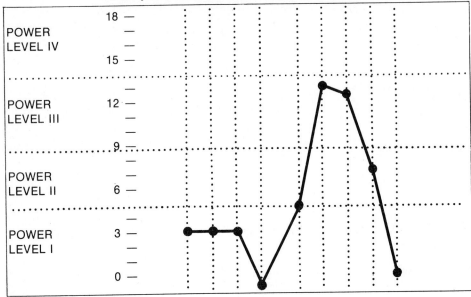

A blank format follows for your use.

Affiliation Power Graph

```
18 —
POWER          —
LEVEL IV       —
            15 —
..........................................................................

               —
POWER      12 —
LEVEL III      —
               —
...........9.—..............................................................

POWER          —
LEVEL II    6 —
..........................................................................

POWER          —
LEVEL I     3 —
               —
             0 —
```

IMPORTANCE TO PROBLEMS

IMPORTANCE TO OPPORTUNITIES

IMPACT OF STRUCTURES

RELATIVE DEGREE OF DEPENDENCY

RELEVANCE OF EXPERIENCE TO LEADERSHIP ABILITY

INVESTMENT

RESOURCE SCARCITY

ERROR MARGIN

INFORMATION FLOW AND CONTROL

If you skipped items 1–9 (because you are not part of a division), then change the scale on the Modified Affiliation Graph on the next page.

Modified Affiliation Graph

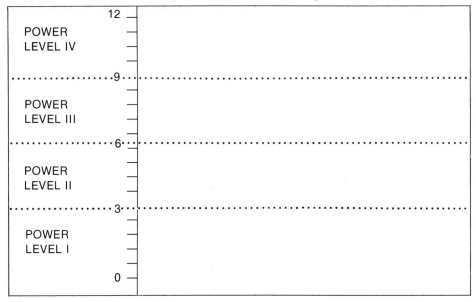

After charting your own organizational affiliation, you might find it interesting to complete the profile again, using another unit or department as your frame of reference. Then, chart your unit in one color, and the other unit or department in another color to get a picture of relative power. Blank profiles and graphing formats are provided in Appendix G.

The Power Level concept can also be useful if you are entering the job market, or are making a career switch and want to evaluate your options. Simply list your options and determine which is most characteristic of Power Levels III and IV. For example, consider Pete Jones. Pete got a degree in chemical engineering, and then his Masters in business administration. His focus in graduate school was on corporate strategic planning. He is especially proud of his research capabilities. Now Pete must choose between four options.

Option A is to join the research department of a chemical manufacturing concern. The company prides itself on its ability to maintain its share of market by introducing new products at a faster rate than its competitors. The research department has the most budget flexibility of any department. The president and chairman of the board of the company both headed up the financial planning department before being promoted. The president holds a degree in chemical engineering. The company's primary competitor has just introduced a number of new products that are threatening to erode the company's market share.

Option B is to join a strategic planning consulting firm as a member of a case team working to improve the internal portfolio of a client. Billing from this client company is among the largest of any accounts currently handled by the consulting firm. It was also among the first accounts handled by the firm, and is the firm's only client in the chemicals area. The majority of the other clients are in heavy manufacturing, and are multinational. (The chemical company is a U.S. company.) Several other consultants in the firm have chemical engineering backgrounds.

Option C is to join the corporate planning department of a firm engaged in heavy manufacturing. The company has grown by 15 percent each year for the past ten years, and it anticipates the same rate of growth in the foreseeable future. The corporate planning function has been in existence for only three years. The president of the company has a marketing background; the chairman of the board is a production expert. The head of corporate planning reports to the chief administrative officer who, in turn, reports to the president. Pete would be one of three planning specialists.

Option D is to assume the position of assistant lecturer in the engineering department of the graduate school that awarded him his MBA. The university relies to a significant degree on grants awarded for research work. Departments that get the most grant monies have the biggest budgets. Most of the research work is done by another department, but the school graduates more engineering majors than any other single type of major. The dean of the university holds an advanced degree in finance. The assistant dean teaches courses in organizational behavior.

Pete considers each of the factors determining Relative Power as follows:

FACTOR	OPTION MOST CLOSELY DISPLAYING LEVEL IV CHARACTERISTICS	OPTION MOST CLOSELY DISPLAYING LEVEL I CHARACTERISTICS
IMPORTANCE TO PROBLEMS	A	D
IMPORTANCE TO OPPORTUNITIES	A & C	B
IMPACT OF STRUCTURES	A & C	D
RELATIVE DEPENDENCY	B	C
PERCEIVED RELEVANCE OF EXPERIENCE TO LEADERSHIP ABILITY	A	D
INVESTMENT	A	D
RESOURCE SCARCITY	A	B & D
ERROR MARGIN	A, B, & C	D
INFORMATION FLOW AND CONTROL	B & C	D

As a result of this analysis, Pete determines that Option A—joining the research department of a chemical manufacturing concern—will affiliate him with the most powerful work group. Doing so will ally Pete with a group whose inherent power base will help rather than hinder him in his efforts to become a highly influential member of the organization.

If becoming highly influential is one of your objectives, and if you, like Pete, are considering a number of options, then I suggest that you spend a few minutes listing your options and then engaging in the same kind of analysis. Blank formats follow for your use.

Job Options

MY JOB OPTIONS ARE AS FOLLOWS . . .

A. _____
   _____
   _____

B. _____
   _____
   _____

C. _____
   _____
   _____

D. _____
   _____
   _____

I would analyze these options as follows:

Power Levels of Job Options

FACTOR	OPTION MOST CLOSELY DISPLAYING LEVEL IV CHARACTERISTICS	OPTION MOST CLOSELY DISPLAYING LEVEL I CHARACTERISTICS
IMPORTANCE TO PROBLEMS		
IMPORTANCE TO OPPORTUNITIES		
IMPACT OF STRUCTURES		
RELATIVE DEPENDENCY		
PERCEIVED RELEVANCE OF EXPERIENCE TO LEADERSHIP ABILITY		
INVESTMENT		
RESOURCE SCARCITY		
ERROR MARGIN		
INFORMATION FLOW AND CONTROL		

Affiliating yourself with the most powerful work group in an organization seems only logical—but beware. **It is wise to do so only if your objective is to become one of the most influential members of the organization, and if the option supports your other important life goals.**

Returning to Pete, let's assume the chemical company was located in New York, and he was eager to live in California. Let's further assume the consulting company and the university are both located in California. Depending on his priorities, Pete might elect to join a relatively less powerful work group in order to pursue his other life goals.

In doing so, is Pete destined to sacrifice his objective of reaching the top level in the organization of his choice? Fortunately not—he can work to change the balance of power in his chosen organization.

Changing the Balance of Power Within Organizations

Changing the balance of power within an organization can be done by increasing the power level of your own work group while simultaneously enhancing the position of the organization as a whole. Some of the factors that determine Power Level lend themselves to change more readily than others: structures, for example, can be changed more readily than strategies. Among the structures, **norms, relationships, conditions,** and **procedures** lend themselves to change more readily than do **policies**.

CHANGING STRUCTURES

A shift in **norms** can be stimulated either by education or by providing alternative models. To take a simple example, one organizational norm might be to dress in three-piece, dark, pinstriped suits. One way to shift this norm is to point out to people the cost of having these suits cleaned, and/or to convince them that the garb restricts spontaneity of action and thought in ways that are detrimental to the work group. This represents an educational approach to normative change. The other approach is less open (and far more expensive!): normative shifts can be made so slowly and subtly that few people are made aware that a change is occurring. To continue with the office apparel example, one work group might decide to begin by maintaining the dark, pin-striped suit while dropping the vest the first week. The second week might see the standard white shirt replaced by a very pale yellow shirt. The third week, a plain dark suit might replace the pinstripe. The fourth, fifth, and sixth weeks the plain colored suits get increasingly lighter while the shirts get increasingly darker. Over time, the definitions of what constitutes appropriate and inappropriate behavior begin to loosen, leaving room for a redefinition that is more compatible with the work group's objectives.

Stimulating shifts in norms relating to dress codes is unlikely to significantly alter the balance of power within an organization. But normative shifts in other areas can have a significant impact. Consider the importance of norms in managerial style, such as the one that says it is appropriate to be directive with employees and inappropriate to involve them in making decisions. This can have a marked impact on employees' ability to contribute to their full potential. Efforts to redefine norms regarding managerial style can thus be very beneficial. Again, the approach can be educational or modeling. Seminars in leadership effectiveness that promote the benefits of participative management can increase management's awareness of style options. Becoming more participative in your own approach, and then letting your results demonstrate the merits of the alternative style can begin to legitimize trying out new approaches. Normative shifts can sometimes trigger reformulations of policies.

Shifting **relationships,** either hierarchical or social, can have a similar impact on policy. Consider a transfer price policy that discourages divisions A and B from "buying" from each other. Further, assume that division C is self-contained; it produces a product that is markedly different from that produced by other divisions, and would not benefit from "purchasing" components from other divisions. Assume the manager of C division believes it is in his interest to retain the transfer price policies that diminish A and B's profits relative to his. It is in A and B's best interest to establish a relationship that diminishes their tendency to compete. In diminishing their adversary status, A and B both "win": it is likely that, in collaborating, they will be able to summon enough clout to alter transfer price policies that benefit C at the expense of the overall organization.

Generally, since shifting norms and relationships have an impact upon **policy,** they also stimulate a rethinking of **procedures.** Procedures describe how policies are to be implemented. In a sense, if a + b = c, then "a" and "b" are the procedures that should yield adherence to policy "c"; shifting procedures can weaken the strength of policy positions. In a telephone company, there is a policy that all emergency calls will be monitored by the floor supervisor. The procedure that makes adherence to this policy possible is that all operators are to stand and put on a red light over their board when they are dealing with an emergency call. If the procedures are not followed, the policy cannot be implemented. To challenge the procedure on the basis of the time it takes to put on the light and to stand when every second counts might be better received than if the operators were to challenge the supervisor's "right" to monitor the calls.

Finally, changing **conditions** can stimulate a rethinking of policies. Consider the organizational policy that states that all purchasing will be performed by a centralized function. Let's further say that this policy was established when available data indicated that centralization of the purchasing function would lead to cost savings. The work group that can prove that, in some locations, local suppliers can offer significantly greater cost savings will probably succeed in stimulating a reconsideration of policy. While the work group did not change the actual condition regarding supply availability, they did change the *perception* of the condition. The impact is the same.

It is sometimes possible to actually modify conditions, and, in the process, to trigger policy or strategic reconsiderations. As an example, consider the head of the new accounts department of an advertising agency. In pursuing and landing accounts all over the world, this manager effectively outdated the organizational policy that stated that no branch offices would be established. In changing a condition (in this case, the nature of the client base), (s)he forced a policy and a strategy into question.

CHANGING PERCEIVED IMPORTANCE

As all of the examples have illustrated, it takes time and energy to create conditions that will force a policy or strategic modification or shift. Having done so, it remains uncertain whether the resulting policy and strategic changes will in fact benefit the work group. That they will do so is more likely when efforts to affect policy decisions are combined with efforts to enhance the perception of the work group as critical to resolving the key problems and responding to the major opportunities facing the organization (i.e., its strategic definition). The steps a work group can take to enhance the perception of its importance to the organization are similar whether we are dealing with problems or opportunities.

As discussed earlier, it is not necessarily actual problems or opportunities that affect the balance of power, but the *perception* of what constitutes a key problem or a vital opportunity. Consider an organization that is losing many middle managers to its competitors. The organization could point to several possible causes of the problem:

- We don't offer our managers enough money or promotion potential.

- We don't give our middle managers enough of a voice in making the decisions that affect them.

- Our middle managers leave because they are not convinced that the company has a sound future.

- Our managers leave because they think the products offered by the competition are of better quality.

In reality, these statements do not define causes; they indicate solutions. To define the problem as lack of money is to indicate a solution—a change in the salary structure. To define the problem as a feeling of lack of participation is to indicate a change in management style.

To indicate the solution at the same time we define the problem is to abort the problem-solving process, and to risk dealing with symptoms rather than causes. Organizations often see their problems in terms of solutions. The definition and the related solutions that are embraced by those most powerful in the organization determine which work groups are regarded as critical and which are regarded as peripheral. Continuing with our example, if organizational leaders define the problem as failure to offer enough money, then the wage and salary department will be perceived as critical to resolving the problem. If the problem is defined as one of product quality, then design engineers, researchers, and quality control people as well as marketing executives may be perceived as the critical units. Training will benefit if the problem is seen as an issue of ineffective management style.

The importance of a unit, then, is largely an issue of how the problem (or the opportunity) is defined. For this reason, the most effective way to enhance the perceived importance of the work group is to modify the way the problem (or opportunity) is stated. In the process of redefining the problem or pointing out causes that had not been considered, you may be pointing the way to solutions or approaches that your work group can help implement. In one family I know, the wife felt powerless to influence family events. She felt her own talents, primarily those in sports, were overshadowed by her husband's ability to earn money. Moreover, the family attributed its tensions to lack of expensive vacations or, more specifically, to lack of money with which to finance such vacations, further disassociating family problems and the wife's strengths. Finally, she convinced the family that their problem was insufficient recreational time together. When they accepted her diagnosis, they also had to accept her power to lead the family towards a solution.

For a business example, assume that management has defined increasing profits as a critical problem. Manufacturing can enhance their position by pointing out that the problem is really one of failure to benefit from economies of scale, and from a failure to take advantage of experience and cost curves. Sales can enhance their position by redefining the problem as one of inadequate call volume. Marketing enhances their position when they define the problem as an ineffective marketing strategy. Design Engineering enhances their position by identifying the problem as one of inappropriate product specifications. **Challenging the definition of the problem or the opportunity is one way to enhance the perceived importance of your work group.**

An alternative method is to surface problems and opportunities relevant to your work group that management has not yet identified. In the process, the work group both benefits itself and the organization as a whole. The work group that seeks to enhance the perception of its importance to the organization highlights problems before they assume crisis proportions, or identifies opportunities while there is ample time to act. The personnel department that identifies the consequences of not hiring or promoting enough minority persons before the Equal Employment Opportunity Commission cites the company's policies is using this strategy; so is the corporate planning department that advises centralized strategy formulation before the competition begins to significantly erode market share in isolated areas.

CHANGING RELATIVE DEGREE OF DEPENDENCY

In the process of redefining a problem or an opportunity, work groups often manage to change their Relative Degree of Dependency. As critical issues shift, so do the objectives of many work groups in the system. With this shift in objectives comes a shift in what is needed from other work groups. When the objective is to get out a large order, and a breakdown would make meeting the objective impossible, Manufacturing's dependence on Machine Maintenance temporarily intensifies. When the corporate objective shifts from reinvestment to acquisition, then dependency on corporate planners intensifies, at least until the acquisition candidate is identified. Labor relations personnel are more critical during contract negotiations than in the months preceding or following negotiations.

One way a work group can alter the Relative Degree of Dependency, then, is to stimulate a rethinking of the objectives of other groups in the organization. The degree to which one group depends on another is a function of their objectives. Changing others' objectives is one way to alter your Relative Degree of Dependency; another way is to restate your own objectives. Dependency exists when a work group needs the resources of another work group; the resource need only exists because of the objectives that are being pursued. If my objective is to get a new car, and I don't have the money, then I become dependent on banks or other loan sources. My dependency would disappear if my desire for a new automobile (my objective) did not exist. When an organization decides not to introduce a new product that requires the purchase of many component parts, it diminishes its potential dependency on certain suppliers.

Frequently, work groups are prevented from changing their objectives because of earlier commitments to plans. When a shift in objectives is not feasible, it is still possible to shift the Relative Degree of Dependency by adopting a group version of the Candy Store Strategy discussed in Chapter 3. Implementing the Candy Store Strategy involves the accumulation of things of value to another work group: a valuable item in most organizations is **time.** If your work group can perform some of another work group's functions, and if it is possible for you to free up resources when another department is overworked, then you are in a position to provide the one critical resource they lack—time. **Information** can also be the thing of value that stocks the group's Candy Store: the personnel department that makes it a point to collect resumes on highly capable people becomes an important resource to other work groups when they need additional talent. The Relative Degree of Dependency, then, can be altered by shifting objectives (your own or others), or by accumulating resources (primarily time or information) desired by others.

In the course of altering the Relative Degree of Dependency, a work group often increases its visibility in the organization. As is true of individuals who seek to enhance their power base, work groups need to be more than expert—they need to be visible. The work group that quietly sets objectives and equally quietly meets them is likely to be taken for granted or regarded as a reliable entity that will continue to function in the face of benign neglect by top management. **A good way to increase top management's understanding and appreciation of the function performed by a work group is to keep the function in the organizational limelight.** This can be done by getting work group members to serve on committees and on ad hoc groups, by publicizing successes, by routing articles of general interest, by using organizational media to introduce special projects, and by writing articles for trade publications that are likely to reflect well on the organization as a whole.

ATTRACTING INVESTMENT

As the work group becomes more visible and in the process stimulates top management's efforts to understand the complexities of its performance, then it also improves its chances of getting management to invest in the function. The data processing/management information systems department that dutifully prints out cost and inventory reports without ever making management aware of the difficulties or complexities involved in doing so is not likely to get a warm reception when it requests a new piece of expensive EDP equipment. The reaction is likely to be, "You've done just fine with the equipment you have. Keep up the good work, and stop this nonsense about sophisticated toys."

Investment requests are more likely to be granted to those who are perceived as scarce resources in the organization than to those whose expertise is not unique in the organization, or to those seen as easily replaceable. One way for a work group to enhance resource scarcity is to master a unique set of skills. Any function becomes a scarcer resource when it blends the expertise of its own field with an in-depth knowledge of the problems, products, and persons in other departments that use their services. Design engineers become a scarcer resource when they add to their functional expertise a unique level of understanding of what is felt to be feasible and infeasible by manufacturing and processing engineering personnel. Sales representatives undermine the myth that they are "a dime a dozen" when they demonstrate that they cannot only sell existing products, but also gather intelligence in the field for new products that will meet an unsatisfied market need.

CHANGING PERCEIVED RESOURCE SCARCITY AND ERROR MARGIN

Resource scarcity can be as much a matter of perception as of reality. Similarly, the impact of error margin is due to both the actual consequences of a mistake and to the perception of the potential severity of error. Make known the risks you take and the consequences of an error: "If we don't handle this complaint right, it could end up costing the company millions," or "If we don't deliver that report within the next six hours, we will lose the account."

A second option open to the work group that wants to benefit from the belief that those who take risks deserve power is to actually take on projects that do have a slim margin of acceptable error. When Manufacturing endorses more comprehensive warranty provisions, they are narrowing their margin of acceptable error, since the cost of product imperfections increases.

Work groups that operate within a slim margin of acceptable error generally have little difficulty gaining access to the information they want. After all, they are in a position to offer a very persuasive argument: "Without free access to information, we will be unable to make the timely readjustments in plan or approach that are required to avoid making costly errors." Living within a slim error margin generally constitutes a convincing need to know.

CHANGING INFORMATION FLOW AND CONTROL

Taking on high-risk projects is not the only way that work groups can better position themselves regarding information flow and control. They can also redefine their function so that it integrates other functions. As a group, supervisors have a great deal of power, functioning as representatives of management to the workers and vice versa. Their function as "integrator" gives them both a need and a right to know intimate details about groups hierarchically below and above them. Counselors in high schools may have a greater power than academic teachers to influence parents. The counselor is paid to act as coordinator between parent, child, and each of the child's teachers. If the objective is to deal effectively with a child having difficulty, the counselor assumes a great deal of leverage due to his or her integrative role.

While some functions naturally bear an integrative responsibility, other work groups need to deliberately seek such responsibility. This can be done by recommending that the company embark on a special project that involves disparate functions, and then volunteering to act as project coordinator. One training department with which I am acquainted has recently succeeded in recommending an organization-wide consumer, prospect, and employee survey with itself named as coordinator. In that role, they are authorized to make decisions about survey content, administration, and feedout. Consequently, they have legitimized their "need to know" details about products, market plans, growth plans, etc. The power of this department has thus increased markedly, at least for the duration of the study.

Another way to begin assuming integrative responsibility is to attempt to get members of the work group appointed to cross-functional task forces. Opportunities for such participation are increasing as compartmentalized organizations find special cross-functional groups necessary to deal effectively in today's complex business environments.

Work groups that succeed in enlarging their functional responsibilities to include integrative activities tend to be those that have the capacity to "speak the language" of a number of diverse and even conflicting functions. When Manufacturing and Quality Control can't resolve their differences, they may both welcome the help of a third party who can understand the viewpoints and needs of both groups. If, indeed, the third party is able to help resolve the conflict to the mutual satisfaction of both departments, chances are their integrative services will be sought out by other groups with similar problems. Intermediators generally end up knowing more than either of the functions they are assisting.

Avoiding Manipulation

In the last few pages, a variety of options available to the work group that seeks to enhance its power relative to other groups in the organization have been explored. The work group can attempt to challenge structures; it can alter management's perceptions of its importance to organizational problems and opportunities; it can accumulate resources to shift the Relative Degree of Dependency; it can take steps to increase top management's awareness of and respect for its function; it can stimulate an increase in the level of investment the organization has in the group; it can develop unique skills and so become a scarcer resource; it can communicate its margin of acceptable error; and it can position itself better regarding information flow and control.

Are these methods foolproof? **The answer is yes if the attempt to enhance the relative power of the work group represents a simultaneous attempt to benefit the organization as a whole.** All of the examples we have discussed thus far represent a win–win outcome—a "win" for the work group and a "win" for the organization.

Many work groups apply a number of other tactics that enhance their power base in the short run, but only at the expense of the larger organization. In the long run, such groups generally end up losing whatever clout and respect they had in the beginning. Manipulations on the part of a work group are as dangerous, and usually as unnecessary, as manipulations on the part of an individual. If your work group is engaging in these manipulations, then you do yourself and your coworkers a service by pointing out nonmanipulative options. The manipulations to look out for include:

- Endorsing or encouraging **policies** and **procedures** that stimulate two other groups to compete inappropriately, and so to spend their energies in nonproductive pursuits that make your work group look better by comparison.

- **Creating problems** in order to convince top management that, since the work group holds the key to the solution, they are indispensable. Witness the labor relations group that sits back and watches a single union consolidate power so that a strike threat assumes increasing significance.

- **Over-investing** as a group in a project with the intention of forcing management to invest more to salvage the original investment.

- **Feigning resource scarcity** by creating an auction climate around your services. "We won't be able to work on your project for at least another two months."

- **Exaggerating negative consequences** to convince others that you operate with a smaller error margin than is the case.

- Getting management to **classify the information you possess as "confidential" or "restricted"** to acquire an informational advantage over others who would also benefit from having access to the data.

All of these tactics represent win–lose approaches, as the perpetrator of the manipulation seeks to gain relative power at the expense of other work groups. Eventually, the organization suffers and the perpetrator along with it.

IN SUMMARY

If your goals lead you to join or stay with a work group whose power base is limited and, therefore, a hindrance to what you want to accomplish, then there are win–win steps you can take to alter the position of your work group, thus improving your chances for success. People who attain their goals are acutely aware of the total system within which they operate. Armed with this overview and an understanding of the politics of the situation, successful people are not constrained by the ability or inability of their own work group to affect the larger organization. Because they are able to adopt a view of the organization as a dynamic system of related parts, they are able to either affiliate with an inherently or potentially powerful organizational unit or enhance the position of their present unit relative to other units within the organization. Effective persons work to further empower others. Their overriding objective is to create outcomes in which everybody "wins."

Appendices

APPENDIX A
Clarification: Minimizing Goal Confusion

Failure to satisfy our values generally indicates that the goals we need to pursue are either unclear or not sufficiently well defined or comprehensive. Minimizing Goal Confusion requires that we define what we plan to accomplish and how we want to accomplish it; the kind of support from others we'll need; and how we hope others will benefit. If you wish to enjoy a high level of Goal Clarity and a high level of value satisfaction, you need to answer the following questions in regard to all the values that you are not currently working to satisfy. (See pp. 20–26 for further information on how to clarify your goals.)

Goal Clarification

1. ACCOMPLISHMENT:
    What products can I make or services can I offer that will contribute to the satisfaction of my value?

    _____

    _____

    Of the product and service options available to me, which appeals to me the most?

    _____

    _____

    _____

2. BENEFICIARIES:
    Who would benefit from my accomplishments?

    _____

    _____

    How will they benefit?

    _____

    _____

    In what ways would their benefiting contribute to the satisfaction of my primary value?

    _____

    _____

    _____

3. LOCATION:
   Where do I hope to work?

   _____

   _____

   How will my choice of location contribute to my ability to satisfy my value?

   _____

   _____

4. METHODOLOGY:
   What methods do I need to master or use?

   _____

   _____

   How will mastery in these areas contribute to my value satisfaction?

   _____

   _____

5. SIGNIFICANT OTHERS:
   How will my efforts affect other persons who are important to me?

   _____

   _____

   _____

   Is this impact consistent with my value?

   _____

   _____

   If not, how can I modify my plans so that they will be consistent with their impact on others?

   _____

   _____

6. FINANCES:
   How much money will I need, and how will I get it while satisfying my value?

   _____

   _____

   _____

7. MATERIALS:

What tools or equipment will I need and how can I secure them in a way that is consistent with my value?

_____

_____

_____

8. SUPPORT:

What kind of support and help will I need from others, and how do I plan to get their commitment, cooperation, or approval?

_____

_____

_____

In the process of trying to gain their support and help, will I be contributing to the satisfaction of my value?

_____

_____

9. COMPETITION:

Who, if anyone, is likely to try to block my efforts, and how do I hope to deal with them?

_____

_____

_____

Are my plans in this area consistent with my value?

_____

_____

_____

If not, what can I do to modify the approach I plan to take?

_____

_____

_____

APPENDIX B
Barriers Analysis

Here are some additional forms for analyzing behavior barriers to your goals. (See pp. 46–49 for a discussion of Barriers Analysis.)

GOAL: _____

_____

BEHAVIORS WHICH I SHOULD BE DISPLAYING AND AM NOT:

1.

2.

3.

4.

BEHAVIOR WHICH I SHOULD BE DISPLAYING AND AM NOT:

_____

_____

WHY NOT (BARRIERS):

1.

2.

3.

4.

BEHAVIOR WHICH I SHOULD BE DISPLAYING AND AM NOT:

_____

_____

WHY NOT (BARRIERS):

1.

2.

3.

4.

GOAL: _____

_____

BEHAVIORS WHICH I SHOULD BE DISPLAYING AND AM NOT:

1.

2.

3.

4.

BEHAVIOR WHICH I SHOULD BE DISPLAYING AND AM NOT:

_____

_____

WHY NOT (BARRIERS):

1.

2.

3.

4.

BEHAVIOR WHICH I SHOULD BE DISPLAYING AND AM NOT:

_____

_____

WHY NOT (BARRIERS):

1.

2.

3.

4.

APPENDIX C
Root Cause Analysis

Here are additional forms for analyzing the root causes of behavior barriers. (See pp. 49–51 for further information on Root Cause Analysis.)

BARRIER: _____

_____

WHAT THIS COULD RESULT FROM (ROOT CAUSES):

1.

2.

3.

4.

5.

BARRIER: _____

_____

WHAT THIS COULD RESULT FROM (ROOT CAUSES):

1.

2.

3.

4.

5.

BARRIER: _____

_____

WHAT THIS COULD RESULT FROM (ROOT CAUSES):

1.

2.

3.

4.

5.

BARRIER: _____

_____

WHAT THIS COULD RESULT FROM (ROOT CAUSES):

1.

2.

3.

4.

5.

APPENDIX D
The Influence Style Profile

This profile is divided into three sections, enabling you to compare how your Influence Style changes as you attempt to influence persons hierarchically more powerful than you, your peers, and subordinates. (See pp. 97–98 for further information on Influence Style.)

As you complete Part I, think of a single subordinate with whom you wish to be more effective, or respond in terms of your entire subordinate group if your relationship with each of them is similar enough to permit generalizing. Whatever person or group you choose to consider should remain constant as you respond to Part I.

While responding to Part II, keep in mind a peer or group of peers as you answer the items. Persons at the same hierarchical level can be considered peers. Choose a single hierarchically senior person (e.g., "boss") as your frame of reference as you respond to the items in Part III.

To complete the questionnaire, read each item and the three responses that follow. For each trio, spread seven points among the three responses to indicate the influence approach you tend to use.

Part I: Influencing Subordinates

I. 1. When it is important to me that my subordinates do a more thorough job of checking their work before submitting it to me, I . . .

    A. Explain the problems that are created when I discover errors later, and ask for their ideas on improving quality control.

    B. Appeal to their sense of pride in improving the quality of their work.

    C. Do nothing, hoping they will learn from work I hand back to them.

I. 2. When my plans require that my subordinates work unusually hard for a sustained period of time, I . . .

    A. Simply tell them what has to be done, exercising my right to give orders.

    B. Ask them what they want in exchange for the extra effort I require.

    C. Hope they'll see the need to put in the extra effort and act accordingly on their own.

	a	b	c	d	e
SUBTOTALS					

I. 3. When I want my subordinates to follow my directions more closely, I . . .

   A. Tell them that I am not happy with their work, that I expect them to listen better, to ask more questions if necessary, and then do exactly as I say.

   B. Tell them what I want, and ask them what I can do to help them.

   C. Try to give clearer instructions, and then assume they have done the best they can.

I. 4. When I want my subordinates to change some aspect of their dress, demeanor, or behavior, I . . .

   A. Tell them that I know they wouldn't voluntarily make me uncomfortable and that I'm sure once they are aware of what is upsetting me, they will change their ways.

   B. Exercise my right to tell them what to do.

   C. Assume they have a good reason for acting as they do, and wait for them to appreciate the desirability of changing on their own.

I. 5. When my plans require that my subordinates work unusually hard for a sustained period of of time, I . . .

   A. Explain the job requirements to them and help them to find ways to do what is necessary.

   B. Ask them what they want in exchange for extra effort I require.

   C. Hope they'll see the need to put in the extra effort and act accordingly on their own.

I. 6. When I want my subordinates to follow my directions more closely, I . . .

   A. Tell them that I am not happy with their work, that I expect them to listen better, to ask more questions if necessary, and then to do exactly as I say.

	a	b	c	d	e
				☐	
	☐				
					☐
			☐		
				☐	
					☐
	☐				
		☐			
					☐
				☐	
SUBTOTALS					

B. Modify the evaluation systems so that those who follow my directions most closely are best rewarded.

C. Try to give clearer instructions, and then assume they have done the best they can.

I. 7. When I want my subordinates to change some aspect of their dress, demeanor, or behavior, I . . .

A. Exercise my right to tell them what to do.

B. Tell them what is upsetting to me and why, and suggest we talk about things we can all do to make each other more comfortable.

C. Assume they have a good reason for acting as they do, and wait for them to appreciate the desirability of changing on their own.

I. 8. When it is important to me that my subordinates do a more thorough job of checking their work before submitting it to me, I . . .

A. Appeal to their sense of pride in improving the quality of their work.

B. Set up a system whereby they are penalized for each imperfect product.

C. Do nothing, hoping they will learn in time from work I hand back to them.

I. 9. When it is important to me that my subordinates do a more thorough job of checking their work before submitting it to me, I . . .

A. Explain the problems that are created when I discover errors later, and ask for their ideas on improving quality control.

B. Set up a system whereby those who make the fewest errors get extra rewards.

C. Do nothing, hoping they will learn in time from work I hand back to them.

a	b	c	d	e

SUBTOTALS

I. 10. When I want my subordinates to change some aspect of their dress, demeanor, or behavior, I . . .

  A. Exercise my right to tell them what to do. ☐ (d)

  B. Tell them that if they will make the change I want, I will do something for them in return. ☐ (b)

  C. Assume they have a good reason for acting as they do, and wait for them to appreciate the desirability of changing on their own. ☐ (e)

I. 11. When my plans require that my subordinates work unusually hard for a sustained period of time, I . . .

  A. Simply tell them what has to be done, exercising my right to give orders. ☐ (c)

  B. Explain the job requirements to them and help them to find ways to do what is necessary. ☐ (a)

  C. Hope they'll see the need to put in the extra effort and act accordingly on their own. ☐ (e)

I. 12. When I want my subordinates to follow my directions more closely, I . . .

  A. Explain the problems that ensue when they only loosely follow my directions, and ask that they try to do more precisely as I say. ☐ (c)

  B. Tell them that I am not happy with their work, that I expect them to listen better, to ask more questions if necessary, and to do exactly as I say. ☐ (d)

  C. Try to give clearer instructions, and then assume they have done the best they can. ☐ (e)

I. 13. When I want my subordinates to follow my directions more closely, I . . .

  A. Tell them what I want, and ask them what I can do to help them. ☐ (a)

  B. Modify the evaluation system so that those who follow my directions most closely are best rewarded. ☐ (b)

a	b	c	d	e

SUBTOTALS

C. Try to give clearer instructions, and then assume they have done the best they can.

I. 14. When it is important to me that my subordinates do a more thorough job of checking their work before submitting it to me, I . . .

    A. Set up a system whereby they are penalized for each imperfect product.

    B. Set up a system whereby those who make the fewest errors get extra rewards.

    C. Do nothing, hoping they will learn in time from work I hand back to them.

I. 15. When my plans require that my subordinates work unusually hard for a sustained period of time, I . . .

    A. Clarify the importance of the project to us and to what we are trying to accomplish, and ask for their cooperation.

    B. Simply tell them what has to be done, exercising my right to give orders.

    C. Hope they'll see the need to put in the extra effort and act accordingly on their own.

I. 16. When I want my subordinates to change some aspect of their dress, demeanor, or behavior, I . . .

    A. Tell them that I know they wouldn't voluntarily make me uncomfortable and that I'm sure once they are aware of what is upsetting me, they will change their ways.

    B. Tell them that if they will make the change I want, I will do something for them in return.

    C. Assume they have a good reason for acting as they do, and wait for them to appreciate the desirability of changing on their own.

SUBTOTALS

a	b	c	d	e

I. 17. When I want my subordinates to change some aspect of their dress, demeanor, or behavior, I . . .

    A. Tell them what is upsetting to me and why, and suggest we talk about things we can all do to make each other more comfortable. ☐

    B. Tell them that if they will make the change I want, I will do something for them in return. ☐

    C. Assume they have a good reason for acting as they do, and wait for them to appreciate the desirability of changing on their own. ☐

I. 18. When it is important to me that my subordinates do a more thorough job of checking their work before submitting it to me, I . . .

    A. Set up a system whereby they are penalized for each imperfect product. ☐

    B. Explain the problems that are created when I discover errors later, and ask for their ideas on improving quality control. ☐

    C. Do nothing, hoping they will learn in time from work I hand back to them. ☐

I. 19. When my plans require that my subordinates work unusually hard for a sustained period of time, I . . .

    A. Clarify the importance of the project to us and to what we are trying to accomplish as a group, and ask for their cooperation. ☐

    B. Ask them what they want in exchange for the extra effort I require. ☐

    C. Hope they'll see the need to put in the extra effort and act accordingly on their own. ☐

I. 20. When I want my subordinates to follow my directions more closely, I . . .

    A. Tell them what I want, and ask them what I can do to help them. ☐

a	b	c	d	e

SUBTOTALS

B. Explain the problems that ensue when they only loosely follow my directions, and ask that they try to do more precisely as I say.

C. Try to give clearer instructions, and then assume they have done the best they can.

I. 21. When it is important to me that my subordinates do a more thorough job of checking their work before submitting it to me, I . . .

A. Appeal to their sense of pride in improving the quality of their work.

B. Set up a system whereby those who make the fewest errors get extra rewards.

C. Do nothing, hoping they will learn in time from work I hand back to them.

I. 22. When I want my subordinates to follow my directions more closely, I . . .

A. Explain the problems that ensue when they only loosely follow my directions, and ask that they try to do more precisely as I say.

B. Modify the evaluation system so that those who follow my directions most closely are best rewarded.

C. Try to give clearer instructions, and then assume they have done the best they can.

I. 23. When my plans require that my subordinates work unusually hard for a sustained period of time, I . . .

A. Explain the job requirements and help them to find ways to do what is necessary.

B. Clarify the importance of the project to us and to what we are trying to accomplish, and ask for their cooperation.

C. Hope they'll see the need to put in the extra effort and act accordingly on their own.

a	b	c	d	e

SUBTOTALS

I. 24. When I want my subordinates to change some aspect of their dress, demeanor, or behavior, I . . .

A. Tell them what is upsetting to me and why, and suggest we talk about things we can all do to make each other more comfortable.

B. Tell them that I know they wouldn't voluntarily make me uncomfortable, and that I'm sure once they are aware of what is upsetting to me, they will change their ways.

C. Assume they have a good reason for acting as they do, and wait for them to appreciate the desirability of changing on their own.

a	b	c	d	e

SUBTOTALS

Part II: Influencing Organizational Peers

II.   1. When I need a peer to influence someone on my my behalf, I . . .

A. Share my problem or my objective with him or her and ask what actions (s)he recommends.

B. Explain why I need his or her help, and ask for it.

C. Modify my objectives to minimize my need for assistance.

II.   2. When I need a peer to modify his or her area's work schedule to give me the support I need, I . . .

A. Indicate ways in which I can make things difficult for him or her if (s)he doesn't agree to do what I want.

a	b	c	d	e

SUBTOTALS

B. Offer to return the favor if (s)he will help me now.

C. Avoid addressing the issue directly, doing whatever I can to minimize my need for assistance.

II. 3. When I want a peer to stop doing something that reflects negatively on the work performed by my area, I . . .

A. Tell him or her specifically what I want done or not done, and make it clear that I will cause trouble if (s)he doesn't do as I say.

B. Express my discomfort, and ask him or her to work with me to make both our areas look better in the eyes of the management.

C. Wait it out, letting my area's performance prove him or her wrong.

II. 4. When I want a peer to share some sensitive information with me, I . . .

A. Tell him or her that I can't get my job done unless I have certain information.

B. Point out that I am in a position to cause negative consequences for him or her if (s)he refuses to tell me what I want to know.

C. Get whatever information I can from printed material or outsiders, and do not address the issue directly with my peer.

II. 5. When I need a peer to modify his or her area's work schedule to give me the support I need, I . . .

A. Openly discuss ways in which we might be more mutually supportive over both the long and the short run.

B. Offer to return the favor if (s)he will help me now.

C. Avoid addressing the issue directly, doing whatever I can to minimize my need for assistance.

	a	b	c	d	e
B		☐			
C					☐
II.3 A				☐	
II.3 B	☐				
II.3 C					☐
II.4 A			☐		
II.4 B				☐	
II.4 C					☐
II.5 A	☐				
II.5 B		☐			
II.5 C					☐

SUBTOTALS

II. 6. When I want a peer to stop doing something that reflects negatively on the work performed by my area, I . . .

    A. Tell him or her specifically what I want done or not done, and make it clear that I will cause trouble if (s)he doesn't do as I say. ☐ (d)

    B. Tell him or her that if (s)he will stop doing and saying things detrimental to me, I will be less tempted to say and do things detrimental to him or her. ☐ (b)

    C. Wait it out, letting my area's performance prove him or her wrong. ☐ (e)

II. 7. When I want a peer to share some sensitive information with me, I . . .

    A. Point out that I am in a position to cause negative consequences for him or her if (s)he refuses to tell me what I want to know. ☐ (d)

    B. Request a meeting to discuss areas in which information could be beneficially exchanged. ☐ (a)

    C. Get whatever information I can from printed material or outsiders, and do not address the issue directly with my peer. ☐ (e)

II. 8. When I need a peer to influence someone on my behalf, I . . .

    A. Explain why I need his or her help, and ask for it. ☐ (c)

    B. Tell him or her that failure to help me would not be in his or her best interest. ☐ (d)

    C. Modify my objectives to minimize my need for assistance. ☐ (e)

II. 9. When I need a peer to influence someone on my behalf, I . . .

    A. Share my problem or my objective with him or her and ask what actions (s)he recommends. ☐ (a)

    B. Ask him or her to talk with the person in question for me and in exchange guarantee to do a similar favor in the future. ☐ (b)

a	b	c	d	e

SUBTOTALS

C. Modify my objectives to minimize my need for assistance. ☐

II. 10. When I want a peer to share some sensitive information with me, I . . .

A. Point out that I am in a position to cause negative consequences for him or her if (s)he refuses to tell me what I want to know. ☐

B. Offer to return the favor, and indicate that I know certain things that could be of use to him or her. ☐

C. Get whatever information I can from printed material or outsiders, and do not address the issue directly with my peer. ☐

II. 11. When I need a peer to modify his or her area's work schedule to give me the support I need, I . . .

A. Indicate ways in which I can make things difficult for him or her if (s)he doesn't agree to do what I want. ☐

B. Openly discuss ways in which we might be more mutually supportive over both the long and the short run. ☐

C. Avoid addressing the issue directly, doing whatever I can to minimize my need for assistance. ☐

II. 12. When I want a peer to stop doing something that reflects negatively on the work performed by my area, I . . .

A. Ask that (s)he modify his or her behavior in the interest of the organization as a whole. ☐

B. Tell him or her specifically what I want done or not done, and make it clear that I will cause trouble if (s)he doesn't do as I say. ☐

C. Wait it out, letting my area's performance prove him or her wrong. ☐

a	b	c	d	e

SUBTOTALS

II. 13. When I want a peer to stop doing something that reflects negatively on the work performed by my area, I . . .

A. Express my discomfort, and ask him or her to work with me to make both our areas look better in the eyes of the management. ☐

B. Tell him or her that if (s)he will stop doing and saying things detrimental to me, I will be less tempted to say and do things detrimental to him or her. ☐

C. Wait it out, letting my area's performance prove him or her wrong. ☐

II. 14. When I need a peer to influence someone on my behalf, I . . .

A. Tell him or her that failure to help me would not be in his or her best interest. ☐

B. Ask him or her to talk with the person in question for me and in exchange guarantee to do a similar favor in the future. ☐

C. Modify my objectives to minimize my need for assistance. ☐

II. 15. When I need a peer to modify his or her area's work schedule to give me the support I need, I . . .

A. Ask him or her to give me the support I need, and trust that his or her respect or friendship will be sufficient reason for cooperation. ☐

B. Indicate ways in which I can make things difficult for him or her if (s)he doesn't agree to do what I want. ☐

C. Avoid addressing the issue directly, doing whatever I can to minimize my need for assistance. ☐

II. 16. When I want a peer to share some sensitive information with me, I . . .

A. Tell him or her that I can't get my job done unless I have certain information. ☐

a	b	c	d	e

SUBTOTALS

B. Offer to return the favor, and indicate that I know certain things that could be of use to him or her. ☐ (b)

C. Get whatever information I can from printed material or outsiders, and do not address the issue directly with my peer. ☐ (e)

II. 17. When I want a peer to share some sensitive information with me, I . . .

A. Request a meeting to discuss areas in which information could be beneficially exchanged. ☐ (a)

B. Offer to return the favor, and indicate that I know certain things that could be of use to him or her. ☐ (b)

C. Get whatever information I can from printed material or outsiders, and do not address the issue directly with my peer. ☐ (e)

II. 18. When I need a peer to influence someone on my behalf, I . . .

A. Tell him or her that failure to help me would not be in his or her best interest. ☐ (d)

B. Share my problem or my objective with him or her and ask what actions (s)he recommends. ☐ (a)

C. Modify my objectives to minimize my need for assistance. ☐ (e)

II. 19. When I need a peer to modify his or her area's work schedule to give me the support I need, I . . .

A. Ask him or her to give me the support I need, and trust that his or her respect or friendship will be sufficient reason for cooperation. ☐ (c)

B. Offer to return the favor if (s)he will help me now. ☐ (b)

C. Avoid addressing the issue directly, doing whatever I can to minimize my need for assistance. ☐ (e)

	a	b	c	d	e
SUBTOTALS					

II. 20. When I want a peer to stop doing something that reflects negatively on the work performed by my area, I . . .

    A. Express my discomfort, and ask him or her to work with me to make both our areas look better in the eyes of the management. ☐ (a)

    B. Ask that (s)he modify his or her behavior in the interest of the organization as a whole. ☐ (c)

    C. Wait it out, letting my area's performance prove him or her wrong. ☐ (e)

II. 21. When I need a peer to influence someone on my behalf, I . . .

    A. Explain why I need his or her help, and ask for it. ☐ (c)

    B. Ask him or her to talk with the person in question for me and in exchange guarantee to do a similar favor in the future. ☐ (b)

    C. Modify my objectives to minimize my need for assistance. ☐ (e)

II. 22. When I want a peer to stop doing something that reflects negatively on the work performed by my area, I . . .

    A. Ask that (s)he modify his or her behavior in the interest of the organization as a whole. ☐ (c)

    B. Tell him or her that if (s)he will stop doing and saying things detrimental to me, I will be less tempted to say and do things detrimental to him or her. ☐ (b)

    C. Wait it out, letting my area's performance prove him or her wrong. ☐ (e)

II. 23. When I need a peer to modify his or her area's work schedule to give me the support I need, I . . .

    A. Openly discuss ways in which we might be more mutually supportive over both the long and the short run. ☐ (a)

	a	b	c	d	e
SUBTOTALS					

B. Ask him or her to give me the support I need, and trust that his or her respect or friendship will be sufficient reason for cooperation.

C. Avoid addressing the issue directly, doing whatever I can to minimize my need for assistance.

II. 24. When I want a peer to share some sensitive information with me, I . . .

A. Request a meeting to discuss areas in which information could be beneficially exchanged.

B. Tell him or her that I can't get my job done unless I have certain information.

C. Get whatever information I can from printed material or outsiders, and do not address the issue directly with my peer.

a	b	c	d	e

SUBTOTALS

Part III: Influencing Superiors

III. 1. When I want my superior to give me more feedback about my work, I . . .

A. Share my own perceptions of my strengths and weaknesses with my superior, and ask him or her whether (s)he agrees with my perceptions.

B. Tell my superior that I value his or her opinions and feel my performance would improve if (s)he would share them with me more often.

C. Say nothing, assuming the feedback will come in time.

a	b	c	d	e

SUBTOTALS

III. 2. When I want my superior to keep me better informed about what is happening in our unit, I . . .

    A. Tell my superior that I cannot function well when I am forced to operate in a vacuum, and that if (s)he values my services, (s)he'll be more open with me.   **[d]** ☐

    B. Ask my superior some specific questions with the understanding that if (s)he provides the answers, I'll content myself with knowing somewhat less than I would like to know.   **[b]** ☐

    C. Assume my superior will tell me what I need to know when I need to know it.   **[e]** ☐

III. 3. When I want my superior to pay me more, I . . .

    A. Tell my boss that I do not feel I am fairly paid for the work I do, and that if (s)he doesn't rectify the situation, I'll seek employment elsewhere.   **[d]** ☐

    B. Tell my superior that I feel that I am underpaid, and ask him or her to discuss the problem with me.   **[a]** ☐

    C. Do not address the issue directly, assuming the raise will come in time.   **[e]** ☐

III. 4. When I feel the demands on my time are unrealistic, I . . .

    A. Formulate my own priorities, and ask that my superior accept them after an explanation of the situation as I see it.   **[c]** ☐

    C. Formulate my own priorities, and tell my superior that unless they are accepted, I'll have no choice but to seek a position in a more flexible and realistic organization.   **[d]** ☐

    C. Do the best I can, not mentioning my feelings to my superior.   **[e]** ☐

	a	b	c	d	e
SUBTOTALS					

III. 5. When I want my superior to keep be better informed about what is happening in our unit, I . . .

    A. Discuss with my superior the areas in which more information would enable me to do a better job. ☐ (a)

    B. Ask my superior some specific questions with the understanding that if (s)he provides the answers, I'll content myself with knowing somewhat less than I would like to know. ☐ (b)

    C. Assume my superior will tell me what I need to know when I need to know it. ☐ (e)

III. 6. When I want my superior to pay me more, I . . .

    A. Tell my boss that I do not feel I am fairly paid for the work I do, and that if (s)he doesn't rectify the situation, I'll seek employment elsewhere. ☐ (d)

    B. Tell my boss I want a raise, and that I would be willing to take on additional responsibility if necessary. ☐ (b)

    C. Do not address the issue directly, assuming the raise will come in time. ☐ (e)

III. 7. When I feel the demands on my time are unrealistic, I . . .

    A. Formulate my own priorities, and tell my superior that unless they are accepted, I'll have no choice but to seek a position in a more flexible and realistic organization. ☐ (d)

    B. Share my perceptions with my superior, asking him or her to work with me to reestablish mutually acceptable priorities. ☐ (a)

    C. Do the best I can, not mentioning my feelings to my superior. ☐ (e)

SUBTOTALS

a	b	c	d	e

III. 8. When I want my superior to give me more feedback about my work, I . . .

A. Tell my superior that I value his or her opinions and feel my performance would improve if (s)he would share them with me more often.

B. Let my superior know that I find working in this environment extremely frustrating, and that I'll consider resigning or requesting a transfer if (s)he doesn't do something to improve communications between us.

C. Say nothing, assuming the feedback will come in time.

III. 9. When I want my superior to give me more feedback about my work, I . . .

A. Share my own perceptions of my strengths and weaknesses with my superior, and ask him or her whether (s)he agrees with my perceptions.

B. Tell my superior that if (s)he'll agree to more frequent formal reviews, I'll stop pestering him or her to share reactions with me.

C. Say nothing, assuming the feedback will come in time.

III. 10. When I feel the demands on my time are unrealistic, I . . .

A. Formulate my own priorities, and tell my superior that unless they are accepted, I'll have no choice but to seek a position in a more flexible and realistic organization.

B. Suggest to my superior that if (s)he will work with me to establish priorities, I will guarantee achieving the critical objectives.

C. Do the best I can, not mentioning my feelings to my superior.

	a	b	c	d	e
8 A			☐		
8 B				☐	
8 C					☐
9 A	☐				
9 B		☐			
9 C				☐	
10 A			☐		
10 B		☐			
10 C					☐

SUBTOTALS

III. 11. When I want my superior to keep me better informed about what is happening in our unit, I . . .

   A. Tell my superior that I cannot function well when I am forced to operate in a vacuum, and that if (s)he values my services, (s)he'll be more open with me.

   B. Discuss with my superior the areas in which more information would enable me to do a better job.

   C. Assume my superior will tell me what I need to know when I need to know it.

III. 12. When I want my superior to pay me more, I . . .

   A. Tell my boss that I feel the quality of my work warrants an increase in pay.

   B. Tell my boss that I do not feel I am fairly paid for the work I do, and that if (s)he doesn't rectify the situation, I'll seek employment elsewhere.

   C. Do not address the issue directly, assuming the raise will come in time.

III. 13. When I want my superior to pay more, I . . .

   A. Tell my superior that I feel that I am underpaid, and ask him or her to discuss the problem with me.

   B. Tell my boss I want a raise, and that I would be willing to take on additional responsibility if necessary.

   C. Do not address the issue directly, assuming the raise will come in time.

SUBTOTALS

	a	b	c	d	e
				☐	
	☐				
					☐
			☐		
				☐	
					☐
	☐				
		☐			
					☐

III. 14. When I want my superior to give me more feedback about my work, I . . .

    A. Let my superior know that I find working in this environment extremely frustrating, and that I'll consider resigning or requesting a transfer if (s)he doesn't do something to improve communications between us.

    B. Tell my superior that if (s)he'll agree to more frequent formal reviews, I'll stop pestering him or her to share reactions with me.

    C. Say nothing, assuming the feedback will come in time.

III. 15. When I want my superior to keep me better informed about what is happening in our unit, I . . .

    A. Appeal to my superior's belief in "participative management," asking him or her to keep me better informed.

    B. Tell my superior that I cannot function well when I am forced to operate in a vacuum, and that if (s)he values my services, (s)he'll be more open with me.

    C. Assume my superior will tell me what I need to know when I need to know it.

III. 16. When I feel the demands on my time are unrealistic, I . . .

    A. Formulate my own priorities, and ask that my superior accept them after an explanation of the situation as I see it.

    B. Suggest to my superior that if (s)he will work with me to establish priorities, I will guarantee achieving the critical objectives.

    C. Do the best I can, not mentioning my feelings to my superior.

	a	b	c	d	e
14.A				☐	
14.B		☐			
14.C					☐
15.A			☐		
15.B				☐	
15.C					☐
16.A			☐		
16.B		☐			
16.C					☐
SUBTOTALS					

III. 17. When I feel the demands on my time are unrealistic, I . . .

    A. Share my own perceptions with my superior, and ask him or her to work with me to re-establish mutually acceptable priorities.

    B. Suggest to my superior that if (s)he will work with me to establish priorities, I will guarantee achieving the critical objectives.

    C. Do the best I can, not mentioning my feelings to my superior.

III. 18. When I want my superior to give me more feedback about my work, I . . .

    A. Let my superior know that I find working in this environment extremely frustrating, and that I'll consider resigning or requesting a transfer if (s)he doesn't do something to improve communications between us.

    B. Share my own perceptions of my strengths and weaknesses with my superior, and ask him or her whether (s)he agrees with my perceptions.

    C. Say nothing, assuming the feedback will come in time.

III. 19. When I want my superior to keep me better informed about what is happening in our unit, I . . .

    A. Appeal to my superior's belief in "participative management," asking him or her to keep me better informed.

    B. Ask my superior some specific questions with the understanding that if (s)he provides the answers, I'll content myself with knowing somewhat less than I would like to know.

    C. Assume my superior will tell me what I need to know when I need to know it.

	a	b	c	d	e
17.A	☐				
17.B		☐			
17.C					☐
18.A				☐	
18.B	☐				
18.C					☐
19.A			☐		
19.B		☐			
19.C					☐

SUBTOTALS

III. 20. When I want my superior to pay me more, I . . .

    A. Tell my superior that I feel that I am underpaid, and ask him or her to discuss the problem with me.

    B. Tell my boss that I feel the quality of my work warrants an increase in pay.

    C. Do not address the issue directly, assuming the raise will come in time.

III. 21. When I want my superior to give me more feedback about my work, I . . .

    A. Tell my superior that I value his or her opinions and feel my performance would improve if (s)he would share them with me more often.

    B. Tell my superior that if (s)he'll agree to more frequent formal reviews, I'll stop pestering him or her to share reactions with me.

    C. Say nothing, assuming the feedback will come in time.

III. 22. When I want my superior to pay me more, I . . .

    A. Tell my boss that I feel the quality of my work warrants an increase in pay.

    B. Tell my boss I want a raise, and that I would be willing to take on additional responsibility if necessary.

    C. Do not address the issue directly, assuming the raise will come in time.

	a	b	c	d	e
20.A	☐				
20.B			☐		
20.C					☐
21.A			☐		
21.B		☐			
21.C					☐
22.A			☐		
22.B	☐				
22.C					☐
SUBTOTALS					

III. 23. When I want my superior to keep be better informed about what is happening in our unit, I . . .

    A. Discuss with my superior the areas in which more information would enable me to do a better job.

    B. Appeal to my superior's belief in "participative management," asking him or her to keep me better informed.

    C. Assume my superior will tell me what I need to know when I need to know it.

III. 24. When I feel the demands on my time are unrealistic, I . . .

    A. Share my perceptions with my superior, asking him or her to work with me to reestablish mutually acceptable priorities.

    B. Formulate my own priorities, and ask that my superior accept them after an explanation of the situation as I see it.

    C. Do the best I can, not mentioning my feelings to my superior.

SUBTOTALS

a	b	c	d	e

Interpretation of your results begins on the next page.

Influence Styles: A Personal Profile
Scoring Instructions

First, add each column of this questionnaire, recording your subtotals at the bottom of each page:

	a	b	c	d	e
	1		6		2
		5	4	1	
	3	0			
					0
Subtotals	4	5	10	1	2

Now, consider Parts I, II, and III separately. Add all the column "a's" together, all the "b's" together, the "c's," and the "d's" for Part I; record these totals under "Part I" on the Scoring Format that follows. Add your "e's" and divide that figure by 2. This is your "e" total for Part I. Do the same for Parts II and III. Use the Key provided to evaluate your final score.

Influence Styles: Scoring Format

KEY:
a — involve   b — negotiate   c — enlist   d — direct   e — no influence

PART I: INFLUENCING SUBORDINATES				
PAGE	a	b	c	d	e
261					
262					
263					
264					
265					
266					
267					
268					
TOTALS					÷ by 2

PART II: INFLUENCING ORGANIZATIONAL PEERS				
PAGE	a	b	c	d	e
268					
269					
270					
271					
272					
273					
274					
275					
TOTALS					÷ by 2

KEY:

a — involve   b — negotiate   c — enlist   d — direct   e — no influence

PART III: INFLUENCING SUPERIORS					
PAGE	a	b	c	d	e
275					
276					
277					
278					
279					
280					
281					
282					
283					
TOTALS					÷ by 2

APPENDIX E
The Behavioral Styles Profile

The Behavioral Styles Profile was designed to help you understand how you behave with others. It is divided into three sections. The first section asks you to respond in terms of how you engage with subordinates: the second, how you behave with peers; and the third, how you behave with your boss. (See p. 158 for further information on Behavioral Styles.)

As you complete Part I, consider a single subordinate with whom you wish to be more effective. You may respond in terms of your entire subordinate group if your relationship with each of them is similar enough to permit generalizing. **Whatever person or group you choose to consider should remain constant** as you respond to Part I.

The same procedure should be followed for Part II. **Keep in mind the same peer or group of peers as you answer these items.** As you complete Part III, choose a single boss as your frame of reference.

To complete the test, read each item and the pair of responses that follow. For each pair, spread five points to indicate the approach you use most often.

If response "a" accurately describes your behavior, and you would never behave as represented by response "b," you would spread points this way:

a.   `5`

b.   `0`

If response "b" provides a slightly more accurate description of your behavior than "a," you would spread your five points this way:

a.   `2`

b.   `3`

If neither response describes of your behavior, you are still asked to spread five points, with the larger number (3) given to the "lesser of two evils".

a.   `3`

b.   `2`

Remember, you are asked to use all five points for each pair, even if you would not be likely to use either response. The response you feel you would be more inclined to use should always receive the most points. Please use whole numbers only.

Part I: Engaging with Subordinates

I. 1. When it is important to me that my subordinates make fewer errors, I . . .

   A. Explain the difficulties they are causing our group, pointing out how poor quality affects us all.

   B. Ask for their ideas on improving quality control.

I. 2. When my plans require that my subordinates do a routine job that is beneath their capabilities, I . . .

   A. Apologize for having to ask them to do the job, and promise to try to avoid having it happen again.

   B. Tell them that every job involves routine and that they should get used to it.

I. 3. When meeting my objectives requires that I reduce the competition among my subordinates, I . . .

   A. Ask what factors are getting in the way of cooperation.

   B. Do not deal directly with the issue, attempting to do the extra work necessary to minimize the negative effects of the competition.

	a	b	c	d
1A	☐			
1B		☐		
2A			☐	
2B				☐
3A		☐		
3B			☐	
SUBTOTALS				

I. 4. When I want my subordinates to show more initiative, I . . .

   A. Tell them that I want them to start doing more
      things on their own.

   B. Let them know that I think their lack of initia-
      tive stems from a lack of purposefulness and
      career dedication.

I. 5. When it is important to me that my subordinates
make fewer errors, I . . .

   A. Explain the difficulties they are causing our
      group, pointing out how poor quality affects
      us all.

   B. Admit that I'm sort of a nitpicker, and ask
      them to bear with me in my efforts.

I. 6. When my plans require that my subordinates do
a routine job that is beneath their capabilities, I . . .

   A. Ask if they mind doing routine work occasion-
      ally.

   B. Tell them that every job involves routine and
      that they should get used to it.

I. 7. When meeting my objectives requires that I reduce the competition among my subordinates, I . . .

   A. Ask what factors are getting in the way of
      cooperation.

   B. Point out that if they were more mature, they
      would understand that their behavior is in-
      appropriate.

I. 8. When I want my subordinates to show more initiative, I . . .

   A. Ask them to tell me about ideas they have for
      making things move more smoothly.

   B. Indicate to them that I'm reluctant to ask them
      to do more, but that I don't have the energy to
      continue all I'm doing.

a	b	c	d
☐			
			☐
☐			
		☐	
	☐		
			☐
	☐		
			☐
	☐		
		☐	

SUBTOTALS

I. 9. When it is important to me that my subordinates make fewer errors, I . . .

   A. Explain the difficulties they are causing our group, pointing out how poor quality affects us all. ☐

   B. Suggest that our error rate stems from their lack of pride in their work. ☐

I. 10. When my plans require that my subordinates do a routine job that is beneath their capabilities, I . . .

   A. Ask if they mind doing routine work occasionally. ☐

   B. Apologize for having to ask them to do the job, and promise to try to avoid having it happen again. ☐

I. 11. When meeting my objectives requires that I reduce the competition among my subordinates, I . . .

   A. Do not deal directly with the issue, attempting to do the extra work necessary to minimize the negative effects of the competition. ☐

   B. Point out that if they were more mature, they would understand that their behavior is inappropriate. ☐

I. 12. When I want my subordinates to show more initiative, I . . .

   A. Ask for their ideas for making things work more smoothly. ☐

   B. Let them know that I think their lack of initiative stems from a lack of purposefulness and career dedication. ☐

I. 13. When it is important to me that my subordinates make fewer errors, I . . .

   A. Ask for their ideas on improving quality control. ☐

   B. Admit that I'm sort of a nitpicker, and ask them to bear with me in my efforts. ☐

a	b	c	d

SUBTOTALS

I. 14. When my plans require that my subordinates do a routine job that is beneath their capabilities, I . . .

   A. Tell them I need their cooperation and ask them to complete the task. ☐

   B. Tell them that *every* job involves routine and that they should get used to it. ☐

I. 15. When meeting my objectives requires that I reduce the competition among my subordinates, I . . .

   A. Point out that everyone in the unit will suffer if *we* don't learn to work together. ☐

   B. Ask what factors are getting in the way of cooperation. ☐

I. 16. When I want my subordinates to show more initiative, I . . .

   A. Indicate to them that I'm reluctant to ask them to do more, but that I don't have the energy to continue doing all I'm doing. ☐

   B. Let them know that I think their lack of initiative stems from a lack of purposefulness and career dedication. ☐

I. 17. When it is important to me that my subordinates make fewer errors, I . . .

   A. Ask for their ideas on improving quality control. ☐

   B. Suggest that our error rate stems from their lack of pride in their work. ☐

I. 18. When my plans require that my subordinates do a routine job that is beneath their capabilities, I . . .

   A. Tell them I need their cooperation and ask them to complete the task. ☐

   B. Apologize for having to ask them to do the job, and promise to try to avoid having it happen again. ☐

a	b	c	d

SUBTOTALS

I. 19. When meeting my objectives requires that I reduce the competition among my subordinates, I . . .

   A. Point out that everyone in the unit will suffer if we don't learn to work together.

   B. Do not deal directly with the issue, attempting to do the extra work necessary to minimize the negative effects of the competition.

I. 20. When I want my subordinates to show more initiative, I . . .

   A. Tell them that I want them to start doing more things on their own.

   B. Ask them to tell me about ideas they have for making things move more smoothly.

I. 21. When it is important to me that my subordinates make fewer errors, I . . .

   A. Admit that I'm sort of a nitpicker and ask them to bear with me in my efforts.

   B. Suggest that our error rate stems from their lack of pride in their work.

I. 22. When my plans require that my subordinates do a routine job that is beneath their capabilities, I . . .

   A. Tell them I need their cooperation and ask them to complete the task.

   B. Ask if they mind doing routine work occasionally.

I. 23. When meeting my objectives requires that I reduce the competition among my subordinates, I . . .

   A. Point out that everyone in the group will suffer if we don't learn to work together.

   B. Point out that if they were more mature, they would understand that their behavior is inappropriate.

	a	b	c	d
19.A	☐			
19.B			☐	
20.A	☐			
20.B		☐		
21.A			☐	
21.B				☐
22.A	☐			
22.B		☐		
23.A	☐			
23.B				☐
SUBTOTALS				

I. 24. When I want my subordinates to show more initiative, I . . .

    A. Tell them that I want them to start doing more things on their own.

    B. Indicate to them that I'm reluctant to ask them to do more, but that I don't have the energy to continue doing all that I'm doing.

a	b	c	d
☐			
		☐	

SUBTOTALS

a	b	c	d

Part II: Engaging with Peers

II. 1. When my plans require that others keep my needs in mind as they plan and execute their work, I . . .

    A. Explain the difficulties they are causing me, asking them to be more responsive to my needs.

    B. Tell them I would like to understand more about their procedures so I can work more cooperatively with them.

a	b	c	d
☐			
	☐		

SUBTOTALS

a	b	c	d

II. 2. When I need to get others to help me deal with a mistake I have made, I . . .

A. Tell them that I've goofed and would really appreciate having them straighten me out.

B. Indicate that such mistakes are bound to happen when people aren't sufficiently available, helpful, or cooperative.

II. 3. When I need others to share some information with me, I . . .

A. Ask if they have any objection to sharing the information.

B. Preface my request with a comment indicating that I feel badly about intruding, and that I hate to bother them with my request, but unfortunately feel that I have no other options.

II. 4. When completing an assignment on time requires that I get additional support from others, I . . .

A. Remind them that if I don't get this assignment out on time, it could reflect badly on all of us.

B. Point out that the timely completion of my project must take priority over their more routine concerns.

II. 5. When my plans require that others keep my needs in mind as they plan and execute their work, I . . .

A. Explain the difficulties they are causing me, asking them to be more responsive to my needs.

B. Avoid creating a hassle, assuming they have reasons for doing things as they do.

II. 6. When I need to get others to help me deal with a mistake I have made, I . . .

A. Ask for their ideas on how to best deal with the kind of situation in which I find myself.

a	b	c	d
		□	
			□
□			
		□	
□			
			□
□			
		□	
	□		

SUBTOTALS

B. Indicate that such mistakes are bound to happen when people aren't sufficiently available, helpful, or cooperative.

II. 7. When I need others to share some information with me, I . . .

A. Ask if they have any objection to sharing the information.

B. Make it clear that my project is important and demands their full cooperation.

II. 8. When completing an assignment on time requires that I get additional support from others, I . . .

A. Ask them for suggestions on ways I might perform my job more efficiently.

B. Mention that I don't seem to be as efficient as they are and that I need their support if I am to avoid falling farther behind.

II. 9. When my plans require that others keep my needs in mind as they plan and execute their work, I . . .

A. Explain the difficulties they are causing me, asking them to be more responsive to my needs.

B. Inform them that their lack of responsiveness to my needs indicates a lack of concern with the needs of the organization as a whole.

II. 10. When I need to get others to help me deal with a mistake I have made, I . . .

A. Ask for their ideas on how to best deal with the kind of situation in which I find myself.

B. Tell them that I've goofed and would really appreciate having them straighten me out.

	a	b	c	d
6.B				☐
7.A		☐		
7.B				☐
8.A		☐		
8.B			☐	
9.A	☐			
9.B				☐
10.A		☐		
10.B			☐	
SUBTOTALS				

II. 11. When I need others to share some information with me, I . . .

    A. Preface my request with a comment indicating that I feel badly about intruding, and that I hate to bother them with my request, but unfortunately feel that I have no other options.

    B. Make it clear that my project is important and demands their full cooperation.

II. 12. When completing an assignment on time requires that I get additional support from others, I . . .

    A. Ask them for suggestions on ways I might perform my job more efficiently.

    B. Point out that the timely completion of my project must take priority over their more routine concerns.

II. 13. When my plans require that others keep my needs in mind as they plan and execute their work, I . . .

    A. Tell them I would like to understand more about their procedures so I can work more cooperatively with them.

    B. Avoid creating a hassle, assuming they have reasons for doing things as they do.

II. 14. When I need to get others to help me deal with a mistake I have made, I . . .

    A. Point out to them the kind of assistance I need, and ask that they cooperate with me.

    B. Indicate that such mistakes are bound to happen when people aren't sufficiently available, helpful, or cooperative.

II. 15. When I need others to share some information with me, I . . .

    A. Tell them what I want to know.

    B. Ask if they have any objection to sharing the information.

Item	a	b	c	d
11 A			☐	
11 B				☐
12 A		☐		
12 B				☐
13 A		☐		
13 B			☐	
14 A	☐			
14 B				☐
15 A	☐			
15 B		☐		

SUBTOTALS

II. 16. When completing an assignment on time requires that I get additional support from others, I . . .

    A. Mention that I don't seem to be as efficient as they are and that I need their support if I am to avoid falling farther behind.

    B. Point out that the timely completion of my project must take priority over their more routine concerns.

II. 17. When my plans require that others keep my needs in mind as they plan and execute their work, I . . .

    A. Tell them I would like to understand more about their procedures so I can work more cooperatively with them.

    B. Inform them that their lack of responsiveness to my needs indicates a lack of concern with the needs of the organization as a whole.

II. 18. When I need to get others to help me deal with a mistake I have made, I . . .

    A. Point out to them the kind of assistance I need, and ask that they cooperate with me.

    B. Tell them that I've goofed and would really appreciate having them straighten me out.

II. 19. When I need others to share some information with me, I . . .

    A. Tell them what I want to know.

    B. Preface my request with a comment indicating that I feel badly about intruding, and that I hate to bother them with my request, but unfortunately feel that I have no other options.

II. 20. When completing an assignment on time requires that I get additional support from others, I . . .

    A. Remind them that if I don't get this assignment out on time, it could reflect badly on all of us.

    B. Ask them for suggestions on ways I might perform my job more efficiently.

	a	b	c	d
16. A			☐	
16. B				☐
17. A		☐		
17. B				☐
18. A	☐			
18. B			☐	
19. A	☐			
19. B			☐	
20. A	☐			
20. B		☐		

SUBTOTALS

II. 21. When my plans require that others keep my needs in mind as they plan and execute their work, I . . .

    A. Avoid creating a hassle, assuming they have reasons for doing things as they do.

    B. Inform them that their lack of responsiveness to my needs indicates a lack of concern with the needs of the organization as a whole.

II. 22. When I need to get others to help me deal with a mistake I have made, I . . .

    A. Point out to them the kind of assistance I need, and ask that they cooperate with me.

    B. Ask for their ideas on how to best deal with the kind of situation in which I find myself.

II. 23. When I need others to share some information with me, I . . .

    A. Tell them what I want to know.

    B. Make it clear that my project is important and demands their full cooperation.

II. 24. When completing an assignment on time requires that I get additional support from others, I . . .

    A. Remind them that if I don't get this assignment out on time, it could reflect badly on all of us.

    B. Mention that I don't seem to be as efficient as they are and that I need their support if I am to avoid falling farther behind.

	a	b	c	d
21.A			☐	
21.B				☐
22.A	☐			
22.B		☐		
23.A	☐			
23.B				☐
24.A	☐			
24.B			☐	

SUBTOTALS

Part III: Engaging with the Boss

III. 1. When I want my boss to give me a chance to do more challenging work, I . . .

   A. Tell my boss that I think I've proven my ability and feel I deserve a chance to really show what I can do. ☐ (a)

   B. Ask my boss how (s)he feels about my ability to handle a more difficult job. ☐ (b)

III. 2. When I want my boss to give me more freedom in deciding how to best approach my work, I . . .

   A. Apologize for questioning his or her methods before asking if (s)he'll consider some new procedures. ☐ (c)

   B. Point out that people have different needs and abilities and that some don't need tight procedural controls. ☐ (d)

III. 3. When I want my boss to let me make more decisions without first checking with him or her, I . . .

   A. Ask my boss how (s)he feels about letting me make more decisions on my own. ☐ (b)

   B. Assume (s)he will give me the chance to make more decisions when (s)he feels I am ready. ☐ (c)

III. 4. When it is important to me that my boss try harder to get some of my ideas accepted by his or her boss, I . . .

   A. Tell my boss that I feel my ideas are worth a hearing and that I lose my motivation when I feel my ideas are being ignored. ☐ (a)

   B. Tell my boss that it's frustrating to work for someone who is afraid to take a risk. ☐ (d)

a	b	c	d

SUBTOTALS

III.   5. When I want my boss to give me a chance to do more challenging work, I . . .

    A. Tell my boss that I think I've proven my ability and feel I deserve a chance to really show what I can do.

    B. Assume my boss knows better than I do how my particular skills fit in with organizational needs.

III.   6. When I want my boss to give me more freedom in deciding how to best approach my work, I . . .

    A. Ask my boss to share with me his or her areas of satisfaction and dissatisfaction with my work.

    B. Point out that people have different needs and abilities and that some don't need tight procedural controls.

III.   7. When I want my boss to let me make more decisions without first checking with him or her, I . . .

    A. Ask my boss how (s)he feels about letting me make more decisions on my own.

    B. Suggest to my boss that part of being an effective manager is encouraging employees to perform to their full potential.

III.   8. When it is important to me that my boss try harder to get some of my ideas accepted by his or her boss, I . . .

    A. Ask my boss what (s)he feels is the best way of getting changes made in the organization.

    B. Preface my request with an apology for always rocking the boat.

III.   9. When I want my boss to give me a chance to do more challenging work, I . . .

    A. Tell my boss that I think I've proven my ability and feel I deserve a chance to really show what I can do.

    B. Indicate to my boss that I don't think (s)he can understand my capabilities.

	a	b	c	d
5.A	☐			
5.B			☐	
6.A		☐		
6.B				☐
7.A		☐		
7.B				☐
8.A		☐		
8.B				☐
9.A	☐			
9.B				☐

SUBTOTALS

III. 10. When I want my boss to give me more freedom in deciding how to best approach my work, I . . .

   A. Ask my boss to share with me his or her areas of satisfaction and dissatisfaction with my work.

B.

   B. Apologize for questioning his or her methods before asking if (s)he'll consider some new procedures.

III. 11. When I want my boss to let me make more decisions without first checking with him or her, I . . .

   A. Assume (s)he will give me the chance to make more decisions when (s)he feels I am ready.

   B. Suggest to my boss that part of being an effective manager is encouraging employees to perform to their full potential.

III. 12. When it is important to me that my boss try harder to get some of my ideas accepted by his or her boss, I . . .

   A. Ask my boss what (s)he feels is the best way of getting changes made in the organization.

   B. Tell my boss that it's frustrating to work for someone who is afraid to take a risk.

III. 13. When I want my boss to give me a chance to do more challenging work, I . . .

   A. Ask my boss how (s)he feels about my ability to handle a more difficult job.

   B. Assume my boss knows better than I do how my particular skills fit in with organizational needs.

a	b	c	d
		☐	
			☐
		☐	
			☐
	☐		
			☐
	☐		
		☐	

SUBTOTALS

III. 14. When I want my boss to give me more freedom in deciding how to best approach my work, I . . .

    A. Tell my boss that I think I could be more productive if I could exercise more of my own judgment. ☐ (a)

    B. Point out that people have different needs and abilities and that some don't need tight procedural controls. ☐ (d)

III. 15. When I want my boss to let me make more decisions without first checking with him or her, I . . .

    A. Tell my boss that I feel I could be a lot more efficient and productive if I didn't have to check with him or her so often. ☐ (a)

    B. Tell my boss that I think I could be more productive if I could exercise more of my own judgment. ☐ (b)

III. 16. When it is important to me that my boss try harder to get some of my ideas accepted by his or her boss, I . . .

    A. Preface my request with an apology for always rocking the boat. ☐ (c)

    B. Tell my boss that it's frustrating to work for someone who is afraid to take a risk. ☐ (d)

III. 17. When I want my boss to give me a chance to do more challenging work, I . . .

    A. Ask my boss how (s)he feels about my ability to handle a more difficult job. ☐ (b)

    B. Indicate to my boss that I don't think (s)he can understand my capabilities. ☐ (d)

III. 18. When I want my boss to give me more freedom in deciding how to best approach my work, I . . .

    A. Tell my boss that I think I could be more productive if I could exercise more of my own judgment. ☐ (a)

a	b	c	d

SUBTOTALS

B. Apologize for questioning his or her methods before asking if (s)he'll consider some new procedures.

III. 19. When I want my boss to let me make more decisions without first checking with him or her, I . . .

A. Tell my boss that I feel I could be a lot more efficient and productive if I didn't have to check with him or her so often.

B. Assume (s)he will give me the chance to make more decisions when (s)he feels I am ready.

III. 20. When it is important to me that my boss try harder to get some of my ideas accepted by his or her boss, I . . .

A. Tell my boss that I feel my ideas are worth a hearing and that I lose my motivation when I feel my ideas are being ignored.

B. Ask my boss what (s)he feels is the best way of getting changes made in the organization.

III. 21. When I want my boss to give me a chance to do more challenging work, I . . .

A. Assume my boss knows better than I do how my particular skills fit in with organizational needs.

B. Indicate to my boss that I don't think (s)he can understand my capabilities.

III. 22. When I want my boss to give me more freedom in deciding how to best approach my work, I . . .

A. Tell my boss that I think I could be more productive if I could exercise more of my own judgment.

B. Ask my boss to share with me his or her areas of satisfaction and dissatisfaction with my work.

Item	a	b	c	d
B (Apologize)			☐	
19 A	☐			
19 B			☐	
20 A	☐			
20 B		☐		
21 A			☐	
21 B				☐
22 A	☐			
22 B		☐		

SUBTOTALS

III. 23. When I want my boss to let me make more decisions without first checking with him or her, I . . .

   A. Tell my boss that I feel I could be a lot more efficient and productive if I didn't have to check with him or her so often.

   B. Suggest to my boss that part of being an effective manager is encouraging employees to perform to their full potential.

III. 24. When it is important to me that my boss try harder to get some of my ideas accepted by his or her boss, I . . .

   A. Tell my boss that I feel my ideas are worth a hearing and that I lose my motivation when I feel my ideas are being ignored.

   B. Preface my request with an apology for always rocking the boat.

	a	b	c	d
	☐			
				☐
	☐			
			☐	

SUBTOTALS

	a	b	c	d

To score the profile, add each column on each page, recording your subtotals at the bottom of each page:

	a	b	c	d
	1		1	
		5	4	1
	3	0		
Subtotals	4	5	5	1

Next, consider Parts I, II, and III separately. Add all the column "a's" together, all the "b's" together, etc., for Part I, then record these totals under Part I on the scoring format which follows. Then do the same thing for Part II and Part III. **Check your addition: the totals for each Part should add up to 120.**

Behavioral Profile Scoring Format

KEY:

a — assertive   b — responsive   c — non-assertive   d — aggressive

PART I: ENGAGING WITH SUBORDINATES				
PAGE	a	b	c	d
288				
289				
290				
291				
292				
293				
TOTALS				

KEY:
a — involve   b — negotiate   c — enlist   d — direct   e — no influence

PART II: ENGAGING WITH PEERS				
PAGE	a	b	c	d
293				
294				
295				
296				
297				
298				
TOTALS				

PART III: ENGAGING WITH THE BOSS				
PAGE	a	b	c	d
299				
300				
301				
302				
303				
304				
TOTALS				

APPENDIX F
Planning the Information-Gathering Meeting

Person from who I need information: _____

My information-gathering objectives are: _____

_____

_____

_____

This person trusts me because: _____

_____

_____

_____

This person doesn't trust me because: _____

_____

_____

_____

This person will want to share the information with me because (perceived benefits):

_____

_____

_____

This person will be reluctant to share this information with me because (perceived risks): _____

_____

_____

_____

I suspect that, as we begin our conversation, this person will be in this mode:

☐ COLLABORATION: (S)he has confidence in me and perceives no danger in talking openly with me. (High Trust/Low Risk)

☐ COOPERATION: While (s)he has no confidence in me, neither does (s)he feel there is any harm in talking with me. (Low Trust/Low Risk)

☐ RESERVATION: (S)he trusts me, but knows his or her answers could jeopardize his or her position. (High Trust/High Risk)

☐ RESISTANCE: (S)he has no confidence in me and has reason to fear talking openly with me. (Low Trust/High Risk)

To meet my objectives, I need this person to assume this mode:

☐ COLLABORATION: To be totally open; to suggest problems and avenues of inquiry; to really make a commitment to the exchange.

☐ COOPERATION: To honestly answer a few predetermined questions.

☐ RESERVATION: To want to talk openly with me despite known and real risks in doing so.

During the conversation, I plan to build trust and diminish perception of risk by:

☐ Making these Positive Assertive-Responsive Statements:

_____

_____

_____

☐ Giving Positive Information on these benefits:

_____

_____

_____

☐ Clarifying my Informal Power base by:

_____

_____

_____

☐ Using these Positive Overheads or Probes:

_____

_____

_____

☐ Using these Negative Overheads or Probes:

_____

_____

_____

☐ Giving these kinds of Reflective Responses:

_____

_____

_____

☐ Giving these kinds of Empathetic Responses:

_____

_____

_____

☐ Making these kinds of Interpretive Statements:

_____

_____

_____

☐ Convincing him or her of the need for mutual support by:

_____

_____

_____

☐ Giving information on these actual risks:

_____

_____

_____

☐ Pointing out how upside gain outweighs risk by:

_____

_____

_____

☐ Taking some risk myself; levelling by:

_____

_____

_____

☐ Offering these personal reassurances:

_____

_____

_____

☐ Offering these "formal" guarantees:

_____

_____

_____

☐ Making this kind of commitment:

_____

_____

_____

☐ Asking for this kind of commitment:

_____

_____

_____

APPENDIX G
Affiliation Power Profile

Instructions: To complete the questionnaire, simply put a checkmark in any one of the boxes to the right of each item. For example, if you are considering the perfume division of a firm that specializes in cosmetics and sees perfume as the company's profit base, you might respond to item 2 this way:

ITEM	True	More True Than False	More False Than True	False
2. As a division, we are in a position or have the resources to enable the organization to respond to those opportunities it regards as most important.	☐	☐	☑	☐

If you are considering a small organization that does not have divisional distinctions, then skip questions 1–9. Respond to the department questions from the point of view of the work group you are considering (e.g., a case team, or an account focus).

If this work group's personnel are members of corporate staff, then skip questions 1–9, and consider "corporate" as a "department" as you answer items 10–18.

Affiliation Power Profile

	True	More True Than False	More False Than True	False
1. As a division, we are in a position or have the resources to enable the total organization to solve those problems it regards as key barriers to its ability to reach its objectives.	☐	☐	☐	☐
2. As a division, we are in a position or have the resources to enable the organization to respond to those opportunities it regards as most important.	☐	☐	☐	☐
3. The structures (i.e., norms, policies, procedures, relationships, and conditions) that are in place give our division complete freedom to decide what we want to do and how we want to do it.	☐	☐	☐	☐

	True	More True Than False	More False Than True	False
4. Other divisions are unable to achieve their objectives without the output or resources of my division.	☐	☐	☐	☐
5. Experience in my division is regarded as critical for anyone who aspires to a top management position.	☐	☐	☐	☐
6. The organization as a whole has invested or is willing to invest sizeable sums in our division, and we have the ability to generate a high rate of return on that investment.	☐	☐	☐	☐
7. People who have responsible positions in our division would be very difficult to replace.	☐	☐	☐	☐
8. It would be disastrous for the organization if our division made a serious error.	☐	☐	☐	☐
9. Our division holds a central position in the information network, knowing most everything and deciding what information other divisions will get.	☐	☐	☐	☐
10. As a department, we are in a position or have the resources to enable the division to solve those problems it regards as key barriers to its ability to reach its objectives.	☐	☐	☐	☐
11. As a department, we are in a position or have the resources to enable the division to respond to those opportunities it regards as important.	☐	☐	☐	☐
12. The structures (i.e., norms, policies, procedures, relationships, and conditions) that are in place give our department complete freedom to decide what to and how to do it.	☐	☐	☐	☐

	True	More True Than False	More False Than True	False
13. Other departments are unable to achieve their objectives without the output or resources of my department.	☐	☐	☐	☐
14. Experience in my department is regarded as critical for anyone who aspires to a top management position.	☐	☐	☐	☐
15. The organization or the division has invested or is willing to invest sizeable sums in our department, and we have the ability to generate a high rate of return on that investment.	☐	☐	☐	☐
16. People who have responsible positions in my department would be difficult to replace.	☐	☐	☐	☐
17. It would be disastrous for the organization, or for the division, if our department made a serious error.	☐	☐	☐	☐
18. Our department holds a central position in the organizational or divisional information network, knowing most everything and deciding what information other departments will get.	☐	☐	☐	☐
19. The function I perform can enable the organization to solve those problems it regards as key barriers to its ability to reach its objectives.	☐	☐	☐	☐
20. The function I perform can enable the organization to respond to those opportunities it regards as important.	☐	☐	☐	☐

	True	More True Than False	More False Than True	False
21. The structures (i.e., norms, policies, procedures, relationships, and conditions) that are in place allow me complete freedom to decide how to perform my function.	☐	☐	☐	☐
22. If I failed to perform my function, others would be unable to do their jobs.	☐	☐	☐	☐
23. The organization regards people who perform my function as having skills that are important to managing the company.	☐	☐	☐	☐
24. The organization or the department has invested or is willing to invest sizeable sums in my function, and we have the ability to generate a high rate of return on that investment.	☐	☐	☐	☐
25. People who perform my function would be very difficult to replace.	☐	☐	☐	☐
26. If people performing my function made an error, the consequences for the organization would be severe.	☐	☐	☐	☐
27. My function holds a central position in the information network, knowing most everything and deciding what information others will get.	☐	☐	☐	☐

To score the Affiliation Power Profile, total the number of checkmarks you recorded and multiply as indicated on the format below:

Total checks in "True" boxes   □ × 6 = □

Total checks in "More True
Than False" boxes   □ × 4 = □

Total checks in "More False
Than True" boxes   □ × 2 = □

Total checks in "False" boxes   □ × 0 = □

TOTAL □

The highest score you could have achieved is 6 × 27, or 162. (If you skipped questions 1–9, the highest possible score is 108.) The lowest score is 0.

The following score ranges should help you interpret the meaning of your scores. Bear in mind, however: the Affiliation Power Profile was designed to provoke thought only. Until statistical tests were performed, the instrument cannot claim to be scientifically reliable or diagnostically precise. Score ranges assume a normal distribution that has not been verified.

RANGE	SIGNIFICANCE
0–40 (if you answered all questions) –or– 0–27 (if you omitted 1–9)	The work group in question has very little power in the organization; individuals in this work group will probably have a very difficult time exerting any measurable influence on the organization; visibility and, therefore, promotion beyond the work group is unlikely.
41–81 (if you answered all questions) –or– 28–54 (if you omitted 1–9)	The work group in question has only a moderate degree of power in the organization. The truly ambitious individual should probably not seek affiliation with this work group. It is unlikely that individuals will have a say in activities or decisions that affect the larger organization or other units.
82–122 (if you answered all questions) –or– 55–82 (if you omitted 1–9)	The work group in question has a substantial amount of power, though other groups at the same level are more powerful. It is likely that this unit can involve or enlist the support of others; directions will go unheeded more often than not, and to negotiate is to risk losing.

RANGE	SIGNIFICANCE
123–162 (if you answered all questions) –or– 83–108 (if you omitted 1–9)	The work group in question is one of the most powerful in the organization. Individuals who belong to this work group will find their organizational affiliation to be an asset in their efforts to achieve their goals within the organization.

To analyze your results, refer back to the profile itself and translate your responses to numerical scores as follows, and enter the scores next to the items.

- If you checked "True," assign a 6;

- If you checked "More True Than False," assign a 4;

- If you checked "More False Than True," assign a 2;

- If you checked "False," assign a 0.

Here is a format for you to use to record your scores:

ITEM	MY RESPONSE/SCORES	MY SCORE
1	☐ True – 6 ☐ More True Than False – 4 ☐ More False Than True – 2 ☐ False – 0	☐
2	☐ True – 6 ☐ More True Than False – 4 ☐ More False Than True – 2 ☐ False – 0	☐
3	☐ True – 6 ☐ More True Than False – 4 ☐ More False Than True – 2 ☐ False – 0	☐
4	☐ True – 6 ☐ More True Than False – 4 ☐ More False Than True – 2 ☐ False – 0	☐
5	☐ True – 6 ☐ More True Than False – 4 ☐ More False Than True – 2 ☐ False – 0	☐

ITEM	MY RESPONSE/SCORES	MY SCORE
6	☐ True – 6 ☐ More True Than False – 4 ☐ More False Than True – 2 ☐ False – 0	☐
7	☐ True – 6 ☐ More True Than False – 4 ☐ More False Than True – 2 ☐ False – 0	☐
8	☐ True – 6 ☐ More True Than False – 4 ☐ More False Than True – 2 ☐ False – 0	☐
9	☐ True – 6 ☐ More True Than False – 4 ☐ More False Than True – 2 ☐ False – 0	☐
10	☐ True – 6 ☐ More True Than False – 4 ☐ More False Than True – 2 ☐ False – 0	☐
11	☐ True – 6 ☐ More True Than False – 4 ☐ More False Than True – 2 ☐ False – 0	☐
12	☐ True – 6 ☐ More True Than False – 4 ☐ More False Than True – 2 ☐ False – 0	☐
13	☐ True – 6 ☐ More True Than False – 4 ☐ More False Than True – 2 ☐ False – 0	☐
14	☐ True – 6 ☐ More True Than False – 4 ☐ More False Than True – 2 ☐ False – 0	☐

ITEM	MY RESPONSE/SCORES	MY SCORE
15	☐ True – 6 ☐ More True Than False – 4 ☐ More False Than True – 2 ☐ False – 0	☐
16	☐ True – 6 ☐ More True Than False – 4 ☐ More False Than True – 2 ☐ False – 0	☐
17	☐ True – 6 ☐ More True Than False – 4 ☐ More False Than True – 2 ☐ False – 0	☐
18	☐ True – 6 ☐ More True Than False – 4 ☐ More False Than True – 2 ☐ False – 0	☐
19	☐ True – 6 ☐ More True Than False – 4 ☐ More False Than True – 2 ☐ False – 0	☐
20	☐ True – 6 ☐ More True Than False – 4 ☐ More False Than True – 2 ☐ False – 0	☐
21	☐ True – 6 ☐ More True Than False – 4 ☐ More False Than True – 2 ☐ False – 0	☐
22	☐ True – 6 ☐ More True Than False – 4 ☐ More False Than True – 2 ☐ False – 0	☐
23	☐ True – 6 ☐ More True Than False – 4 ☐ More False Than True – 2 ☐ False – 0	☐

ITEM	MY RESPONSE/SCORES	MY SCORE

24
- ☐ True – 6
- ☐ More True Than False – 4
- ☐ More False Than True – 2
- ☐ False – 0

☐

25
- ☐ True – 6
- ☐ More True Than False – 4
- ☐ More False Than True – 2
- ☐ False – 0

☐

26
- ☐ True – 6
- ☐ More True Than False – 4
- ☐ More False Than True – 2
- ☐ False – 0

☐

27
- ☐ True – 6
- ☐ More True Than False – 4
- ☐ More False Than True – 2
- ☐ False – 0

☐

Next, transpose your scores onto this format:

FACTOR	ITEM/SCORES	TOTAL ALL ITEMS
IMPORTANCE TO PROBLEMS	1 _____ 10 _____ 19 _____	☐
IMPORTANCE TO OPPORTUNITIES	2 _____ 11 _____ 20 _____	☐
IMPACT OF STRUCTURES	3 _____ 12 _____ 21 _____	☐

FACTOR	ITEM/SCORES	TOTAL ALL ITEMS
RELATIVE DEGREE OF DEPENDENCY	4 _____ 13 _____ 22 _____	☐
RELEVANCE OF EX- PERIENCE WITH GROUP TO LEADER- SHIP ABILITY	5 _____ 14 _____ 23 _____	☐
INVESTMENT	6 _____ 15 _____ 24 _____	☐
RESOURCE SCARCITY	7 _____ 16 _____ 25 _____	☐
ERROR MARGIN	8 _____ 17 _____ 26 _____	☐
INFORMATION FLOW AND CONTROL	9 _____ 18 _____ 27 _____	☐

After recording your totals, graph them by putting a point above the factor and across from the number representing your total for that factor. For example, assume you had these scores:

FACTOR	ITEM/SCORES		TOTAL
IMPORTANCE	1	4	10
TO PROBLEMS	10	4	
	19	2	
IMPORTANCE	2	4	
TO OPPORTUNITIES	11	2	6
	20	0	

Your graph would look like this:

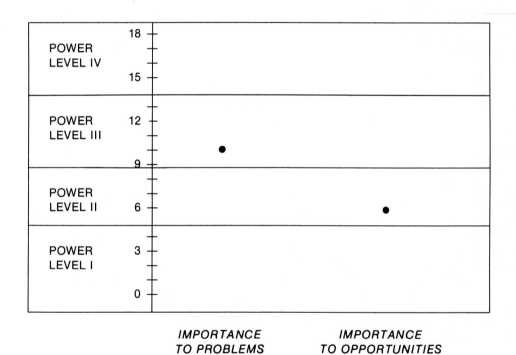

IMPORTANCE
TO PROBLEMS

IMPORTANCE
TO OPPORTUNITIES

After recording all your totals, connect them. Your completed graph might look something like the graph on the next page.

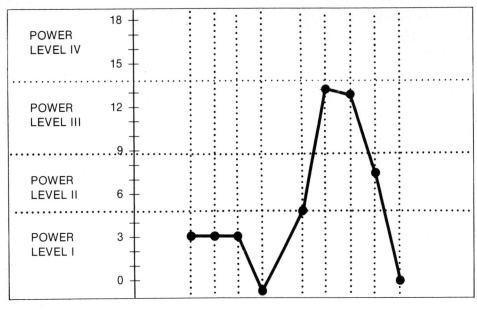

A blank format follows for your use.

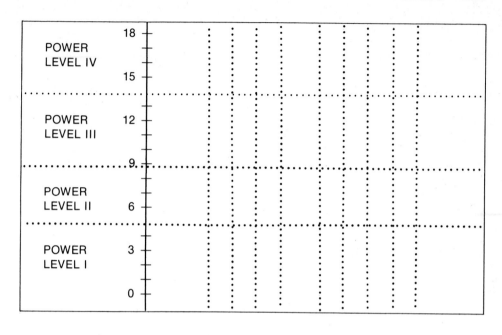

If you skipped items 1–9 (because you are not part of a division), then change the scale on the graph as follows:

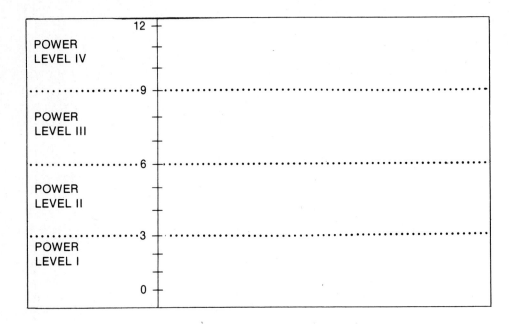